C000121415

THE OLD FIRM IN THE NEW AGE

THE OLD FIRM IN THE
NEW AGE

Celtic and Rangers Since the Souness Revolution

BILL MURRAY

MAINSTREAM
PUBLISHING PROJECTS

Copyright © Bill Murray, 1998
All rights reserved
The moral right of the author has been asserted

First published in 1998 by
MAINSTREAM PUBLISHING PROJECTS
Edinburgh

ISBN 1 85158 948 4

No part of this book may be reproduced or transmitted in any form or
by any means without written permission from the publisher, except
by a reviewer who wishes to quote brief passages in connection with a
review written for insertion in a newspaper, magazine or broadcast

Photographs courtesy of *The Scotsman*

A catalogue record for this book is available from the British Library

Typeset in Garamond
Printed and bound in Great Britain by Butler & Tanner Ltd

*For Else in Holland, who is somewhere there at
the beginning of it all,*

*and Liz (Morag) in Paris, who has lived through
so much of it*

Contents

Preface

Since *The Old Firm* came out in 1984, the changes in world football, and not just Scottish football, have been little short of revolutionary. In Scotland the arrival of Graeme Souness at Ibrox and his subsequent signing of the Catholic player, Maurice Johnston, have been two of the most hysterical media events in Scottish sport, and since then Rangers have gone on to equal Celtic's record of winning nine Scottish League Championships in a row. Since the arrival of Souness and the signing of Maurice Johnston several people have suggested that I update *The Old Firm*, as its central theme is the way in which Celtic and Rangers have developed as champions of their respective communities, Celtic of the Catholic-Irish, Rangers of the Protestant-Scots. In the last two chapters of that book I was critical of Rangers for their refusal to play Catholics, and suggested that signing a Catholic would no more upset their Protestant identity than Celtic's many Protestant footballers had affected their Catholic identity.

Writing an updated or revised edition of *The Old Firm* would have been a daunting task, and in any case that book has taken on a life of its own – and is still in print. I thought of adding a new chapter to bring it up to date, but it was soon apparent that only a book could do the subject justice. Moreover there is a certain poetic wholeness in the period covered, beginning with a Rangers team that refused to play Catholics and ending with a Rangers team that could contain more Catholics than Protestants in its first eleven: a revolution indeed – and in the strictest sense of the word.

The Old Firm was my first foray into sports history, a long way from my original research speciality, the French Revolution, but since then I have merged my interests in French history and sports history by studying the relationship between sport and politics in France in the years before the Second World War, particularly workers' sport and the Nazi Olympics. I was diverted from this when I was asked to write a history of football and that took up several years and resulted in two books on the subject. In the course of this research I became even more aware of the importance of the part played by the Scots in the spread of the world game than I had originally thought, and had no qualms about

9

emphasising this; and throughout it all the unique relationship of Celtic and Rangers came into ever clearer focus.

The present book takes up the story of Rangers and Celtic where I left off in 1984, but it is more an impressionistic work than a long haul involving years of research. I have tried to avoid going over ground covered in *The Old Firm* (and *Glasgow's Giants*), but I cannot assume that all readers of this book will have read the earlier works, and so where necessary I have recapitulated or referred to what was said there.

All those who helped me with these books have helped with this one. As always I must thank La Trobe University: terrible things are happening to universities at the moment, but I have been left free to pursue my interests; Carol and Heather in the History Office; the staff of the university library; and my colleagues who have all been as sympathetic as ever to what for many of them is still an esoteric topic. In Germany, Arnd Krüger and Ulrich Matheja offered their usual support; and in Holland, Else Bongenaar, someone who plays an unspoken part in this book (as in *The Old Firm*) most kindly found the material in the Dutch press relating to Pierre van Hooijdonk. Friends and colleagues in the Australian Society for Sports History have tolerated my eccentricities and sharpened my thoughts. Anthony Bidgood kindly copied several issues of his collection of *Tiocfaidh Ar La* for me. Don Ferrell continued to help me through the mysteries of electronic communication, easing the onset of panic when I thought I might have lost a file. I have also continued to enjoy the encouragement of family and friends in Adelaide, where Rosemary McKay flies the Scottish flag with inexhaustible pride; and my daughter Morag, better known as Liz, now in France but who spent a year in Scotland caught up with one side of the Old Firm.

Others have helped by sharing their knowledge of the Old Firm and the Scottish football scene. I must first record my thanks to Jack Webster who, although he has not had much to do with this particular book, has been a constant source of encouragement and help to me since he first read the original manuscript of *The Old Firm* back in 1983. Others were generous with their time in a two-week period in November 1997: of those who expressed no objection to being named it is my pleasure to thank Gerry Dunbar, Roddy Forsyth, Michael Kelly, David Low, Kevin McCarra, Archie McGregor and Gerry McNee. I wrote to the chairmen of both clubs and was accorded a long and productive discussion with Fergus McCann. Peter McLean, Celtic's public relations manager, provided me with a mountain of relevant material, while Joe Sullivan made helpful comments on what I had written. John Greig, public relations manager of Rangers, took time out from a busy schedule to answer many of my queries and very kindly arranged for me to join a tour of Ibrox stadium at short notice. Rangers director Ian Skelly invited me to watch an Old Firm match from the rarefied atmosphere of the Club Deck, after which I had a long conversation with former Rangers manager David White. The editor of *Follow, Follow* did not reply to my letters. At the University of Strathclyde I had further illuminating conversations with Callum G. Brown, Richard J. Finlay and Rangers fan John Young. At Mainstream, my thanks to Bill Campbell for permitting a rescheduling of the deadline, and to the editorial department who handled all the consequent changes with good humour and professional skill.

My most immediate and greatest debts go to three people who have given more of their time to my work than any individual has a right to expect. Graham Walker, an unwavering Rangers fan through the darker days into the recent triumphs, has discussed many aspects of Scottish football with me, before, during and after matches, and made many incisive comments on an early draft. Roy Hay, grandson of a Celtic great from early in the century and who is still suffering from his beloved Ayr United's rejection of David Murray in 1988, has constantly tried to beat sense into me at the same time as he improved what I have been trying to say. He also read an early draft, but it is not his fault if some of my excesses remain uncurbed. Once more, however, my greatest debt is to Pat Woods, in this book more than any other. Quite simply I could not have written it without Pat, as he has kept me constantly supplied with information on the Old Firm in between my trips to Scotland since 1984. Again he has read the drafts with meticulous care and saved me from many errors. My judgements are my own, as is my way of expressing them, and from these, in this book more than in any other, Pat remains totally absolved.

Bill Murray
January 1998

Introduction

On the evening of 7 May 1997, Rangers Football Club beat Dundee United by a single goal from Brian Laudrup to win their ninth consecutive Scottish League Championship title. It was the culmination of a frenetic season in which the champions and their eternal rivals, Celtic Football Club, collectively known as the 'Old Firm', fought out what was virtually a private battle, with the eight other teams in the Scottish Premier League acting as little more than a backdrop. It was a historic victory for Rangers, who thus equalled the nine consecutive League flags won by Celtic under Jock Stein in the years between 1966 and 1974, a period in the shade of their Glasgow rivals that had haunted the Rangers faithful ever since. In the course of laying that ghost to rest Rangers had also laid to rest another ghost from their past: their refusal to play Catholics, which the club once thought was necessary to preserve its Protestant traditions. This sectarian policy was already an anachronism in Scotland of the mid-1980s, but in the world of global television and the financial rewards that went with this, sectarianism was not only an irrelevance, but a potential barrier to playing in the ever more lucrative European competitions. The first steps in modernising Rangers and setting them on the road to domestic success and regular entry into the top European competition came with the appointment of Graeme Souness as player-manager on 7 April 1986.

Souness's arrival at Ibrox Park, the famous ground of the Glasgow club, created an unprecedented buzz of interest from a media for which the arrival and departure of football team managers to the rhythm of success and failure had become a routine event. Certainly Rangers was not a club that made a habit of sacking managers, although there had been five in the two decades before the arrival of Souness, a reflection of the falling fortunes of the club, above all its failure to keep up with Celtic. All but David White of these managers had been from 'traditional' backgrounds, committed to the club's Protestant past and prepared to maintain the old values. The new man had no such previous connections, and this suggested that something new was in the air. Those expecting, or fearing, great changes, were not to be let down.

Souness was brought from Sampdoria in Italy in a coup that was carried out swiftly, cleanly and in remarkable secrecy, despite the fact that on three separate occasions he had said that the only thing that might bring him back to Scotland would be as a manager of Rangers. No one took him seriously – except David Holmes of Rangers. He was a world-class player who had represented Scotland on many occasions, but he was also known to be tough and ambitious, a man who liked to get his own way. In signing him Rangers were clearly intent on revolutionising a club that had been labouring well below its potential, its reputation clouded over by its unspoken tradition of never playing a Catholic footballer. In modernising Rangers Souness's success was shattering, and as the 'sleeping giant' aroused itself and adapted to the rapidly changing economics of British football, their traditional rivals Celtic were left floundering in their wake. Worse, one of the pedestals on which they had based their moral superiority was about to be knocked from under them.

When *The Old Firm* was published in 1984, I thought it would be only a matter of time before Rangers gave in to the pressure to break with their past and sign a Catholic. Those closer to the pulse of Scottish football dismissed this as unlikely. Then came Souness with his cosmopolitan background and well-publicised boast that he was a football mercenary, interested only in winning. For many Rangers die-hards winning was not the only thing; more important was to win without playing Catholics. This was an attitude that took Souness three years to break down, but even before then he had embarked on changes at Ibrox that were nothing short of revolutionary.

For Rangers, 1984 was not a particularly auspicious year, and certainly not a particularly happy one. For their supporters, who were failing to turn up at Ibrox by the tens of thousands, there had been little to lighten the long darkness since the triple Championships of 1976 and 1978. Other clubs would have been happy enough with the successes Rangers had in these intervening years; but Rangers are not another club. In 1984 the man who had won them these successes was back, although the much revered Jock Wallace was not to be the miracle-man the faithful hoped he would be. Celtic during this time were also still in the shadow of the great teams that had set them on the way to nine successive League titles, called the Lisbon Lions after their even more memorable feat of winning the European Cup in 1967 against Inter Milan in the Portuguese capital.

A 'New Firm' was said to have come into being in the early 1980s, as Aberdeen won three League Championships and three successive Scottish Cups, as well as a European trophy in 1983, while Dundee United played some sparkling football, won the League in 1983 and came within an ace of European success in 1987. Together they challenged the dominance of the two big Glasgow clubs. It was a short-lived challenge, and their failure to draw crowds as large as those who came to watch even a mediocre Rangers or Celtic game, showed that it was not just the quality of the football that drew Scottish supporters to watch the Glasgow giants.

In 1984 the disasters at Bradford, the Heysel and Hillsborough were in the near future, and the hooliganism that played a role in the second of these disasters was a blight on the game – less so in Scotland, where the strict laws against alcohol at matches introduced after the 'Hampden Riot' of 1980 went a long way to easing this problem. Attendances at football matches throughout most of the football world in the early 1980s were on the decline, and in Scotland Rangers and Celtic were playing to well below their usual crowds. Football was said to be in a crisis, and although a cure was at hand it had many features worse than the disease. Football in 1984 was on the brink of a revolution, as independent television companies fought the state monopolies and used football as a bait to attract subscribers or customers to watch their pro-grammes. In this they were assisted by the new cable and satellite technology that brought football instantaneously to a global audience, a new market, exposure to which the owners of the advanced technology sold to eager sponsors.

In the aftermath of the disasters at Bradford and Brussels, football was snobbishly dismissed by one newspaper as a slum sport played by slum people in slum conditions. Within a decade the image of the game had changed, as a new class of spectators came to watch matches from the comfort of the completely renovated and all-seated stadiums that were one of the outcomes of the report into the Hillsborough disaster of April 1989. Some of the richest football clubs accepted the Taylor report with the ideological spur that in this way they would get rid of the fans some of them regarded as scum, attracting instead to their corporate boxes a clientele who found through football a means of pursuing their com-mercial interests. Football was becoming fashionable, attracting people who could afford the steep increases in prices that went along with creating the new stadiums. By the 1990s football stars were sought after as never before to sell products on television to people who might never have been inside a football ground. This was not new, but it was on an unprecedented scale; footballers from the earliest days had given their names to help sell products in which they had had little interest, such as the non-smoking Stanley Matthews who used to sell cigarettes in newspaper advertisements in the 1950s, while the late Denis Compton appeared on billboards throughout the country selling Brylcreem. But these were exceptional sports stars and Denis Compton was better known as a cricketer than an international footballer. And neither

Compton nor Matthews enjoyed the hero-worship of the stars of stage and screen, a gap that has closed slightly in the 1990s.

Football in the 1950s was still seen as the game of the working class; and while it has never been a completely working-class game, it has always had an appeal to the less well-off, as an avenue of escape for those with talent in their toes and as a cheap form of entertainment for those who could only afford to watch from the terraces. The condition of the working class itself changed steadily in the years from the 1950s, and the changes in football grounds reflected this in part. But there were other forces at work, as those who have always seen a commercial advantage in the game's popularity took advantage of its global reach to recreate it in an image closer to their corporate ideal: from the late 1980s football had to be made fit to set before the new class of yuppies (to use a favourite term of the time) who had just discovered the game.

The 1980s, the decade of Thatcher in Britain and Reagan in the United States, has been praised or denounced as the decade when the rich were taught to despise the poor with an easy conscience, the 'greed is good' philosophy that reigned supreme as individuals, companies and corporations set out to market and make a profit from anything they (or someone else) owned. Football teams were to the fore in this as they sold their jerseys, their names and their traditions in the pursuit of more wealth. In the new post-modern world bigotry was a nuisance if not an irrelevance, and there was no way that a modern company could operate out of a 'biscuit tin', as was said disparagingly of Celtic – mainly by their own supporters. Rangers and Celtic, so often partners when it suited their commercial interests, came to separate terms with the new age, the one with considerably more success than the other, to such an extent that the growth of Rangers in financial terms and their success on the domestic front threatened to put an end to any serious rivalry from Celtic.

It had been otherwise in that other tumultuous decade from the mid-1960s when the cultural revolutions convulsing the western world left Rangers exposed as a sectarian sore in a world where bigotry in all its forms was coming under attack. Blacks in the United States rejected the racism that was their daily lot; indigenous peoples revolted against their colonial masters, women set out to claim an equal place alongside their menfolk, and soon homosexuals would come out of their closets. It was the decade of peace and love-ins, of protest marches against the Vietnam War and in favour of a world in which the rights of the community were upheld against the greed of the individual or the privileges of the few. In Northern Ireland marchers protesting the violation of basic civil rights were met by the forces of Protestant privilege, sparking a virtual civil war in which the British Army had to be brought in to protect the Catholics.

In Scotland, the continued refusal of Rangers to employ Catholic players came under attack, increasingly as they refused to admit they had such a policy and the situation in Northern Ireland worsened. During this time the public image of Celtic continued to improve as they won the European Cup in 1967 and bestrode the Scottish domestic scene with flair and panache through to 1974. More significantly Pope John XXIII, with the reforms of Vatican II (1962–65), brought the Catholic Church into the twentieth century and a new period of ecumenism was opened up. In this period, too, from the late 1950s to the early 1970s, the number of Catholic students at Glasgow University increased three-fold and comprised one of the largest student bodies in the United Kingdom. For the first time ever, perhaps, Celtic were openly praised by all sections of the Scottish press, although the paranoia that had been nurtured over the century could not be erased so easily.

Celtic's success on the field and a series of setbacks to Rangers on and off the field, brought their sectarian practices in regard to not playing Catholics increasingly under criticism. Celtic, who had always played Protestants, although they refused to let the direction of the club fall into non-Catholic hands, were able to occupy the moral high ground. All this was challenged with the arrival of Souness, irrevocably so when he signed the Catholic player Maurice Johnston in July 1989. A historic breach had been made in the Old Firm rivalry, but two individuals could not dissolve the hatreds of nearly a century overnight, and one of the world's great football derbies proceeded into the glitzy new age of global sport with its own challenges to face.

1. The Greatest Club Game in the World?

Anywhere in the world where Scots have gone – and that is just about everywhere – you will find Celtic and Rangers supporters. The big clubs of Spain, Italy and England have their fans around the world, but it is doubtful if any of them have such a devoted and widespread following: few have had such unbroken loyalty over the decades, and none of them owe their popularity to the polarisation that exists between the two sets of fans over religion.

A South American *hincha* (fan) is said to have been the first to make the claim that you can change your wife or your religion, but two things you can never change are your mother and your football team. He was speaking of football fans in Argentina, but he could have been speaking for fans all around the world: not least those of Celtic and Rangers. In the years before the Second World War, when the British game was still held in awe throughout the football world, Rangers or Celtic could at various times lay claim to being the best club team in the world, although it is a claim that has no solid foundation, as the club games played on the continent at that time were not treated seriously by the British and foreign clubs very seldom visited Britain. In Britain itself, the Celtic team that won six Championships in the first decade of the century could hold its own with any English team; and the Rangers team that dominated the inter-war period usually came out on top in their regular glamour friendlies with Arsenal in the 1930s. In the decade after 1966 Celtic and Rangers set up a remarkable record for a country as small as Scotland, by then reduced in football terms to a size more commensurate with its population, the rest of the world having taken over the game the British had invented and done so much to promote.

During this time Scotland held two European trophies: in 1967 when Celtic won the European Cup and in 1972 when Rangers won the European Cup-Winners' Cup. A week after Celtic won the European Cup in Lisbon, Rangers came within a toe-poke of making it a Scottish double of European trophies when they lost by a single goal in extra time in the European Cup-Winners' Cup to a Bayern Munich side that included three young stars who would take it to world acclaim – Sepp Maier, Franz Beckenbauer and Gerd Müller. Three years later Celtic again reached the final of the European Cup, but fell to Holland's Feyenoord, arrogantly believing they had won the trophy after they had outclassed England's Leeds United with victories in both legs of the semi-final – in the second leg in Glasgow before a record 133,961 spectators. In the evening of 19 April 1972 Glasgow hosted two European semi-finals: in the European Cup-Winners' Cup a crowd of 80,000 at Ibrox saw Rangers eliminate Bayern Munich on their way to a confrontation in the final with Moscow Dynamo in Barcelona, while 75,000 at Celtic Park saw the home team eliminated on penalties by Inter Milan. Celtic reached another European semi-final, in 1974; but despite the changes at Ibrox after 1986 there has been only one lonely season (1992–93) when Rangers revived memories of the glory days of Scottish participation in Europe.

It was Rangers and Celtic who were to the fore in pioneering the armies of travelling supporters for away games in Europe. Celtic fans travelling to Lisbon for the 1967 European Cup final supplied enough stories to fill a book (which the journalist Gerry McNee duly wrote), many of which involved the ingenious stunts thought up about how to get there – and then get back. With Europe a regular part of the football calendar some fans of the two clubs had to work out complicated itineraries on how to get to the midweek game on the continent and then back to Scotland for the League game on the Saturday – and in some cases convince their boss that they had good reasons for absences from work. By the 1980s cheaper air travel eased some of these difficulties, but others could still arise. When Rangers were scheduled to play Dynamo Kiev in the first round of the European Cup in September 1987, some of their fans overcame the visa restrictions by joining the Scottish Communist Party and signing up for an official tour that conveniently coincided with the Rangers visit.[1]

Despite the glamour of Europe, however, it is their games with each other that most fire the passions of the Bears of Rangers and the Bhoys of Celtic – also known as the Huns and the Tims, the former an unfriendly reference to the Rangers supporters, the latter accepted by the Celtic supporters. The relationship between the two teams mystifies the minds of more rational mortals, but is real enough to keep up a constant stream of anecdotes and reminiscences. Two stories from Stephen Walsh's *Voices of the Old Firm* highlight the peculiar relationship between the two teams: Rangers were playing a League match at Ibrox on 23 October 1971 when it was announced that Partick Thistle were beating Celtic 4–0 in the League Cup final at Hampden Park. Joyous Rangers fans immediately left Ibrox, commandeered all the taxis they could and made their way across Glasgow to join the Jags supporters in exulting at the humiliation of a Celtic team more used to sweeping away all before it.[2]

The other comes from the end of the 1982 season when Celtic were playing St Mirren at home, and needing a point to win the League. Aberdeen were playing at home to Rangers that same day, and if they won by a four-goal margin and Celtic did not pick up the point they needed, the Dons would win the League. When the half-time score came through from Pittodrie that the Dons were winning 4–0, instead of angst at Parkhead, where the score was 0–0, Celtic fans started to cheer, hoping the Dons would pile on the agony, even, it would appear, at the cost of their own League flag.[3] As it was, they won 3–0 to take the title in comfort.

LOCAL DERBIES AROUND THE WORLD

Local 'derbies', the particularly tense confrontation of two teams in close geographical proximity, are part of the life-blood of football. They are almost as old as the game itself, spreading out from villages to towns and then within towns, and ultimately to nation against nation or nations within nations. From the earliest times, local heroes have emerged for their sporting skills, carrying the hopes of those without their abilities but only too willing to identify with them. From the late nineteenth century followers of football teams were devising ingenious ways of supporting their local heroes and wearing their colours, and loyalty soon took precedence over the quality of play. Today teams of exquisite skill, be it in Africa, South America or elsewhere, have played before half-empty stadiums while sell-out crowds have watched more boring or blood-and-thunder encounters involving their national or local teams. In Scotland from the 1890s, Rangers and Celtic thrived in opposition to each other, attracting support from all over Scotland and even beyond its borders, leaving other teams in the competition far behind. The basis for the success of the two clubs certainly included skill, but the passions that inspired the fans were tribal at worst, pride in their communities at best. The Rangers/Celtic club game, the Old Firm, has been called (by Scots) the greatest club game in the world; but leaving aside what is meant by 'great', it is unique in its religious basis.

At the turn of the century football in Britain was far in advance of the rest of the world, although Europe and most of Latin America would eventually catch up. From the beginning of the century Argentina and Uruguay in South America, and Hungary and Austria in Europe, played the most ferociously contested national rivalries outside the United Kingdom. Uruguay, with a population of two to three million, shares with Scotland a small population and a totally disproportionate impact on the world game – Uruguay through to the 1960s was arguably the world's most successful football nation. Uruguay also shares with Scotland a domestic league dominated by two big city rivals: Nacional and Peñarol. However, unlike the Old Firm, who have occasionally been dislodged from the top spots in Scotland, the stranglehold of the two big Montevideo teams is almost complete. Neither has a clear-cut ethnic identity, Peñarol having long since lost any Italian origins that might have set them against a 'purer' Uruguayan Nacional. In Argentina the Boca Juniors–River Plate derby has no ethnic base: both began in the poor Boca district of Buenos Aires, but when River moved further west into a more affluent suburb they attracted a slightly wealthier support. Long before Rangers started the fashion in Scotland in the 1980s, the Argentines were prepared to spend a fortune to attract star players, and River Plate became known as The Millionaires for their free-spending on players in the 1930s; in the 1940s they produced arguably the best forward-line in the history of the game, known as 'La Máquina'.

Football flourished later in Brazil than it did in Argentina, Uruguay or Chile, and it came with the acceptance of blacks into the all-white socially exclusive teams who had run the game before the 1920s. Vasco da Gama, of Portuguese origins, first broke the ban, and their success through playing blacks was soon followed by other clubs, most notably Flamengo, founded as an independent football team in 1911 when they broke away from the Boating Club of which they had been a part. Fluminense, founded in 1902, also from a Boating Club, signed a few blacks in the 1930s, but they were treated in a most patronising way and the club never sought nor won the support of the poor in the way Flamengo did. The Fla–Flu derby, however, became the biggest in the world, with regular crowds of over 150,000 to see their games, and a record 177,656 spectators in 1963. This was made possible by the construction of the Maracaná in 1950, to house the World Cup of that year. Some Scottish crowds came close to 150,000 in the late 1930s; but the most an Old Firm game attracted was 118,730 to a Ne'erday game (the name given to the traditional New Year's Day game between Rangers and Celtic, now more often played on 2 or 3 January) at Ibrox in 1939 – thousands, however, were locked outside that day. The previous Ne'erday game had seen a record 83,500 squeezed into Celtic Park, while at Ibrox in the late 1930s and late 1940s, Old Firm games attracted crowds of up to 95,000, with 105,000 for a League Cup game on 16 October 1948. These were the peak days of attendance at football matches in Britain, when safety was taken less seriously than it is today, although crowds for the big games were usually limited by ticket to 134,000 for Hampden, the national stadium.

In Britain and Europe there are equally tense local derbies, but as in South America and outside Northern Ireland, few of these are based on opposing ethnic, cultural or religious foundations as was the case in Scotland between Rangers and Celtic. Players of Nürnberg and neighbouring Furth in Germany in the 1920s refused to travel in the same train to play for the national team, and the Czech teams Slavia and Sparta have been rivals throughout their one hundred-year history. In Belgium, where the linguistic divisions are the source of savage enmities, no team emerged as champion of the Flemish-speaking regions in opposition to a team representing the French-speaking Walloons. In the beginning, all teams had French names and the national and most local administrations conducted their affairs in French. But from early in the century a process of 'Fleminising' the game and converting clubs back to Flemish titles has restored the linguistic and cultural predominance of the Flemish teams. Moreover, the Belgian national team that has performed some minor miracles in recent years, is one of the few Belgian institutions which has won the support of the entire nation.[4]

Italy is another country where regional differences have been overlooked when the eleven men of the Azzuri take the field; but at the local level the confrontations can be bitter: teams from the wealthier north against those from the south, but more importantly two teams from one town or a town close by. In Rome, Lazio are sometimes seen as having a slightly more middle-class following than their eternal rivals, Roma. When Lionello Manfredonia arrived at Roma in 1987 after ten years with Lazio and two with Juventus, a club almost as hated as Lazio by Roma fans, the Ultras of the Southern Curve split in two between those who wanted to accept Manfredonia and those who hated him for having worn the colours of the enemy. It was a split much worse than any that developed at Ibrox after the arrival of Maurice Johnston to play for Rangers, a man of alien faith who had also worn the colours of the enemy.

HAKOAH AND THE MUSCULAR JEWS

Most local derbies are cross-town rivalries with little class, ethnic or above all religious antagonisms. Before the Second World War, however, there were several prominent Jewish clubs which had to live with the anti-Semitism of their rivals, but no single rival emerged to champion the anti-Semitic cause – others on the political stage performed this task only too successfully. In Spain, clubs representing provinces with different ethnic bases, especially Castilians, Catalans and Basques, have set up bitter rivalries, but they all share the same religion.

The association of religion and football goes back to its early days, when the 'muscular Christians' sought to win over the souls of would-be converts by encouraging their enthusiasm for football. Churches, along with pubs, were often at the origins of clubs that are still well known today; Aston Villa and Everton in England, Queen's Park, Hibernian and Celtic in Scotland, are just a few of those prominent today that had religious origins. Jewish clubs were founded in the 1890s in Europe, but it was not until 1909 and the founding of Hakoah in Vienna that a Jewish club came to challenge the élite continental clubs.

Hakoah was founded as a refuge from the anti-Semitism that scarred the city of dreams, a multi-disciplined sports club devoted to demonstrating that Jews were neither weak nor water-shy, as popular prejudice had it. The club produced some brilliant swimmers who were often accompanied by their wrestlers and weight-lifters who stood ready to battle with or dump in the pool those who were too vocal in their anti-Semitism. But it was the football team that was the pride of the Jewish community, winning games with a bruising style that deliberately set out to deny the weakling stereotype. Hakoah have since lost the glamour they had in the mid-1920s, when they won the first professional Austrian League Championship in 1925, much to the anguish of the many anti-Semites in the Austrian capital. They lost many of their best players to 'the rich uncle in America' after tours of the USA in 1926 and 1927, and struggled in the 1930s, finally to be crushed when the Nazis absorbed Austria in 1938. Along with FK Austria, which was seen as the team of the liberal Jews, they were faced with the general anti-Semitism so prevalent in Austria at this time, although no specific team emerged to challenge them on an anti-Semitic basis.

In view of the fate that awaited them, it is impossible to overestimate the reality of race hatred against the Jews of Europe, and ridiculous to claim that the insults at football matches involving Jewish teams was no more than '90-minute racism', but there were occasions when winning rose above prejudice, giving pause to question the depth of feeling behind the chants and slogans voiced at sports meetings. One fan whose team was saved from relegation by a Hakoah victory, and who was more used to expressions like 'filthy pigs' when referring to Jews, congratulated Hakoah with a mumbled, 'Well done, Herr Jew.' And it was not unknown in games between two Jewish teams for the followers of one or other to let loose insults that in any other situation would have been denounced as anti-Semitic.[5]

The closest Europe came to a local derby based on anti-Semitism was with Ferencvaros and MTK in Hungary. Ferencvaros, or 'Fradi' as they are popularly known, were a Catholic and more working-class team, and their rivalry with MTK, one of Hungary's first clubs, had a strong anti-Semitic streak. MTK went the way of other Jewish teams in Europe when the Nazis and their allies came to power, and when the Communists took over in the years following the defeat of the Nazis, neither MTK nor Fradi was in favour, the one for its bourgeois origins, the other for its association with fascism. In the Netherlands, several Jews were involved in the founding of Ajax Amsterdam, but they have never been a particularly Jewish team, no more so than Tottenham Hotspur in England, whose Jewish connections are incidental. In the contemporary fashion for football hooligans to take on Nazi postures, Ajax have been denounced as 'Yids', a title that many Ajax supporters have been happy to accept, even though they are not Jewish. And no team in the Netherlands ever looked like gaining fame because it hated Jews. In Hungary Ferencvaros fans have renewed full-throated anti-Semitism in their terracing repertoire, an indication as much as anything of the sad state into which a once great football nation has sunk. And so far as Jews having to disprove that they are physical or moral cowards is concerned, the establishment and subsequent history of the state of Israel in 1948 has put paid to that stereotype.

CATALANS AND BASQUES

It is in Spain that the most intense football rivalries based on ethnic identity have been formed, particularly with those clubs that represented the separatist ambitions of the Catalans and the Basques. These reached a new intensity when General Franco, whose one redeeming grace was that he genuinely loved football, promoted Real Madrid as the regime's ambassador abroad and the champion of Castilian centralism at home. He was much more successful in convincing the innocent abroad that his regime was a reflection of the all-white purity of one of the greatest teams in the history of the game; but at home the Catalans and the Basques were not won over to the regime that came to power, after three years of civil war, in 1939.

Franco, especially through his friend Santiago Bernabeu, who had devoted all of his adult life to the club, favoured Real Madrid. He fed his impoverished subjects a constant feast of football: non-stop games from South America on television on May Day, the traditional day for workers' celebrations; newspapers using up to six times their space on sport in preference to politics; and overall a general policy of 'foot-ballising' the masses in the hope that their minds might be taken up with matters other than their misery. Against the rebellious provinces Franco was pitiless in his attempts to impose his dictatorship. He banned the

Catalan and Basque clubs from displaying symbols of their ethnic identities, forced them to change their names, usually from the English origins to Spanish, and forbade the use of the Catalan and Basque languages. This was impossible to carry out in the culture of football, and under the protection of the crowds at the stadiums FC Barcelona (CF Barcelona under Franco: that is Club de Fútbol instead of Fútbol Club – originally Foot-Ball Club) in Catalunya and Athletic (Atlético under Franco) Bilbao flaunted the colours and chanted their provincial slogans and hatred of Madrid. Since Franco's death in November 1975, however, much of the Barcelona/Real Madrid rivalry is based on sporting success. Under the dictatorship – and even before – it was not so, and provincial pride underscored all games between El Barça and El Madrid.

FC Barcelona's community identity with Catalunya is one of the most deep-seated and mutually supportive in the game, although not all of its supporters would agree with the goals of the more extreme separatists, especially since the restoration of local privileges to the 'autonomous provinces' in the new Constitution of 1978. The Catalan national identity can be compared more readily to Scottish national ambitions than to those of a local club, and unlike Celtic who refused to have their jerseys numbered because it sullied the hoops, but surrendered when it came to commercial graffiti, Barcelona have refused, despite the millions this would bring in, to have the colours of Catalan pride besmirched by a sponsor's name. The makers of the shirt have an identifiable logo, however, and in the world of commercial exclusives this played a role in the astronomical sums offered to the young Brazilian superstar, Ronaldo, where a rival shirt maker was involved in subsidising the fortune that could have taken him to Rangers, except that he chose the less lucrative but more competitive Italian League and Inter Milan.

If Barcelona's identity can in some way be compared to that of Scottish nationalist ambitions, those of the Basque clubs perhaps bear some resemblance to that for a united and republican Ireland: certainly that is how the Irish Republican Army like to see it, and in February 1996 an IRA spokesman appeared at a meeting in support of Basque independence at the stadium of Athletic Bilbao, a meeting in which Basque terrorists (ETA) were to the forefront with their familiar black hoods and guns. It is also how the pro-IRA Celtic fanzine *Tiocfaidh Ar La* sees it, praising their militancy and the killings that have accompanied their struggle for independence – presumably down to the murder in July 1997 of the young politician held as a hostage and whose death brought millions of angry Spaniards together as no other event had done. *TAL* encouraged Celtic supporters to take an interest in the Basque struggle, and when watching Basque clubs on television to give them a shout of

'Gora ETA Militar', the equivalent to 'Up the 'Ra' (Militar (M) being the equivalent of P for Provisional in the IRA).[6]

Basque claims to independence are stronger than those of either the Scots, the Irish or the Catalans, in that their culture is based on a language totally different from that of the Castilian centralists. Not surprisingly then, the Basque clubs are even more fiercely independent, and for a long time most of them refused to employ anyone who was not a Basque. Unlike Rangers, who surrendered their all-Protestant identity in 1989, Athletic Bilbao refused, even under threat of relegation, to bring in non-Basque players to help the club.

Bilbao's strict Basques-only policy began in 1919, 21 years after the foundation of the club, and not only was it restricted to Basques, but Basques born in the province of Vizcaya, that is to say players born within 80km of the club, a population of about three million. Not only that, but the players had to have parents and grandparents born in the region. Despite this policy, they have never been out of the Spanish First Division and have been the most successful of the Basque clubs; in recent years, however, when they have been threatened with relegation, they have relaxed their policies and play Basques without restriction, even French Basques.

The other powerful Basque club, Real Sociedad de Saint Sebastian, had a Basques-only policy, but this included anyone born in the Basque country, so that the son of an immigrant could be accepted. This has relaxed even further in recent years, and like Bilbao they have always been prepared to employ foreign coaches or managers, which they see as an honour to the club. (Even in the more enlightened commercial days in Scotland one might wonder whether Rangers supporters would regard the appointment of a Catholic manager as an honour.)

FC Barcelona, on the other hand, have welcomed foreign players and coaches since their inception in 1899, and despite teams that have included few Catalans over the years, this has in no way affected the club's Catalan identity. The club has nurtured a healthy relationship with the community, and once a week the stadium and its magnificent museum are open for free to the public. In Scotland, Celtic found early in their history that Protestants playing for the club did not dilute their Catholic identity; it is only in the past decade or so, however, that Rangers have found out what others had been telling them for years: that Catholics or even Englishmen in the team's colours would not destroy what they stood for.

The Spanish game has other notable reflections of the situation in Scotland. Although one of the wealthiest regions in Spain, and although FC Barcelona has for a long time been one of the richest football teams in the world, it has suffered from a persecution complex developing into a paranoia that goes back to 1911 and has lasted even into the time of Johann Cruyff. There are no cries of 'masonic conspiracy' here, as regularly accompany setbacks to Celtic in Scotland, especially as the most prejudiced treatment against Barcelona came in Franco's time, when freemasonry was crushed with a fanatical fury. 'Political refereeing' even gave rise to a new word in the Spanish language: a *'Gureceta'* for an outrageous refereeing decision. It came from a quarter-final second leg Cup game in June 1970, when Emilio Gureceta, the referee in charge of the game, awarded a penalty to Real Madrid against Barcelona for a foul committed well outside the penalty area.[7]

In recent years, presidents of Barcelona and Real Madrid have refused to be seen inside each other's stadiums, but while Rangers and Celtic directors have often felt uncomfortable as guests at away games, and at the beginning of 1998 antagonisms between the owners of the two clubs surfaced in the press, the closest either club has come to a ban on the other was on one occasion when David Murray, the Rangers chairman, refused entry to Celtic supporters.

One thing the Basques, Catalans and Castilians have in common, however, is their faith. They have private chapels in their grounds; the players can cross themselves to their heart's content anywhere they like, and they are even proud to have the Pope as one of their members. Only in Scotland (and to a lesser degree Northern Ireland) did a team of specific ethnic, in this case religious, origins, draw a single rival based on opposition to these origins. The strength of Glasgow Rangers grew and fed on its anti-Catholicism, which in turn stoked the fires of Irish nationalist and religious passions, to create the aptly named business based on bigotry. For a long time, indeed until the 1980s, this was a profitable concern. Now it is the business that comes first and the crowds who are filling the remodelled stadiums at Ibrox and Parkhead come for the spectacle and not to satisfy some basic tribal urge. Or so the new management hopes.

THE HATE THAT SURPASSES ALL UNDERSTANDING

Even if the religious divisions of Celtic and Rangers were to become irrelevant, the rivalry between the two big clubs would continue to be accompanied by a mutual hatred: it seems to be the way of the world and an inescapable element in the human spirit. Count Otto von Bismarck, the Prussian architect of a unified Germany in 1871, once remarked that he was sustained in his life by two things: the love of his wife and his hatred for Ludwig Windthorst, the leader of the (Catholic) Centre Party.

For all the devotion that fans claim to have for a particular team, this is a love that often has to be nurtured by hatred of a close rival. At times this can reveal a sickness that has more to do with the psyche than football: Torino fans praising those of Liverpool for killing Juventus fans at the Heysel in 1985; Liverpool fans abusing those of Manchester United with reminders of the dead bodies on the runway in Munich in 1958; Nigerian players taunting Ethiopians with gestures to their mouths and stomachs mocking their hunger; London fans in the 1980s flaunting pound notes and designer underwear at the fans of clubs from the north of England; Italians from the north dismissing those from the south as 'niggers'; the list could go on, through to the Dutchman who claimed that the happiest moment in his life was after the World Cup final in 1974 when he heard that a German celebrating his country's victory over Holland had fallen from a balcony and killed himself.

Not so very far removed from Bismarck, then, was the Hearts fan with whom I shared 90 minutes of a Hearts–Hibs game shortly after the appearance of *The Old Firm* in October 1984. I was introduced to him soon after the game began as he urged Hearts to 'Get stuck into them fuckin' Taigs!' ('Taig' is an insulting word for a Catholic; 'Fenian' is more common in the West of Scotland) – and eyeballed me provocatively when I turned to see who was bellowing in my ear. This invitation to discuss the nature of sectarian rivalry took up much of the remainder of the match, and at some time in our debate the Taigs became Catholics. But as my new associate concluded, somewhat at a loss to explain in any positive way his attachment to Hearts (whom he saw as the capital's anti-Catholic equivalent to Rangers): 'You've got to hate somebody.'

Hitch your hatred to religion and you have a holy cause, and it doesn't matter whether you attend a particular church or are terribly concerned about the nature of the Trinity or the real presence at the mass. But it would also be wrong to ignore the religious elements in the support for the two teams: religion has always been about more than matters spiritual, and the hand of history that has hung over most countries is not so much dead as a source of sustenance in large parts of Scotland. The vast bulk of the Rangers support is Protestant, as that of Celtic is Catholic. That these terms should be used in a secular sense is not a contradiction in terms: logic or even sociological discourse over the nature of religion or class holds very little interest for most football fans, above all those of Celtic and Rangers. Few fans would want it otherwise.

2. A Catholic Comes to Ibrox

For some people the 'Glorious Twelfth' is in August and marks the opening of the grouse season; for those who know better, the 'Glorious Twelfth' is in July and commemorates the anniversary of the Battle of the Boyne, when King William of Orange defeated the deposed Catholic King James VII and preserved the kingdom from popery. It is an event remembered by some with more fervour than Independence Day in the United States, the famous Fourth of July, or the Fall of the Bastille in France, and all three were drawn together in 1989 for different reasons. In that year the Americans were still paying homage to the bicentenary of the introduction of their Constitution, while in France the nation was celebrating the bicentenary of the French Revolution which was about to reach its climax on 14 July; in Scotland, however, minds were fixed on other things as the sporting world still reeled from the events of 10 July, when the Rangers Football Club presented to an astonished media gathering their latest signing: former Celtic player Maurice 'Mo' Johnston, who claimed to be a Catholic and as such was of the faith that some Rangers fans, encouraged by the board, vowed should never darken the Protestant soul of the Ibrox club. He was not, as most reports said, Rangers' first Catholic signing, or even their first major signing who was a Catholic, but apart from two Catholics signed by accident and a couple of junior signings, one of whom, John Spencer, was on the brink of first team selection, he was Rangers' first Catholic player since the First World War.

The Scottish media duly concentrated on the actions of the extremists who demonstrated their disgust at the club's surrender of its principles and vowed never to have anything to do with the club while the Fenian played in its colours. But the media were also only too happy to praise Rangers for finally coming through on the promises they had been making for nearly two decades. Few stories in living memory had evoked such interest, and all that was lacking was the timing of the event: two days later, the 12th instead of the 10th, and the Rangers manager, no stranger to mischief-making, could have had more reason to smile at the furore all around him. Indeed the only story that had aroused comparative media attention had been the arrival at Ibrox just over three years previously of the manager himself: Graeme Souness, the man responsible for Johnston being signed.

SOUNESS VERSUS THE PAST

Graeme Souness's arrival as player-manager on 7 April 1986 heralded great changes at Scotland's biggest football club, as the new man wasted no time in preparing Rangers to join the ranks of the great teams not only in Britain but the rest of the world. He was given money to do so that surpassed the spending power of all previous Rangers managers combined. He signed Englishmen, including a black, then moved out to foreign fields to capture talent wherever it could be found. But, until Johnston, no Catholics. Souness was regarded with some suspicion on his arrival. His life abroad and his expensive tastes in clothing and toiletries were not what Glaswegians were used to; but suspicion about his taste in toiletries was as nought compared with the fears held by some that he was not a Rangers man and might take seriously his promise to sign players regardless of their religion.

Previous Rangers managers, like Willie Waddell, Jock Wallace and John Greig might have said they were willing to sign Catholics, but the faithful knew this was a smokescreen to confuse the media and keep the world body FIFA quiet, and that even if a Catholic were to be signed, as one of them said, there would be no way he would play for the team. Apart from his continental airs, Souness was married to a Catholic, and although she was divorced and as such in breach of the faith, she was bringing her children up as Catholics: there was no doubt that when Souness said he would sign players regardless of their religion, he was serious. He soon learned that this was not going to be as easy as he thought, and the word was passed gently to him to look in other directions. Faced by the dead hand of Scotland's religious past, Souness looked elsewhere, at least until the Rangers following could be prepared for the hammer-blow of 10 July 1989. Those unfamiliar with the situation in Scotland (and Northern Ireland) could only be amazed that such an apparently trivial matter could take on such titanic proportions, but it was merely the tip of an iceberg concealing a long history that had to be navigated with care.

It had begun nearly a century before, in the early 1890s, when the long-established Rangers became the first team to put a stop to the triumphal progress of the Celtic Football and Athletic Club, which had been founded just a few years earlier, following a meeting in St Mary's Hall, Calton, on 6 November 1887. From this moment the Catholic community of Glasgow invested their inexhaustible energy in the project, from the Archbishop who, as patron, headed the first appeal for subscriptions in January 1888, to the hundreds of unsung volunteers who constructed a playing field before there was even a team to play on it. Success on the field ensured the support of Catholics throughout Scotland and beyond. It was all the brainchild of Brother Walfrid, a Marist determined to keep the poor free from the temptations of Protestant soup kitchens and to provide a leisure occupation that would save them from apostasy in the dangerous years when they left school and had too much idle time on their hands. The club's pioneers were mainly first- or second-generation Irish, Scots who were happy to be called Irishmen, and the spectacular success of the Catholic club in its early years was a source of great joy to those Catholics of Irish origin who still had not been accepted into the bosom of Scottish society, and indeed often felt rejected by it. By the early 1890s many such Scots were already succeeding in the professions, but in football-mad Scotland, which had known many Catholic teams before the advent of Celtic, it was the triumphant successes of the new team from the east end of Glasgow that most boosted the pride of those who felt like outcastes in their own homeland.

Protestant Scots whose vision of the world was disturbed by the interlopers looked on with some concern, and when a saviour came in the shape of the Rangers Football Club, many of them, taking advantage of improved public transport – trams to take people across the city, ferries to cross the Clyde at Govan and Whiteinch, eventually a subway system that dropped them off right on the Ibrox doorstep – deserted their own teams to follow the one team capable of putting the Irishmen back in their places. That came in the 1893–94 season, when Rangers beat Celtic on four occasions out of the six games they played, losing only once. Rangers, founded in 1872, had progressed rapidly to challenge the giants of the time, Vale of Leven, Renton, Dumbarton and even Queen's Park, but at the time of the founding of Celtic they had struck a low ebb. However, under the growing influence of William Wilton, who was appointed match secretary in 1889, and with their success against the Irishmen, Rangers never looked back.

Both clubs soon saw the financial advantages in playing each other in games where the ethnic edge was clear cut, and it was this commercialism, which the amateur sports writers of the day found repellent, that led to the two clubs being branded 'The Old Firm' in a *Scottish Referee* cartoon of 1904. In the early days it was Celtic who were the more ethnically distinct, for while they were prepared to play Protestants, indeed could not have succeeded without them, the entire ambience of the club was Irish and Catholic: the first patron, whose appeal launched the club, was the archbishop of Glasgow, all the directors, as they would be until the 1990s, were Catholic, and the vast bulk of its supporters were Catholic. The club saw little need to conceal this, any more than it did the support of several of its leading players and directors for Irish nationalism, some of whom were to be found on public platforms supporting the cause. More publicly, the players' jerseys proclaimed the origins and ethos of the club: originally a white shirt with a green collar and the Celtic cross as a logo, this changed to vertical green and white stripes before the famous green and white hoops took over at the beginning of the 1903–4 season. Then there was the Irish flag flying over the ground, green with a gold harp until it was replaced by the tricolour of the Irish Free State after its bloody birth in 1921. Like the players' strips, it was an open proclamation of what the club stood for.

There was nothing religious in the origins of Rangers, and they were Protestant only in the sense that the vast majority of clubs in Scotland at this time were made up of Protestants. They began, as was the case with so many other clubs in the 1870s, out of a boys' kickabout. Like Queen's Park, Scotland's premier club, their founders came from the Highlands, but unlike Queen's Park who were associated with the Young Men's Christian Association, they had no particular religious connections. Rangers' founders came from the Gareloch, with just that bit more talent and organisational ability than the hundreds of other clubs springing up all over Scotland in the 1870s and 1880s. Games on the Glasgow Green, where they had to compete for space with dozens of other enthusiasts, gradually changed to more prestigious locations in the more prosperous south side of the Clyde before they built their own ground, called Ibrox Park, in 1887. They relocated to the present site in 1899, having built one of the finest sports stadiums in the land.

Being Protestant at this time did not necessarily mean being anti-Catholic, but it was frequently the case, and when this was linked to opposition to Irish Home Rule, the two could come together in a potent mix. Rangers were no more anti-Catholic than most clubs in Scotland in their early days, although some of their more prominent directors were freemasons and Unionists. The most notable of these was John Ure Primrose, an active freemason, Unionist and militant opponent of Irish Home Rule, who had a near lifelong relationship with the club and was chairman from 1913 until 1923, the year before he died. He is said to have committed the club to the masonic cause.[1] The year before Primrose became chairman, the anti-Catholic aspects of the club were given a boost when the Belfast shipbuilders Harland and Wolff, with their predominantly Protestant workforce, set up a yard in Govan. Like other giants of the heavy industries in Scotland, the owners were happy to appoint foremen who favoured fellow Protestants when employment was scarce. It was about this time that Rangers' practice of not signing Catholics gradually became a policy.

In the early years of the twentieth century Celtic had the best team in Scotland, possibly Britain, winning the League Championship six times in a row between 1905 and 1910. It was in an attempt to break this deadlock that Rangers signed several Catholics between 1906 and 1908, while Archie 'Punch' Kyle, who played for the club between 1904 and 1908, remains the longest-serving Catholic in Rangers' history, a fact omitted from all the histories of the club until recently. Eventually, from the time of the First World War, Rangers found that they could beat Celtic without Catholics – and in any case the dream of any young Catholic footballer was to play for Celtic. Similarly most young Protestant hopefuls set their sights on playing for 'the mighty Glasgow Rangers'.

In the inter-war period the 'no Catholics at Ibrox' policy strengthened: it never appeared in written form nor was it officially acknowledged by the club, but it was an open secret indulged by the media and welcomed by the supporters, a ban on Catholics that applied not just to players but to any employee of the club. Games between Celtic and Rangers became overlain with quasi-religious overtones and supercharged by the politics of Ulster, so that much of what happened on the field spilled over into the streets, and while the rest of Britain could enjoy its football in conditions of comparative calm, games between Rangers and Celtic became battles – not just rhetorical, and not just of days of yore (1690) – reflecting the tensions in Northern Ireland.

Little of this was to be reported in the secular (that is Protestant) press, which cherished Rangers as one of its own, and Catholics were left to express their grievances in their own papers, but before the reforms of Vatican II, most Catholics failed to see the ways in which their own Church discouraged too close relations with the Protestant community. Catholics certainly had to face prejudice in many areas and often suffered in terms of progress in certain professions, but it was the Vatican that set up the barriers to normal social interaction between Catholics and Protestants, because of its strictures on interdenominational marriages and through its insistence that young Catholics be educated in isolation from Protestants. Much of this was to change with the reforms of Pope John XXIII at Vatican II, when the Counter-Reformation, a relic from the past going back to the Council of Trent (1545–63) was finally brought to an end. The first duty of Catholics was still to follow the faith of their fathers and convert the heretic, but they were now free to travel the road to God along with other Christians, to be judged on what they were in themselves and not as children of the martyrs.[2] More practically, many married Catholics gave up the wearisome game of Vatican roulette and convinced themselves that they could engage in conjugal relations without having to pretend that their aim was to produce a child. It was confusing for the more conservative Catholics, but when later popes tried to crush the liberalism that had been unleashed, they found that it was too late to close the door to the modern world.

It was against this background that Rangers' refusal to sign Catholics began to come under criticism, especially as the Scottish game broadened out into Europe and British football fans showed the world a new brand of hooliganism. In cases involving Rangers fans the sectarian element added a new ingredient. In 1969 the troubles in Ulster, beginning with simple demands for basic human rights for Catholics, exploded into virtual civil war, and Rangers' anti-Catholic image as well as its well-publicised links with Ulster, became a target for a Scottish press that until then had effectively accepted Rangers' ban on Catholics. The matter was compounded when Jock Stein, himself a man of deep Protestant convictions, with family and friends of Orange sympathies (some of whom never spoke to him again after he joined Celtic, a fate shared by other Protestants who wore the colours of the Catholic club), took Celtic from 1965 into their glory days in domestic and European competitions.

In the meantime, the escalating violence in Ireland, and the highly publicised incidents of hooliganism involving Rangers fans, brought the club under a barrage of criticism from all quarters. Apart from a few principled shareholders at annual general meetings, however, the club did nothing about its anti-Catholic image, and the fans who objected to being branded as bigots because of this had to keep their collective anger to themselves. In the early 1960s some Celtic fans, in the spirit of the fanzines to come, published *The Shamrock*, a magazine with a pro-IRA stance that criticised the bumbling way in which the club was being run. Rangers, too, had had magazines put out by the supporters, most notably the *Rangers Review* that came out from April 1947 and then the *Rangers FC Supporters Club Annual* that virtually replaced it from 1950. But these fan magazines were generally deferential to the club, in complete contrast to *The Shamrock* and the fanzines that started to proliferate from 1987. Rangers fans were generally muzzled by the club tradition that silence was the best response to controversy, that the club, being bigger than the man, was always right. Indeed when the break with the past came it was from the club itself: the bigotry expressed in the Ibrox terracing was merely a cruder and more vociferous expression of the views in the boardroom, and the Rangers revolution had to begin there, with the clearing out of the old guard as a first step in modernising the club.

AWAKES THE GIANT FROM ITS SLUMBER

The fortunes of the Rangers Football Club on the eve of the Souness signing were about as low as they had ever been. Under Jock Wallace, who had become manager in 1972, Rangers broke the Celtic deadlock in 1975 and won two trebles in 1976 and 1978. But Wallace left in May 1978 after a bust-up with another of the club's stalwarts in upholding the 'traditions' of the club, the former star player and manager, Willie Waddell. Wallace was replaced by another dyed-in-the-blue Rangers man, John Greig, who in his first season came within eight minutes of achieving Rangers' third treble in four years, before a ten-man Celtic team scored twice to pip them for the 1979 Championship. But the burden was to prove too much for a young man thrust from being captain of the club to managing-director overnight, and all Rangers gained in the rest of the Greig years was a Scottish Cup victory against Dundee United in a replay in 1981 and a League Cup victory the following season. Greig resigned on 28 October 1983, saying he was finished with the game, but he could never leave Rangers and returned in 1990 as their public relations manager.

The first two choices for Greig's replacement were the men behind the remarkable resurgence of the New Firm of Aberdeen and Dundee United: Alex Ferguson and Jim McLean. Neither could be tempted, Ferguson it was said because he was married to a Catholic and had many Catholic friends, and as a former player was only too well aware of the club's feelings on this matter. The man most disappointed by McLean's rejection of the job was Walter Smith, his assistant, who was to have been part of the deal. Smith's time would come, however. In the end Rangers had to settle for Jock Wallace, who had always been the people's choice, a no-nonsense guts and determination manager whose attitude to Catholics playing for Rangers was well known. The second coming of Wallace was to offer no salvation, however: that would have to come from out of the deserts on the other side of the Atlantic, from Nevada, where Lawrence Marlborough, grandson of John Lawrence (the self-made millionaire known as 'Mr Rangers' who was chairman of the club from 1963 until he resigned for health reasons in 1973) had gone to live in 1983.

Lawrence Marlborough had little interest in football as a game, but he was a businessman and this was reflected in his decision to live in the United States. There he became attracted to the American sporting ethos, where clubs operated as money-making franchises owned by a single individual. It was a different world from that operating in Scotland, but from whatever angle he viewed the club in which he was a major shareholder, it was not maximising its commercial potential. And so he completed a share deal with the Rangers director, Jack Gillespie, in November 1985 that gave him a narrow majority on the board; in return, Gillespie was promised a place on the board for life. Marlborough went on to buy further shares that lifted his control to nearly 66 per cent. It was not done without a few cross words, but his power now allowed him to bring about a bloodless coup whereby three directors were removed in February 1986 and the chairman since January 1984, lifetime Rangers man John Paton, was replaced by David Holmes, an employee from Marlborough's own company, John Lawrence (Glasgow) Ltd. Holmes, who combined the posts of chairman and chief executive, was in his private life a Falkirk supporter, and in the revitalised Ibrox business credentials rather than the traditional faith were the first prerequisites. As Holmes set about modernising the club, however, he insisted that 'Rangers belong to the people'. His greatest success was his first: the signing of Graeme Souness, then playing for Sampdoria in Italy.

SOUNESS TAKES UP THE CHALLENGE

Souness came out of the east, like several of his most distinguished forerunners: the legendary Bill Struth himself came from Edinburgh and later moved to Fife; Willie Woodburn also came from the capital, as did John Greig, who as a youngster of 16 when he signed for the club was in tears that it was Rangers and not his own club Hearts that had signed him. Souness, too, came from the capital, but his was a different world, even from that of Greig, who had been born a mere eleven years before him. Born on 6 May 1953, he was endowed with a fair football talent but even more a deep faith in his own abilities. His career became that of the fabled prefab to penthouse, as he left behind his humble beginnings to bestride the international stage with arrogance and class, making an independent fortune that was further boosted when the glazier's son married the daughter of a Liverpool retail millionaire in 1980. His playing career before 1986 was entirely outside Scotland: he openly professed that he was a football mercenary who would play for whoever offered him most money, and in this regard he was quoted as saying he wished he had been born in England.

As a youngster Souness was a lukewarm Hearts supporter with little interest in Rangers. At barely 17 he constantly criticised the manager of Spurs for not playing him in the first team and as a result was sent to Middlesbrough where he had an unhappy spell before signing on in 1978 for a Liverpool team about to reach the peak of its outstanding progress. There he gained a reputation as a world-class player, and following

Liverpool's victory on penalties over Roma in the European Cup final in 1984 he went to Sampdoria, not, as most players unctuously claim, to take on new challenges, but as a tax exile. In Italy, unlike many British footballers before him, he felt very much at home in wine bars and classy restaurants rather than drinking in pubs and eating take-away kebabs. In a Scottish jersey he was as committed to the colours as any home-based Scot, a skilled player whose physical approach was in the tradition of Sammy Cox, 'Tiger' Shaw and Bobby Shearer, added to which was an elegance and a cynical violence that made even his own team-mates wince.

Souness made no secret of his Conservative and royalist opinions, and this would cause no trouble inside the walls at Ibrox or among a large number on the terracings. But he was a winner, so committed to coming out on top that it did not matter to him even if he did so with the help of Catholics – he had even played alongside them, at Liverpool and in Italy, while they were not unknown in the Scottish team. Like anyone with an experience of the game beyond Scotland, he knew that the religion or politics of the men wearing the jersey was irrelevant, and as the entire history of the game has shown, with the exceptions of the isolated cases of Rangers and the Basques, the fans of any team are above all concerned about victory: English clubs had welcomed the foreigners from north of the border in the 1880s, and those that queried the social or national origins of their players were soon left behind; Italy and Spain had always signed foreigners with abandon, and the socially sensitive clubs of South America in the 1920s and 1930s had had to swallow their racism and accept blacks. Today, to the benefit of the player if not the country he has left, Europe is home to the best footballing talent of the world, an expression of the desire of individuals to compete at the highest level and the technological changes that make it possible for them to reveal their talents on a global basis.

In 1986 this was not as obvious as it would become even a few years later, so that when Souness went across the border to plunder players from England he took the Scottish sporting public by surprise. Not only did he sign Englishmen, but he signed top-class Englishmen, two of them current internationalists, willing to play for a recognised inter-national manager, on higher salaries than they could earn in England, and above all with the prospect of playing in Europe from which they had been banned after the Heysel tragedy of 1985. Until Souness the traffic had been virtually all one way across the border, and many Scots took some delight in the process being reversed: never since Falkirk signed Syd Puddefoot from West Ham in 1922 for £5,000 had any Scottish club paid such a fantastic sum of money for an English player.

Several Catholic players were on the market at this time, and the grape-vine quivered with rumours as to who had been approached and who would be the first one to sign.

One of the first was Alistair Dick, a Scottish youth internationalist then with Spurs, but his family leaked the story to the press, complete with a picture of the young Dick wearing a crucifix around his neck, and so the club dropped the idea. Glasgow-born Catholic, Ray Houghton, then playing for Oxford United, was the first Catholic to be made an offer by Souness, but he was only too well aware of the situation in Glasgow, and went on to sign for Liverpool, while on the international stage he chose to play for Ireland rather than Scotland – his father came from Donegal. Souness also admitted trying to sign Derek Statham of West Bromwich Albion and another Catholic whom he would not name. This was probably Ian Rush, the deadly Welsh striker and former team-mate of Souness at Liverpool, but who was also known at Ibrox to have admitted that one of his lifelong ambitions was to have an audience with the Pope. Rush was then having an unhappy time with Juventus, and when he returned to England in 1988 it was to his old club, despite an offer of £3 million from Souness, by far the most he had offered for a player until that time. Among other Catholics rumoured to have been linked to Rangers were Liam Brady, one of Ireland's finest ever players and later to become a Celtic manager, and Mirandinho, a Brazilian playing for Newcastle, who claimed that Rangers had approached him. And a month before the signing of Mo Johnston Souness tried to secure the signature of John Sheridan of Leeds United and Ireland.[3] Souness was perplexed at this refusal by the more vociferous fans to countenance Catholic players at Ibrox and asked in exasperation while on World Cup duty in Mexico in 1986: 'Do they want a sectarian team or a successful one?'[4]

By signing Englishmen, Souness eased the fears of the faithful, although some of the new arrivals, such as Mark Falco and Trevor Francis, were scrutinised for any giveaway signs that might reveal deep-felt beliefs, such as the parts of their body they touched or the school to which they sent their children. In Rangers' first major signing, Terry Butcher from Ipswich for £750,000, they had no such fears, although even he had to quash any lingering doubts with a public pronouncement that he was not a Catholic: Butcher was a Conservative, implacably opposed to the IRA and anything to do with 'Southern Ireland'. He refused to listen to the Irish pop group U2 for this reason, and when he found out that Jim Kerr of Simple Minds was a Celtic supporter he threw his collection of the band's tapes out of the window.[5] More to the point he was a great central defender, the captain of England who had knocked back an offer from Manchester United to play for Rangers. Along with the goalkeeper Chris Woods, who arrived at the same time from Norwich for £600,000, he formed the backbone of the new Rangers team. Others came and some went, for transfer fees that seemed outrageous at the time but which would appear like peanuts ten years later, while local Rangers stars, Ally McCoist and David Cooper, cursed that they had committed themselves to long-term contracts: Cooper had re-signed the year before Souness arrived and McCoist committed himself to a four-year contract in 1986. By the summer of 1989 Souness had spent nearly £12 million on 28 players, four of whom, Gary Stevens and Trevor Steven from Everton, Richard Gough from Spurs and Maurice Johnston from Nantes, each cost over £1 million.

THE NEW RANGERS

The English imports were welcomed, and Mark Hateley when he arrived in 1990 from Inter Milan – after a failed attempt to get him from Monaco in France in 1987 – soon found that his rumoured comparison of Glasgow with Beirut was as ridiculous as others knew it was – Brian Laudrup would later comment on how much friendlier the Rangers fans were compared to those of Fiorentina, who were as quick to abuse as they were to idolise. Hateley, after a troubled start, mainly caused by injury but not helped by suspicions that he was a Catholic, soon set up a match-winning partnership with Ibrox favourite Ally McCoist, and won over his critics in the East Enclosure with many match-winning performances. None of these players, however, touched the hearts of the Rangers fans the way certain other English players did: above all Graham Roberts, who came from Spurs for £450,000 in December 1986, and won over the fans with wholehearted displays that owed as much to physical commitment as skill. Like some other English imports he cheerily adopted what he saw to be the culture at Ibrox, and lost no friends for the rumoured stories of how he mimicked the Pope in post-match frolics. Above all he won undying fame when, deputising in goal for Woods, who had been sent off in an infamous Old Firm match in October 1987, he conducted the crowd behind the goal in a few choruses of 'The Sash', a piece of pantomime that would not be lost on Paul Gascoigne when he joined the club a few years later. Butcher was also instructed in how to win over the fans, and received an ovation when he visited the Larkhall Rangers Supporters Club and opened with the immortal phrase: 'No Surrender!'

Souness might have been a Unionist and a royalist, but he could make no sense of the anti-Catholicism that hung around the club. Shortly after he arrived, he could not believe the despondency of the players in the

41

dressing-room when in the last game of the 1985–86 season Rangers won a UEFA place in Europe, but then the news came through that Celtic had won the League. About the same time he made a statement he had to go back on in the official *Rangers News* a couple of years later, when he said: 'I don't care if we lose four times a year to Celtic as long as we still win the League.'

Despite all this, the Rangers fans were returning to Ibrox in droves. On 9 May 1986, the night before the Scottish Cup final between Hearts and Aberdeen, Rangers played in the Glasgow Cup final, a fixture that would normally attract a few thousand out to see the club's young hopefuls, but on this occasion it was a sell-out. That it was against Celtic was one of the reasons for this, but more important was the possibility that the new man might make an appearance on the field that night. The pre-season friendlies in the summer of 1986 had to be made all-ticket games, but not only were the fans coming back, they were coming back with a commitment to the club that denied frequently repeated accusations – and by Rangers people themselves – about them being fickle. Nowhere was this better demonstrated than when thousands stayed behind to cheer the club after defeats in Europe, but above all at the end of the 1989 Scottish Cup final when Rangers lost 0–1 to Celtic and the Rangers support refused to leave the ground. So enthusiastic was their support for their losing team that the post-match interviews with the Celtic captain had as a musical background the sound of the massed choir from the terracing belting out 'The Sash' and other songs of joy.

Souness's first two signings were among his best. One was to end transfer speculation surrounding the fate of Ally McCoist by securing the young star to a four-year contract. The other, not strictly speaking a Souness 'signing', but which needed his approval when he was suggested by Holmes, was the appointment of Walter Smith as assistant manager. Smith, whose dream as a youth was to play for Rangers, had to make do with a career with Dundee United, first as an iron-clad defender then as an assistant to Jim McLean, a manager whose success with the limited financial resources at his disposal must entitle him to be ranked among the greatest managers in Scottish football. Smith was 18 when he signed for the Tannadice club in 1966, and completed an apprenticeship as an electrician while playing part-time football. After 18 months with Dumbarton from September 1975 he returned to Dundee United where McLean took the thoughtful young footballer under his wing. Smith was desperately disappointed when McLean knocked back the Ibrox offer in 1983, and when the second opportunity came he had no hesitation in accepting it. In February 1986 Smith was approached about partnering

Souness in the new Rangers, and although he had ambitions to become a manager and had indeed been approached regarding the top job at Motherwell, St Johnstone and St Mirren, he had no hesitation in joining Rangers. Souness could not have succeeded without the right-hand man who knew the Scottish game intimately, while the calm and outwardly affable Smith offered a counterweight to the volatile and confrontationist Souness. Smith's salary as assistant was much greater than he could ever have expected at Dundee United, and more than he would have received even as manager of most Scottish clubs, while his partnership with Souness paid off when he succeeded him in April 1991 and went on to lead the club to its historic nine League titles in a row.

There was one other signing that in a different sense was more significant than that of the two Rangers stalwarts: Mark Walters. In most countries in the Anglo-Saxon world a 'mixed marriage' is one between people of different races: it is perhaps only in Scotland and Ireland that the notion of a mixed marriage is immediately taken to be one between people of different religions, religious bigotry often being regarded in Scotland as stronger than racial prejudice. However that may be, Scotland is no more immune to racial prejudice than other countries, and while racial chants fouled the air at many English grounds in the early 1980s as more and more teams took advantage of the skills of native-born players of Afro-Caribbean background, there is little ground to believe that the situation would have been any different in Scotland. The reception of blacks playing for English teams in pre-season friendlies was at times poisonous, and it is for such reasons that Souness's signing of black player Mark Walters from Aston Villa for £500,000 in late 1987, must go down as one of his bravest signings. Securing the signature of two Jews, the Israelis Avi Cohen and Bonni Ginzburg from Macabbi Tel Aviv, was of no great moment.

Walters was a gifted player, but this would not have protected him from his colour if he had not been wearing a Rangers jersey, or if the club had not given Souness its complete backing. As it is, Rangers fans who did abuse the newcomer were immediately banned from the ground, while the official *Rangers News* came out strongly against anyone who criticised the signing. Unofficially, the new Rangers fanzine, *Follow, Follow*, placed Walters on the cover of its first number with an editorial saying that 'Blue is the only colour that counts', a policy that it would follow in all subsequent editions. In his first game against Celtic at Parkhead on 2 January 1988, Walters was met by monkey chants and a shower of bananas, but at Ibrox he was protected by the club and its supporters, and those whose neanderthal tendencies urged them to join in the chants of the opposition just had to contain themselves.

Some transposed their racism to the 'one of ours' variety, as in the Skol Cup final against Celtic in October 1990, when Celtic's coloured player Paul Elliott fouled a Rangers player and was met by the tirade from a Rangers fan to the effect that: 'You're no' even a real black! You're no' even a real darkie! At least we've got a proper nigger! Mark Walters is black! You're just coffee-coloured!'[6] Among Celtic fans a similar racism could be found in the woman at a Celtic–Hibernian game some years later who pointed at Hibs player Kevin Harper and asked her companion in a matter of fact way: 'Who's the wee coon?' only to be told that there was nothing to worry about as 'Wee Harper's all right. He's a Mick.'[7] Signing Catholics was another matter. And given Scotland's history, understandably so. But the time had to come. Most people expected a highly rated foreign Catholic – it had long been a joke about what would have happened to a Maradona or a Pele or any of the big Italian or Spanish stars who were Catholics, if Rangers had wanted to sign them. In the 1970s this was not on, by the late 1980s it was, and it was from the ranks of one such foreigner, English or Latin, that most observers thought that Rangers would bow to the inevitable. Instead Souness dropped a bombshell. It was one thing for him to pick a Scottish-born Catholic, and one with a well-publicised hatred of the club, but to sign one who had played for Celtic and claimed to be a true Tim, a Bhoy to his bootstraps, was going beyond the pale. But there he was before the TV cameras on 10 July 1989, looking somewhat sheepish beside a smirking Graeme Souness. As well might Souness have been grinning, for not only had he taken the Scottish public by surprise, he had put one over Celtic. Indeed there was more gnashing of teeth outside Celtic Park than there was burning of scarves outside Ibrox.

MO SURRENDER

On 12 May 1989, as Celtic prepared for their coming Scottish Cup final against Rangers, Johnston appeared before the cameras at Celtic Park in a Celtic jersey professing his love for the club his heart had never left throughout his spell with French club Nantes. The board and the Celtic fans were delighted, but over the next few weeks there developed 'snags' which deteriorated into bickering and threats of legal action over whether or not Johnston was a Celtic player. There were rumours of him going to Rangers and some bets were even taken on this, but on 25 June Johnston categorically denied that he would join them. On 1 July his contract with Celtic was withdrawn, and it was then that Souness moved in for the kill. The Celtic board was shown up in a bad light, acting like amateurs and giving the appearance that they had lost the player because they would not meet his financial demands, conditions that Rangers had no trouble in agreeing to.

Johnston was not what many Catholics would be proud to accept as one of their own, as his observance of the faith was minimal and his behaviour not that of which the devout would be proud: in this regard he was no Paul McStay or Tommy Burns. Indeed his father was a Protestant, a lifelong Rangers supporter, but he had married a Catholic and had allowed his son to go to a Catholic school. Tainted by his education, Johnston had taunted Rangers fans when he crossed himself in front of them after being sent off in the final of an Old Firm League Cup final on 26 October 1986, and in a biography published in 1988 he declared his hatred of Rangers for their policy on Catholics. In Rangers terms, then, he was a Catholic, and as such a standing insult to the hard core of the Rangers support; worse, he had worn the colours of the Irish/Catholic club, and in the eyes of some Rangers supporters this was as bad as being a Catholic. But against this the more rational Rangers supporters could rejoice in the way Souness had once more embarrassed their rivals, having snatched their prize catch from under their noses. And even among some diehards this not only made the signing more palatable, it was a consolation devoutly to be savoured: the Tims had been stuffed again!

The more immediate reaction was less philosophical, and the TV cameras lined up to see the more outraged Rangers fans arrive at Ibrox to perform the anticipated rituals of scarf-burning and tearing up their season-ticket books; among the other moments of high drama was when a car pulled up outside the ground and laid a wreath mourning the loss of '116 years of tradition'. There were some angry scenes, especially when Souness appeared, but most of the fans milling around were simply stunned. Union Jacks appeared with 'No Mo Here' on them, and a sign saying 'Traitor's Gate' was hung over the main entrance to Ibrox. On the wall near the M8 motorway, FUCK YOUR MO SURRENDER was painted in big, block letters by Celtic fans for the benefit of passing motorists – in the press the expletive was removed out of respect for their more gentle readers.

In fact there were only about 30 calls by fans asking for refunds on their season tickets, while others called in anxiously inquiring about a new season book to replace the one that had either been lost or accidentally damaged. David Miller, secretary of the Rangers Supporters Association, who was shocked by the signing, expressed his disapproval in a less than convincing statement that this was more for it being Johnston than for him being a Catholic. At the club's AGM held in the Broomloan Stand at Ibrox in August, however, the angry interjections

45

were outdone by the applause from the 2,000 shareholders when the chief executive, Alan Montgomery, blamed separate schools for religious bigotry, and the biggest cheer of all went to Graeme Souness when he explained why he had signed Johnston: he wanted Rangers to be the best. Some Rangers supporters clubs promised never to appear at any game in which Johnston played, while other Rangers fans ludicrously refused to recognise the results in games in which he played – and therefore that Rangers did not win the League in the 1989–90 season. More rationally, a few Rangers fans refused to go back to Ibrox while Johnston was there, but this proved too much for some, who later went along in disguise: the pain of staying away was too much. Rangers continued to play before a full house and there was no serious trouble between pro- and anti-Johnston Rangers supporters such as greeted the signing of Manfredonia for Roma in Italy. At Ibrox it hardly got worse than one section of the East Enclosure singing: 'Mo, Mo, Super Mo, Super Maurice Johnston', while another part sang: 'Mo, Mo, Fuck your Mo, Fuck your Maurice Johnston'. The whole saga was perhaps best summed up seven years later by the Rangers fan in the Rosevale pub in Partick who told the reporter of the London-based magazine *Shoot*: 'My great-grandfather wouldn't have been able to imagine such a thing. My grandad would have been furious. My dad was uneasy about it. Myself? I don't mind who we sign as long as they can play football. And for my son it won't even be an issue.'[8]

The most outspoken opposition to the Johnston signing came from the 'traditional' areas, although they were depleted as the hardliners had already left for Ireland and the big celebrations on the Twelfth. In Northern Ireland itself a meeting of the Glasgow Rangers Supporters Clubs was held in the Whitehead Rangers Club on 23 July 1989, with invitations for two representatives from each of the 97 clubs in Ulster to attend. The packed meeting placed an immediate ban on travel to Ibrox while Johnston was with the club, which affected the 400 regulars who went to the games; they also called on their 6,000 members to boycott Rangers' commercial products and participation in the Rangers Pools. The meeting was anxious to clear itself of any charge of bigotry, claiming reasonably enough that Johnston had treated Rangers with contempt and they were just returning the compliment, but went on to make the rather contradictory statement that their opposition was not to Johnston being a Catholic, but to the breaking of one of Rangers' main traditions.[9]

Among Rangers' Scottish players there was some resentment. A few years later Terry Butcher told how the Rangers kit-man refused to set out Johnston's gear with the other players', or to give him the chocolate bars that were distributed to them. These duties then fell to Butcher as captain, who also noted that the Scottish players found it harder to accept Johnston than the English, above all for the reaction among their friends.[10] Johnston had had troubles enough living in Glasgow before he left Celtic for France, and so he was provided with a safe house in Edinburgh, in fact Graeme Souness's which was empty at the time, with minders to ensure his safety when he made any public appearances. Unlike Salman Rushdie, who at this time was in hiding from the Ayatollah's *fatwa*, Johnston was in hiding from both sides of the religious divide.

Johnston was immediately branded a Judas by the (more polite) Celtic supporters, and a host of jokes appeared along this theme, although one of the best appeared in *Follow, Follow*, where the Rangers fanzine had a cartoon of Johnston confessing before a priest: 'Forgive me, father, for I have signed'.[11] The Celtic fanzines, in honour of his time in France, dubbed Johnston '*le petit merde*' (the little shit), and 35 members of the New Stevenson Celtic Supporters Club, near Motherwell, petitioned to have its name changed to the 'We Hate Mo Johnston CSC'. A *Herald* photographer caught the Union flag at half-mast at Celtic Park on the day of the deed, and asked, tongue-in-cheek, whether this was inadvertence, recognition of the death of Laurence Olivier who had just died, or just a sign of the general distress at the club.[12] And the *Rangers News* was surely not being serious when it reminded its loyal readers in a front-page editorial that Johnston 'was a player who had entertained the Ibrox faithful in the past with his on-the-field skills'.[13] The readers of *Follow, Follow* were evenly split on the matter, but the Major, one of the fanzine's regular contributors, was not amused. In signing 'the wee beggar rat-bag' he claimed some years after the event, the club had 'broken the mould' and for that he could never forgive Souness.[14] On the other hand, the history of the club, co-authored by one of its most devoted fans, makes the enigmatic statement that Souness 'failed to change the nature of things. He was bucking the Scottish establishment, and the Scottish establishment is blue.'[15]

The fans at Ibrox tried to get behind Johnston, and it helped when he scored the only goal against Celtic two minutes from the end of an otherwise undistinguished Old Firm game on 4 November 1989. It also helped that Johnston had a phlegmatic personality with no serious interest in religion or issues beyond the most basic. In this he was like the black American baseball player, Jackie Robinson, who was used to break down the racial barrier in the game in the US when he was signed by the Brooklyn Dodgers in 1947. Robinson had the necessary temperament to withstand the abuse he would expect to receive, in his case from his team-mates as much as from his opponents, as well as the fans from both sides, *all* of whom would be against him. Johnston's problems were minor in comparison and in 1989 the vast majority of the Scottish football public welcomed the Ibrox breakthrough.

But Johnston never really fitted in: singing 'The Sash' or mimicking a flute-player would have done little to help his particular reputation, and in November 1991, having lost his first team place, he left for Everton and subsequently a host of other teams. His departure from Ibrox was without any regrets, but nor were there any recriminations: he had, after all, been one of Souness's most successful signings after his first year. Above all, and to the surprise of none but those who had held bitterly to the exclusion of Catholics before Souness, Rangers had signed and played a Catholic and the world continued to turn on its normal axis.

A NEW BEAR AT IBROX

On a regular basis after the arrival of Souness, Rangers supplied the press with a continuous stream of stories, on the field, off the field and behind the scenes. The most startling of these was when it was announced in November 1988 that Lawrence Marlborough's shares in Rangers had been bought up by a hitherto little-known financial genius called David Murray. Like Souness, the 'whiz kid who snapped up the Gers' had had no previous association with the club, but he soon established his personality in such a way that he won over the most cynical of the Rangers followers as he acted in accordance with his claim to hold Rangers in a custodial relationship, rather than as a property from which he would make a profit.

Murray was born in Ayr, and was rejected twice by his home town club, first when he played in a trial match as a youngster (after which he went on to play rugby), then with an offer to buy it early in 1988, rejected because he was deemed 'too volatile'. Failing to buy Ayr and take them to who knows what heights, he had to make do with a second choice and buy Rangers. His interest in Rangers came through his friend and neighbour, Graeme Souness, who alerted him to the possibility of the Marlborough shares becoming available, and who later claimed Murray as his best-ever signing. On 18 November the first steps were taken and the deal was completed within the week, a certain urgency entering the negotiations when it was heard that the grasping hands of Robert Maxwell were closing in. This was the second time that the fate of Rangers and the criminal then posing as a public benefactor crossed; before Holmes, Maxwell had offered the position of player-manager at Oxford United to Souness.[16] For £6 million Murray had a bargain, although the club was in the red to the same amount, and Souness showed his faith in the future by pledging £600,000 of his own money: in his own words this was his pledge of a lifelong commitment to the club. It was an ideal partnership to keep Rangers to the fore in the world of international finance and, hopefully, on the international football scene.

Murray's father had been a coal merchant and a gambler, which had led to a divorce and his son having to move from Fettes College in Edinburgh back to the state system, so that while he became one of Scotland's richest capitalists he did not fit easily into a conservative right-wing mould. He was named as a likely chairman of the Scottish Conservative Party, but has stated that none of his companies, including Rangers, has ever contributed funds to the Tory Party; he has also retained a social conscience that saw him defend public utilities in the face of privatisation. Moreover, although a convinced Unionist he has remained committed to the development of specifically Scottish businesses.

Murray's business career began in 1969 when he started work for £7 a week in his uncle's metal dealing firm in Edinburgh, but four years later he had branched out on his own. By 1976, when he was seriously injured in a horrific car accident that put paid to any of his sporting ambitions, his firm, Murray International Metals was turning over £2 million annually with a £100,000 profit. In 1982 Murray sold 10 per cent of his steel-broking firm for £1.5 million and two years later won the Scottish Business Achiever's Award. When Murray International Holdings (MIH) bought Rangers the company controlled a network of 36 companies with an annual turnover of £90 million. Murray by then had branched out into several fields, including the leisure industry, but made money mostly on buying and selling property – in view of his father's experience, however, not as a gambler, but by taking calculated risks.

Murray's upbringing in Ayr had given him a liking for football. But at Fettes College in Edinburgh he found rugby more suitable to his social tastes and his financial ambition: there were more useful contacts to be made in rugby than in football circles. Many of his old rugby mates work for MIH, and the deal with Rangers was nothing great in commercial terms, but like Berlusconi with his multi-million dollar empire and a football team that accounted for only a fraction of his profits, there was more esteem to be gained from the ownership of a club that was the pride of the neighbourhood than the ownership of any number of television stations, retail outlets or metal businesses.

The new Souness-Murray partnership was the public face of Rangers, and while it gave most of the club's supporters a sense of pride in a stadium and players who could match the best from anywhere in the world, there were doubts held by some about how far the club had been taken from its roots, not just in the dilution of its Protestantism, but the way in which it was getting away from the ordinary fan with whom the club had always associated itself. Some at the club were happy to get rid of what they called the scum, and the finances of the club dictated that it pander to the new-found middle-class clientele who like to be associated with success, but misgivings were felt by the true Bears whose territory in the East Enclosure was about to be converted to seating. In the battle between the Camel Coats with season-tickets and the Bears who could only afford to pay on the day, there was no contest. Murray insisted that the fans had to be part of his ambitions for Rangers and Ibrox, but in practice this meant the richer fans, and increasingly so as the years went on. But whatever the rumblings of discontent from those who saw themselves as the true fans, there was always consolation to be found in the embarrassment that Rangers' success caused the Tims at the other end of the city, not only in the players who bestrode the Ibrox turf, but the ever-improving Ibrox stadium. Scarcely was Murray in control of the club than he was announcing new plans for the stadium which would take the club well into the twenty-first century. At Celtic Park concern about the failure to match their rivals was stilled by success on the field in 1988 and 1989, but the respite was little more than a lull in what for a long time was a one-sided battle.

3. The End of the Biscuit Tin

Celtic completed their centenary season in triumphant fashion, with a League and Cup double on the field, and off it a brilliant stage production of the club's history, 'The Celtic Story', which played before enthusiastic audiences at Glasgow's Pavilion theatre throughout most of May and June 1988. The following year they won the Cup again, but thereafter a resurgent Rangers swept all before them. Celtic were about to enter the lean years that they had not known since the early 1960s, and, as in the years on the eve of the Stein era, the board came under attack for failing to meet the supremacy of Rangers. This time there was no Stein to inspire the players; nor was there on the board a figure of the stature of Robert Kelly or even Desmond White to lead directors who seemed more intent on preserving their own privileges than building a winning team. Or buying one, which was the essence of the new ethos. The immediate reaction of the Celtic board to the big spending of their rivals was to protest that they would not be stampeded into trying to buy success, and Tom Grant grumbled at the end of 1986 that Celtic would not 'splash out outrageous sums of cash, just because people see Rangers do it'.[1] Celtic were then at the top of the League, playing before large crowds, but by the end of the season they were no longer at the top and four of their best players were seeking their fortunes elsewhere: Maurice Johnston, Brian McClair, Alan McInally and Murdo MacLeod. In income from gate money and transfer fees Celtic had gained much more than they had spent, but, to use the sarcastic phrases that were fast becoming clichés, the 'family club' was ill-prepared to meet the demands of the new age as they continued to work out of the 'biscuit tin' and to expect the players to 'play for the jersey'.

By the 1980s the entire sports world had undergone a commercial revolution that saw its stars earn money on a scale never before thought possible. The dollar rush began with the individual sports in the 1960s, above all in golf where Arnold Palmer and Mark McCormack of IMG (International Management Group), the world's largest sports management business, showed how sports stars could become millionaires through sponsorship and lending their name to a host of commercial products. At this time Wimbledon, still a haven of amateurism, paid for the balls it used, but from 1968 along came the acceptance of professionals, soon to be earning as much as the golfers, and the manufacturers of balls had to outbid their rivals to pay for the privilege of supplying balls for the world's premier tennis tournament. Cricket in Australia was hijacked by the TV mogul Kerry Packer in the late 1970s, the players having been easily seduced from the bosom of the conservative Australian Cricket Board by offers of vastly increased payments compared to the pittance they had been paid previously. Packer's main aim was to replace the government television monopoly with a hyped-up game tailored for his own Channel Nine television audience. By this time the Olympic Games, always a showpiece for the hypocrisy of amateurism, were put on sale to the highest bidder. The world body for football, FIFA, also underwent a transformation when the Brazilian multi-millionaire, Joao Havelange, replaced the former English schoolteacher and referee, Stanley Rous, as president in 1974. It was a shift away from the more honest, but stuffy and conservative British approach to that of a man who had made millions in the midst of scandalous poverty – a metaphor, perhaps, for the changes about to befall the game.

RISING WAGES, FALLING VALUES

The increases in the salaries of British footballers came slowly, even after the abolition of the maximum wage in England in 1961 and the end of the retain and transfer system in 1963. The odd player was immediately promised £100 a week, but few were paid as much as that and even more were sacked to keep the wage bill down. Three of the greatest coaches of this time, all Scots, Matt Busby at Manchester United, Bill Shankly at Liverpool and Jock Stein at Celtic, men revered by their players and each of whom had known hard times in his earlier life, did what they could to keep players' wages depressed: the Lisbon Lions were on £40 a week, much the same as the stars of Manchester United and Liverpool. In Scotland, Rangers and Celtic also believed that players should be on modest wages: Rangers are said to have lost Jim Baxter because they would not depart from the principle of paying all players the same and give him an extra £40 a week, although this was only one of the factors that sent the Rangers hero south; in the 1970s Rangers' spending on players was curtailed by the expense of rebuilding Ibrox; by the 1980s they were falling well behind what players could get in England, losing John McClelland to Watford and Gordon Smith to Brighton, lowly English clubs that were prepared to pay twice that of Scotland's richest club. Before Souness, Rangers' record signing fee was £235,000, to bring

Craig Paterson from Hibs to Ibrox in 1982, while no player was paid more than £240 a week. Jock Wallace left Rangers because he was not given the money to spend on players that he wanted, and Waddell, Wallace and Greig together received less money to spend on players than was given to Souness in his first years in the club. Despite this it is Celtic that have earned the reputation of being a Scrooge, of operating a 'multi-million-pound business out of a biscuit tin'. The label stuck as they fell behind the free-spending Rangers after 1986.

Rangers' and Celtic's ability to call on loyalties denied other clubs has been the source of their playing strength through the years, although the tug of the jersey and the appeal of the dollar have never been clearly disentangled. It was an issue that went back at least to 1893, when the *Irish Weekly Independent* ridiculed the notion that Celtic players played for the jersey ('faith and fatherland' were the words actually used) when everyone knew that they played 'for 30/- a week'. There is much to admire in a player whose commitment to a club is a loyalty beyond that which is owed to a paymaster, but it is a loyalty that has often been abused, and before the 1980s even the most loyal servant could well ask why he should play for the price of a fish supper when champagne and fancy cars were on offer elsewhere. The days of Jimmy McGrory playing for a club that took advantage of his devotion were long over, although Danny McGrain may well have wondered about his rewards after a lifetime devoted to the same club. He was freed shortly after his last appearance at Celtic Park, in a League game against Falkirk on 2 May 1987, without as much as a handshake from the board or the chance to say a proper farewell to the fans.

Celtic lost Kenny Dalglish in 1977, but Scotland was never going to provide a stage big enough for one of the greatest players ever to grace its grounds. They lost Charlie Nicholas in 1983, a one-time denizen of the Jungle, the Celtic equivalent to the Kop at Liverpool or the East Enclosure at Ibrox, who was unhappy with the terms he had been offered. They tried to sell another brilliant graduate from the Jungle against his wishes in 1982: this was when Tommy Burns' contract ran out and Celtic tried – shades of McGrory and Maley in the 1920s – to tempt Arsenal to buy him for £1 million as a replacement for Graham Rix. In the end Rix stayed with Arsenal and Burns, a future Celtic manager then at the peak of his career, signed a four-year contract on £300 week (£100 more than before) and a signing-on fee of £18,000, to be paid in instalments over the period of the contract.[2] Even with the inflation of the 1970s this was a considerable advance on the wages paid to the Lisbon Lions, and more than what was paid at Ibrox – but a paltry sum in comparison with the explosion in wages that was to come.

It was not only the players who had reasons for complaint at what the centenary history of Celtic called 'fiscal restraint': Celtic's managers found it a constant source of frustration. Billy McNeill, who spent his entire playing career at Celtic and who was captain of the team throughout the Stein years, was dismissed as manager in June 1983 because he had asked for a contract and indicated that he was not satisfied with his salary. A man of the older generation, he nevertheless felt frustrated by the restraints placed on him so far as buying players was concerned, and he had several battles with Desmond White who had weightier matters to consider, such as the amount of money the club was spending on youth trips, scouting, travel expenses and petrol consumption – while less kindly fans would add the amount of money coming through a particular turnstile. Even in the 1990s, as Michael Kelly tells us of his days as a Celtic director, the club's financial largesse did not extend to car phones and decent catering.[3]

McNeill and White devoted their lives to the one club, but their running battles finally led to a parting of the ways. McNeill's successor, David Hay, ran into similar problems, and when he travelled south in the 1986–87 season in search of players to bolster the defence he was told by chairman Jack McGinn through the columns of *Celtic View* that if he wanted them he would have to finance them out of his own pocket. When the club asked him to resign so that they could maintain the fiction that they had never fired a manager, Hay refused and was discarded, as one of his family said, 'like a piece of garbage'.[4]

McNeill was reappointed to the club at the end of May 1987, in a cloak-and-dagger affair in a Clydebank carpark that excited the imagination of the tabloids, but which was too late to prevent the departure of four class players who were Celtic to the core, but who now headed for more profitable pastures down south or across the Channel. This time around McNeill was given some money to spend on players, but in trying to counteract the spending spree at Ibrox, Celtic were trumped at every turn: on the same day as they bought Frank McAvennie from West Ham in October 1987 for a record £800,000, Rangers paid nearly double that amount to bring Richard Gough from Tottenham Hotspur. It was a story that would be repeated many times over the next few years.

FAITH OF THE FAMILIES

There is much to admire in a club whose board sees itself as the custodian of a set of ideals rather than of being the trustees of a profit-making conglomerate, but none of this means anything if they fail to satisfy the appetite of the fans for titles and trophies. Before Souness, the Rangers board comprised a small group of men who had often been successful businessmen but who were above all devoted to the club – for a long time they were all former players. These men saw themselves as the keepers of a trust, a sacred trust even, of a Protestant heritage which was interpreted by their fans as much as by their enemies as being anti-Catholic. The Celtic board on the other hand, was dominated by a few families devoted to upholding the cause of the Catholic/Irish community and their descendants and friends. By playing Protestants and employing Protestants in various capacities they were able to claim that they were not a Catholic club: what this means is 'exclusively' Catholic, for the entire ethos of the club is steeped in its origins. No one exemplified this more than Robert Kelly, a man of deep principle, justly proud of his club's role in Scottish society, who at the time of the great flag flutter in the early 1950s urged Catholics to become better organised and to wield an influence in proportion to their numbers as the early pioneers had done. In a speech to the Glasgow Province of the Knights of St Columba in February 1952 he praised that body as an example of how Catholics could fulfil their duties 'to make sure that Catholic laymen, in whatever profession they have been called, exert their influence to the fullest possible extent'.[5] According to his nephew, Michael Kelly, there were suspicions in the early 1960s that he was trying to create an all-Catholic team;[6] and through to the modern era being a Catholic was a plus for any player who came to Celtic Park.

Of the two families that have dominated Celtic since its earliest days, the Kelly name goes back to the signing of star player James Kelly from Renton in 1888. This is often given as the basis for the club's early playing success. Kelly went on to become a director and chairman of the club from 1909 to 1914, staying on as a director until his death in 1932. His son, Robert, took his place on the board and became chairman from 1947 until shortly before his death in 1971. The Kelly name was carried on by his nephew, Kevin, who joined the board on his uncle's death and became chairman in 1991. 'Bob' Kelly was succeeded by Desmond White as chairman, and when the latter died in 1985 the White name was carried on on the board by his son, Christopher.

The Whites were not original members of the club, but in some way they can claim this through John Glass, who more than any other individual was responsible for establishing the club's success off the park in the early years. Glass, who never missed a committee meeting and who was chairman of the club before it became a limited liability company in 1897, died in 1906. He was replaced by his protégé, Tom White, who at 22 years of age was one of the youngest ever directors of a football club. White also inherited Glass's shares. He took over as chairman from James

Kelly in 1914 and remained in that position until 1947, when his son Desmond joined the board. The other name that made up the Celtic family was Grant, represented on the board at the time of the Souness takeover by young Tom, who was brought onto the board in March 1985 in a move to ensure that the power he wielded through his large shareholding was used in the proper way.

Tom's great-grandfather, James, had been one of the original directors, a businessman from Northern Ireland who had made his fortune in the drink trade, but who had been better known in his day for his forays into stadium construction than for anything to do with the team. James Grant died in his native Ireland in 1914, leaving his large shareholding to his son, John, who later emigrated to Canada. When he died the shares were inherited, among others, by his sister, Felicia Grant who lived in Toomebridge, Northern Ireland, and who through a complicated succession of inheritances, including those of Tom Colgan who had been a Celtic director, ended up in the 1960s with the biggest block ownership of shares in Celtic: 1,705 fully paid and 1,752 half-paid. Although this did not pose a direct threat to the Kelly/White block ownership, Robert Kelly in particular was careful to court her friendship. Although she never threatened to use her share power, she never relinquished it. When she died in Belfast in 1973 her shares passed to Tom Grant's father, from whom he inherited half on his father's death in 1979, with voting control over the other half. There were other Grant shares in Canada, and they would play a key role when moves were undertaken in the 1990s to seize control of the Celtic board from within.

Celtic shares were closely controlled by the majority shareholders, who did not allow them to be traded on the open market, a precautionary measure taken by Tom White in 1933 to keep out 'undesirable outsiders' – more specifically to stall what he feared might have been a threat to the board from the growing shareholding of Willie Maley. The directors ran the club as a family trust, and while that 'trust' was seen to be in the interests of the larger Celtic 'family', and the team did well, there were few complaints. During this time Bob Kelly and Desmond White studiously and honestly portrayed the image of a club that cared about its supporters, many of whom had come from impoverished social circumstances. Against this background, Celtic baulked at expensive moves on the transfer market or grandiose schemes of stadium development, and the club did what it could to ensure that its poorer followers could afford games at Parkhead. Neither Kelly nor White seem to have made any money out of the club, and Kelly in particular was more interested in its traditions than its bank balance. In 1956 he expressed concern, in view of the way the game was expanding into floodlighting and international club football, that 'the big clubs will grow bigger and the middle and smaller clubs smaller, with the possible weakening of the whole structure'.[7] He was appalled by the abolition of the maximum wage in England in 1961, and how this would lead to excessive demands by the players. Faced during this time by one of the best Rangers teams of any era, he refused to match them by entering the transfer market. In doing so, however, but even more so by trying to manage the team by using Jimmy McGrory as a front, he committed the inexcusable sin of letting the club fall behind Rangers. This he expiated, faced by growing fan discontent, with the appointment of Jock Stein as manager in 1965.

With the unprecedented success of Stein, the Celtic board was under no pressure to modernise the club, and Desmond White continued to treat the supporters as the same battlers who had followed Celtic from wind-swept terraces and rudimentary facilities for decades. By the 1980s the Catholic community in Scotland was no longer that of the immigrants seeking roots and a place in society as was the case with their predecessors a century before, nor even that of those in the inter-war period suffering the worst of a depressed economy in which Protestant bosses looked after their own and were respected for it. By the 1960s 'The Grip' was more an excuse than a barrier to promotion and Catholics were firmly entrenched throughout the professional and managerial layers of Scottish society.

The situation of the average fan was changing throughout Britain and other advanced capitalist countries, where class lines were no longer as clear as they had been before the consumer revolution began in the late 1950s. The ranks of the middle classes were swelling as more people depended for their living on white collar jobs and technology took over some of the more onerous tasks performed by manual labour. On the domestic front dishwashers, electric blankets and other appliances were within the reach of most and cars were no longer a luxury. Living standards were improving, for most people, but not all, and the gaps were widening between those in work and those out of work. In less than two decades from 1970 employment in many of Glasgow's engineering enterprises was devastated, including 40 per cent of the jobs in shipbuilding and marine engineering, and while the new shopping centres with their coffee shops and wine bars added a welcome touch of class to the city, the peripheral housing estates with their rootless youths and the country's cheapest heroin remained an urban desert to remind the better-off that all of Glasgow was not smiling better in the 1980s: the rich were becoming increasingly richer and the poor more desperately poor – and forgotten.[8] But there were enough people who saw themselves as better off to support governments committed to helping the rich.

Celtic and Rangers of the 1980s then, still had supporters who found in football a passion and a leisure pursuit that suited their pocket. But there were others who were not so willing to put up with the conditions that had been borne so stoically by their fathers. This was a reality that Rangers, with their all-seated stadium and the higher prices that went with it, grasped more readily than Celtic. Even Celtic supporters on meagre incomes themselves called out for the club to match the spending at Ibrox, above all on players, as a life of eternal torment at the hands of the Huns was too horrible to contemplate.

THE 'GERS GO MARCHING ON

In Souness's first full season at Ibrox, 1986–87, Rangers won the League for the first time since 1978; they also won the League Cup, but went out of the Scottish Cup in a sensational 0–1 home loss to Hamilton Accies in the first round. Celtic won nothing that year, although they came second in the League and lost the Skol Cup final to Rangers in controversial circumstances. David Hay was replaced by Billy McNeill, in Celtic terms the equivalent of John Greig and Jock Wallace put together. 'Caesar' made a triumphant return to his old club with a team that was as close to being all-Catholic as any in Celtic's history. Unlike his Ibrox rivals with all their high profile Englishmen, McNeill's team in its first year was the embodiment of the Celtic ethos – although they too had their Englishmen, the Yorkshireman Mick McCarthy and Chris Morris from Cornwall (both of whom were Catholics).

The Rangers 'mercenaries' adapted quickly to their new environment, and welcomed with exaggerated fervour the passions of the Old Firm games. Nowhere was this more enthusiastically demonstrated than at the second Old Firm game of the second Souness season, at Ibrox on 17 October 1987. It was in this game that two Englishmen, captain Terry Butcher and goalkeeper Chris Woods, were ordered off and Graham Roberts, who had deputised in goal, was reported after the game for incidents missed by the referee. Celtic's import from England, the Scot Frank McAvennie, but playing in his first Old Firm derby, was also sent off. It was a dramatic confrontation where Rangers pulled back from 0–2 down to draw 2–2 in the last minute with their depleted team. The major sensation was still to come, however, when the matter was brought before the Procurator Fiscal of Glasgow, Sandy Jessop, and Rangers and Celtic jointly employed Len Murray (a Celtic supporter in his private life) to defend the players against charges that they had engaged in conduct 'likely to provoke a breach of peace amongst spectators'. In addition to the offences for which the players were sent off and for which

Roberts was reported, incidents involving Roberts and Peter Grant of Celtic were noted, but not acted on: this was when Roberts, deputising in goal for Woods, 'conducted' the Rangers players in singing sectarian songs when Rangers equalised, and when Grant crossed himself 'provocatively' after he had scored his goal. In the cases that went to court, Woods and Butcher were convicted and fined: McAvennie was discharged and the case against Roberts was adjudged 'not proven'. For Archie Macpherson, a veteran reporter of Old Firm games, this one was no worse than many of those he had seen in his day: there was never any serious danger of the crowd becoming involved and the Crown had overreacted. Football, he claimed, was being taught a lesson and the four players brought before the court, far from being 'a threat to law and order, were being made scapegoats in a politically hostile environment'.[9] The blundering of Prime Minister Thatcher into football in the wake of the Heysel disaster was a temporary glitch in the game, but the use of television cameras to pick up incidents on the field missed by the referee, and the intervention of the police, were to become a regular part of the landscape.

In the meantime, Rangers were saved from a barren 1987–88 season on the strength of a penalty shoot-out against Aberdeen in the final of the Skol Cup on 25 October 1987. A late equaliser when the score was 3–2 for Aberdeen climaxed a pulsating encounter and sent the game into a scoreless extra time. Iain Durrant scored the all important goal from the spot. Celtic made an early exit from the Skol Cup, but went on to win the League and then added icing to their 100th birthday cake with a 2–1 victory over Dundee United in the Scottish Cup. They won the Cup again in 1989, 1–0 against Rangers in a scrappy game in which a late goal by Terry Butcher was mysteriously disallowed. Celtic reached the Cup final the following year but were deprived of a third successive Cup victory when after a scoreless draw with Aberdeen, the Dons won on penalties, 9–8.

On such a slender thread hung the fate of manager Billy McNeill, whose problems on the field were complicated by the growing turmoil off it. He was not helped by events on the other side of the city where Rangers were beginning to strike a winning combination and Souness at last started to curb the appalling behaviour on the field that had marked his first two seasons with the club. In 1988–89 he set Rangers on the way to their successive League flags, and repeated the Skol Cup triumph against Aberdeen, this time with a more convincing 3–2 victory. The Dons had their revenge the following year, in 1989, but then Rangers won the League Cup in 1990 with a win over Celtic. The elusive Scottish Cup would have to wait until 1992. In games between the two clubs,

Rangers outclassed Celtic in the first Old Firm game of the 1988–89 league season with a 5–1 victory at Ibrox in August 1988 that sent the fans into delirium. A few of the more historically aware, however, regretted that Souness eased up on Celtic quarter of an hour after the interval, being content to stroke the ball around with arrogant disdain of the opposition rather than increasing the pressure and wiping out the memory of Celtic's 7–1 League Cup victory of 1957. Some fans, including Walter Smith, tried to remind the players of the need to score more goals, but Souness and the English imports knew nothing of bitter memories past and as a result Celtic's victory at 'Hampden in the Sun' remained unexpunged. Celtic won the second league game, but did not win another Old Firm league game until 24 March 1991. A long winter of bitter discontent had set in for Celtic.

Off the field Celtic lagged even further behind. Shortly after the Mo Johnston signing, the accounts to be presented to the Rangers' Annual General Meeting (3 August) for the year ended 31 May 1989 revealed that Souness was earning at least £4,000 a week, Butcher was on well over £3,000 and eight other players were on about £2,000. It was a massive leap in salaries from even a few years previously, and a millennium away from the day back in 1935 when Bob McPhail and Jerry Dawson made their way up the marble staircase to complain about their bonus for an upcoming prestige friendly against Arsenal at Ibrox. The players had been promised a canteen of cutlery if they won, evoking from McPhail the imperishable protest: 'There's no much use having a knife and fork, Boss, if ye canny afford a steak.' Players travelled to games on public transport in those days, but this was changing in the 1950s and by the early 1960s Rangers players could be seen posing proudly outside Ibrox flaunting their wealth with their Hillman Imps and Ford Zephyrs. Nevertheless, like their Celtic counterparts, they were paid little more than double the salary of a skilled worker: they were still part of the world of the people who watched them each week. By the 1990s the football stars were in a different firmament.

For Rangers fans who had invested in the club there was good news off the field as well as on it. Shares in Rangers had shot up from £16 in September 1988 to £40 in July 1989. That no dividend was recommended was of no consequence: Rangers shares were not a vulgar commodity but a source of pride to be shared with others of the faith. Nor were too many people at Ibrox worried about the £7 million overdraft; apart from the club's assets being valued at £23 million, money was tumbling into the club from all directions.

Alan Montgomery, from a working-class background and unlike Souness and Murray a fanatical Rangers fan from his childhood, was appointed as chief executive of Rangers at the beginning of March 1989. His job was to convert the loyalty associated with the Rangers brand name into commercial reality in a variety of fields that would wander far beyond the Ibrox turf. Montgomery came to Rangers from Scottish Television, and the money to be made from the most lucrative of the media was high on the new executive's list. Ian Archer pictured a future that even he no doubt thought he was exaggerating at the time, but which now seems like an understatement. Archer envisaged Rangers in two years time owning golf courses, cinemas, hotels, strings of restaurants and perhaps even old folk's homes. The club already had interests in the sports goods industry, but there was no reason why it should be restricted to the leisure field. Archer went on to suggest that:

> . . . the day may come when you book your holiday through a Rangers travel agency, fly on a Rangers aeroplane to the Costa del Rangers somewhere in the Med, where the skies are always blue.
>
> If you are a Rangers fan, when you settle the bill the bad news will be lessened because the profits will be handed over to Graeme Souness to buy even bigger and better players for the club.[10]

In the meantime the club was about to embark on an ambitious programme to make one of the grandest football stadiums in Britain even grander. On 30 March 1990 the club unveiled plans for a two-year £11 million facelift, more than half of which would come from the sale to the public of bonds costing between £1,000 and £1,650. These would give the purchaser a lifetime right to purchase a season-ticket in the Top Deck that was to be added to the Main Stand. In addition, executive boxes could be bought for £50,000 each. The standing areas would be converted to seating. It was all a long way from the days when David Hope's plans to introduce executive boxes had been stymied by the protests of those who thought such luxury repugnant to the Rangers tradition. In 1989 the fans had a voice they did not have in the 1960s, but the spirited campaign of *Follow, Follow* to try to save the enclosure from seating was doomed by the new ethos of the club and the number of fans able to pay the new fees, or who were prepared to put themselves in hock to do so.

The bond scheme came into operation at the beginning of June 1990, for the well-heeled by a straight payment, for the less well-heeled it was made affordable with easy payments spread over three years on a low-interest credit scheme. By the end of 1992 Ibrox had three tiers in the Main Stand and all-seated accommodation for 45,000 spectators. Inside were catering facilities supplying anything from Bluenose Burgers and

True Blue Crisps in the fast-food sections to top-quality restaurant meals in the thickly carpeted Top Deck, where a myriad of business deals could be completed without any undue distractions from what was happening on the field.

Fans in the still-standing East Enclosure could be heard chanting: 'You can stick your season-tickets up your arse', but their cries were lost in the air. In the pages of *Follow, Follow* the hike in prices was criticised, whether it was of the club for suggesting that a £4 enclosure ticket would not allow Rangers to buy players like Mo Johnston, or of the journalist Dixon Blackstock as a 'cheeky bastard' for sneering at people who wanted to buy a Savile Row suit at fifty-bob-tailor prices, especially when, as in his case, he got into all the games for nothing. Such fans showed more logic than realism, and when *Rangers News* on 6 September 1989 tried to justify a hike in prices for a European game against Bayern Munich, in part by pointing out how much it cost to attend a Diana Ross concert, the retort from the fans was that Diana Ross played Glasgow once every four years, while Rangers, apart from playing domestic games at Ibrox at least 22 times a year, had played many European games.[11]

The fans fighting the rising cost of entering Ibrox had as much chance as King Canute against the waves. They eased their frustration by taking it out on Alistair Hood, Rangers' newly appointed police liaison officer. 'Herr' Hood, with many variations on the SS image, became a much hated figure for taking his duty as overseer of fan behaviour somewhat zealously: according to the fanzines he conducted a reign of terror on wee boys who sang loyalist songs and waved patriotic flags.

THE STADIUM: THE SORROW AND THE PRIDE

The changes at Ibrox were spurred on by the Taylor Report on all-seated stadiums following the Hillsborough disaster of April 1989, and by the example of the stadiums that had hosted the World Cup in Italy in 1990. Sadly, it had been a stadium disaster that led to Rangers reconstructing Ibrox to make it the imposing stadium it is today.

Before the majestic new stadium was erected at Celtic Park in the summer of 1996 and completed two years later, Celtic's ground could never compare with Ibrox Park, except perhaps in its earliest days. But from 1899, and above all from 1929, when the redbrick main stand designed by Archibald Leitch was completed, the Ibrox stadium could be seen on the Glasgow horizon, preserved by an order declaring it a building of historical importance in 1980. Celtic Park is affectionately known as 'Paradise'. A popular story attributes the name to an ironical allusion comparing the move from an enclosure adjoining Janefield cemetery in August 1892 to being like 'leaving the graveyard to enter Paradise'; but the more authentic reason is the comment by John McLaughlin that the club was constructing a Garden of Eden out of a desert.[12] For the times this was an impressive, even palatial ground, with its two tracks, one for athletics and one for cycling, whose high banking gave spectators an excellent view. But it would soon be surpassed by Ibrox.

Despite the imposing main entrance to Ibrox before the 1970s, the bulk of the spectator accommodation, like that of most grounds in Britain, was deplorable, but less deplorable than most and infinitely less so than Celtic Park. Celtic chairman, Desmond White, justified his refusal to spend money on ground improvements by claiming that he did not want to put the game beyond the reach of the ordinary supporter. An admirable sentiment, and based on a social reality when a few shillings or a lift over for wee (and not so wee) boys allowed tens of thousands of people to watch their favourite pastime at reasonable cost – and perhaps to be infected by the football obsession. It was also a reflection of the social attitudes of the owners of the grounds that simple facilities like adequate lavatories and protection from the wind and rain were seen as luxuries wasted on the poor. Nor was safety a prime concern. The rebuilt Ibrox of the 1930s was at one stage designed to hold 200,000 spectators, crammed together like sardines; in fact for the record crowd of over 118,500 who came to see the Rangers/Celtic Ne'erday game of 1939, thousands clamoured to get out, but the police refused because of the trouble likely to ensue from the thousands still trying to get in if they opened the gates. Some never saw the ball that day, others only when it was hoofed into the air. And on that day, as on innumerable occasions before and after, and in grounds throughout Britain, tragedy was averted by the crowds, unencumbered by spectator fencing, being allowed to spill out onto the track.

It took the tragedies of Bradford in 1985 and Hillsborough in 1989 to force a radical restructuring of the football grounds of Britain. Long before the Taylor Report, however, Rangers had embarked on plans to renovate Ibrox, also, alas, as a result of a tragedy on the scale of Bradford and Hillsborough. This was on 2 January 1971 when 66 Rangers fans were crushed to death and 145 injured on the infamous Stairway 13 at the end of the first Old Firm game of that year. It was not the first tragedy at Ibrox, or on Stairway 13: the first great tragedy in modern sporting history took place at Ibrox in April 1902 when a wooden terracing specially built to take additional standing spectators to hold the Scotland v England international collapsed, plunging 25 to their deaths and leaving more than 500 injured, many seriously. The game continued, a mere charade when the players saw the dead and dying bodies stretched out before them at half-time, while until the final whistle fans continued to watch the game clinging perilously to the structure from which others had so recently fallen to their deaths.

From that time on standing accommodation was built only over solid earth. Unlike cinemas and dance halls, which became with football the most popular sources of public entertainment through to the late 1950s, football grounds were not subject to state regulation until the Safety of Sports Grounds Act of 1975.[13] Because of this Rangers were able to ignore the three incidents involving deaths and injuries that fore-shadowed the tragedy of 1971: in 1961 (2 dead, 44 injured), 1967 (11 injured) and 1969 (30 injured) on a staircase that was too narrow and did not allow for funnelling, and whose steps were too steep. Ironically the deaths of 1961 resulted in a measure that added to the deaths in 1971, when the wooden palings that had allowed hundreds to burst through to safety was replaced by solid concrete and wooden sleepers which did not give way in 1971. Whatever the faults of the Rangers Football Club before the tragedy – and these were pointed out in pitiless detail by the sheriff at the inquest – the club's response thereafter was swift and to the point, with money from Rangers Pools being poured into the stadium rather than into players. The result was the new Ibrox that ranks as one of the best in Britain today. The Centenary Stand was built in 1973 and complete redevelopment began in 1978 with the razing of Stairway 13 and the erection of what was to become known as the Copland Stand. The Broomloan and Govan Stands then arose as all-seated edifices to surround the pitch along with the imposing old Main Stand.

A plaque was erected to the memory of the victims on the 20th anniversary in 1991. Willie Waddell, former player and manager at the time of the disaster, who performed heroically when he was the first to realise the scale of the disaster, claimed that the new Ibrox was itself an eternal memorial to the victims. The disaster can never be erased from the minds of those who were affected, and aspects of its reporting have troubled other Rangers fans who were never satisfied with the accepted story of what had triggered off the disaster: a late equalising goal by Colin Stein that had fans rushing back up the stairs to see what had happened. No serious observer could have attributed the blame for the tragedy to Stein: the tragedy of 1971 was one that was waiting to happen and all Stein did was to do what he had been paid – and idolised – for. Other Rangers fans simply wanted the truth of the disaster to be known, and spoke up on the 20th and 25th anniversaries, claiming that the accident took place at least five minutes and anything up to ten minutes *after* Stein's goal.

The popular account certainly rings true. With only a minute to go in a goalless game Celtic's Jimmy Johnstone scored what everyone thought had to be the winner. There was jubilation at the Celtic end, and disgust at the Rangers end, where to a chorus of mumbled and not so mumbled expletives Rangers supporters made for the exit at Stairway 13. While they were still making their way down the steep stairs, some with their feet not touching the steps, as had happened on countless occasions before, a roar from the ground signalled that Rangers had equalised. There was an immediate attempt to make sense of the roar: a hesitation, perhaps some tried to get back up the stairs, although this would have been impossible, but in the confused joy, because the triumphant roar was coming from Rangers supporters, someone tripped and the momentum from above set up an avalanche of human flesh.

What now seems more likely is that thousands of Rangers supporters stayed on at the top of the terracing dancing and singing, and it was from their numbers some minutes later that someone stumbled on the steps – there are several references to a man with his wee boy on his shoulders suddenly disappearing. Even among those celebrating so close to the ill-fated stairway, many went home that gloomy night unaware until they heard about it on the radio or television that they had been so close to what was until then the worst disaster in British sport.

Long before the building of the new Ibrox got under way a religious truce blanketed a shocked city as Catholics and Protestants came together in mourning for the victims. It was not to last, and a new level of depravity was struck 20 and 25 years later when silences in memories of the victims, one at Ibrox, one at Celtic Park, were broken by morons unable to be silenced by the bulk of the fans whose attempts to shut them up would only have made the situation worse – as happened when Aberdeen supporters tried to do something about the cretins among their supporters who were ridiculing the silence in memory of the recent death of the Ibrox legend, big Geordie Young, on 10 January 1997.

THE DYNASTIES DO IT THEIR WAY

As the new Ibrox continued to grow in glory, even those who were finding it difficult to get inside were happy to mock the problems at Parkhead, the Rangers fanzines referring to Celtic Park as 'The Piggery' and its fans and players as the Scum, the Beggars, the Bead-rattlers or the Soap-dodgers. This was the modernised version of the odd cartoon from early in the century that had depicted Celtic as the bog Irish and Rangers as being handsome and elegantly attired. It was an image of Rangers that was to be carefully fostered by William Struth, whose attention to detail and smartness in dress amounted almost to a fetish, but along with the arrogance, it did give the Rangers players a certain pride in themselves and the club.

Celtic, on the other hand, cultivated the image of a club that was founded on charity, caring for the poor and disadvantaged. But in actual fact, its directors from the earliest days showed a dedication to making the club a commercial rather than a charitable organisation, much to the despair of the stalwarts who had built the club from nothing in its first years. Most notable of these was John H. McLaughlin, Celtic's first chairman when the club became a limited liability company in 1897, a man who had an outspoken contempt for the 'street corner loafers' and 'soup kitchen cranks' who thought that they should run the club. These were the people whose voluntary efforts had built the ground and formed the brake clubs, the supporters associations of the time, and who as a consequence thought they deserved some privileges at the club, such as concessions on season-tickets and a say in how the club was run. These same fans also revealed another aspect of their idealism when they asked for a limit to the number of Protestants the club played. This and other social considerations were overthrown by the hard-headed businessmen who converted Celtic into one of the first limited liability companies in football, ensured that shares on offer to the public did not threaten the control of the board, and paid themselves some of the largest dividends of any football club in Great Britain.

It was McLaughlin, too, who, supported by Rangers, was behind the formation of the League in Scotland in 1890 and its logical and intended consequence in the introduction of professionalism three years later. One of his main reasons for doing this was to curtail the financial demands of players who as amateurs were bound by no contract – it was Celtic, after all, whose amateur players went on strike for better wages in 1891. He also thought that professionalism would stop money from the big clubs being redistributed to the poorer. It was also McLaughlin who stood against those who wanted to create a clearer-cut Catholic image at the club and who condemned the Irish community in Scotland for its opposition to the Boer War. No seeker after popularity, he weathered the contempt of those who feared the club was falling into the hands of 'a few moneyed speculators'. In short, Celtic's first chairman would have been very much at home in the football of the 1980s, where money and not social responsibility was the prime concern. By the time of his death in 1909, the club's origins in charity had become, in the words of one of the club's first historians, paraphrasing Shakespeare, 'sicklied over with the pale caste of gold'.[14]

A football team on an all-conquering run can get away with almost anything off the field, and Celtic had had enough successes over the years to cover the fact that the family club was in fact a narrow patriarchy in which the fans had little say. There had been widespread discontent against the board in the 1940s when the club underwent one of the worst periods in its history, and there were protests against Robert Kelly on the eve of Jock Stein's appointment. By the late 1980s the fans were again on the edge of revolt as Celtic fell behind Rangers and the board seemed unwilling or unable to do anything about it. It was apparent that the club would have to throw away the biscuit tin and attract new millions to the club, either through a private individual or by opening the club up to the fans with a share issue. Faced by such unpalatable alternatives, the board at Celtic Park retired into a defence of their own private interests. Tom Grant had been brought onto the board because his potential power through his shares threatened the incumbents – 70 years after the last Grant had been on the board. Jack McGinn's appointment to the board as first commercial manager in 1982 seemed to be a departure from the control by the 'families', and the official centenary history marked his appointment as 'indicative of a new era in football'.[15] In fact, as Michael Kelly tells us, McGinn was appointed to look after Desmond White's son, Christopher, who had joined the board at the same time.[16] Desmond died in 1985 and the following year Tom Devlin, another long-standing member of the board, having joined it in 1949, died. The fate of the club was in the hands of three young scions of the 'families', to whom would be added Michael Kelly in 1990; but far from displaying the adventurousness of youth they proceeded to put a shell around themselves as protection from the outside world.

Celtic marked their centenary year with an official history which, superb though it is in many ways, still has several blind spots. Its author, Brian Wilson, a former left-wing journalist and now a Labour politician, took to task those who depicted the Celtic directors as bumbling but well-intentioned incompetents: on the contrary, he claimed, writing from the vantage point of the directors' box, they had led the club through a 'century of honour'. This was not the interpretation of an un-official history that came out a year before Wilson's book. Tom Campbell and Pat Woods, writing with the faith of the faithful for the faithful, but from outside the official sanctum, told the tale of a club with a certain gritty grandeur, but painted in the warts, most of which were on the faces of the club's directors.[17] This the board of the 1980s found unacceptable; they refused to recognise the 'rogue' history and any other books by the rogue historians, which were banned from being sold through any Celtic outlet. Like the works of Trotsky in the Soviet Union under Stalin, at least two of the best books on Celtic became non-books.[18]

Other devoted fans of the club were rebuffed by the board for their criticisms. In 1989 Gerry Dunbar of the Celtic fanzine *Not the View* offered the club a bust of Jock Stein, commissioned from funds raised by donations to the fanzine. Refused by the 'Politburo' because of the fanzine's uncompromising attacks on the board, Dunbar took the bust to the People's Palace where it was welcomed into what the fanzine considered a place more fitting as a tribute to the 'People's manager' – among the ordinary fans of the club.[19] With the renovations undertaken by the new owner after 1994 a grander monument was promised with the naming of the Jock Stein Stand behind the western goal, completing the improvements to the spectator accommodation at Celtic Park.

One other reason that the 'rogue' history was banished from Celtic outlets was that it represented a threat to the profits of the official history, a minor manifestation of the biscuit tin mentality with which the club was increasingly being associated. By 1990 a coterie of family friends was in no position to meet the demands of a game that was now a global phenomenon, with riches through sponsorship that were beyond the dreams of the most insatiable even a couple of decades previously. Celtic and Rangers were among the last clubs to adopt commercial graffiti on their jerseys, but even they soon succumbed to the financial blandishments of having their once sacred shirts besmirched by a sponsor's logo. By 1984 they were bowing to the inevitable, and ironically the only thing that held this up was the fear by advertisers that their name on one jersey would alienate half their potential customers. The solution, unique in the unlovely history of turning sportspeople into mobile advertising boards, was for the double-glazing firm of C.R. Smith to advertise on both sets of jerseys. This was before Souness, and shortly after he arrived the commercial balance of the two clubs was so disturbed that Rangers sought another advertiser and found one much more lucrative in the brewer McEwans when the agreement with the double-glazier ran out in 1986. From 1988 David Murray swept the club along on his own commercial wave, leaving Celtic washed up on the shore. Help was at hand, but it was disdainfully spurned.

In 1988 an expatriate Scot, who had gone to Canada in 1964 and made himself into a millionaire, offered Celtic a massive financial injection that would have helped the club out of its problems. Fergus McCann was the son of a high school teacher, an avid Celtic supporter who had been one of the most active members of the Croy Celtic Supporters Club. The bulk of his fortune came from organising golf tours from North America, thus cashing in on a leisure pursuit that was another of his passions. His offer to Celtic in 1988 was for a low-interest loan of £5 million to increase the seating capacity of the stadium with a two-tiered stand and provide standing accommodation for 48,000, in return for which he would receive a percentage of the increased revenue this would generate. Although at this stage McCann was not seeking control of the club, his offer was rejected.[20]

After several meetings with the directors, McCann felt he was getting nowhere, and the following summer he wrote to them offering to buy a 51 per cent shareholding at £110/£120 per share. In addition he would invest capital of £3 million in the club and put up the collateral for a further £2.2 million loan. He now wanted the position of executive director, and although he promised the directors that their positions would be safe, the thought of someone outside the families having a controlling interest in the club terrified them. And so the offer of effectively £7.2 million pounds was rejected, while the directors promised to block any attempt McCann made to purchase shares. McCann, having been rebuffed by the board in what he considered a 'rude and unbusinesslike way', approached Michael Kelly in his capacity as a public-relations officer. Kelly was not then a director, but he refused to take on the job: he was too much in sympathy with what he saw as the 'aspirations' of the board. Kelly believes this soured McCann against him.[21] Given the diametrically opposed position of the two men in regard to the question of power the possibility of friendly co-operation between them was highly unlikely, and so it is pointless wondering how a union of Michael Kelly and Fergus McCann might have saved Kelly himself and the bulk of the Celtic faithful from the traumas that were about to befall them.

Other offers came in to help the club, but they were all rejected. Paul Green, a property millionaire living in Jersey, offered to buy the club for £6 million in August 1989 by buying up enough shares to gain a 51 per cent majority. He intended to build a new stadium in the vacant land near the Parkhead Forge complex in which he had an interest, but his offers were never taken seriously. Gerard Eadie, owner of the double glaziers, C.R. Smith who were Celtic's major sponsor, also thought of buying the club, but decided to back Fergus McCann instead.

While Celtic remained marooned, Rangers went their own way, as the revolution begun by Marlborough and carried forward by David Murray continued to bring success on the field. Rangers fans who had lived through the shadow of the Stein years and beyond rejoiced in the glory of the new-look Bears and the regular trouncing of the Tims, besides which any faults in the Rangers hierarchy were mere peccadilloes. Celtic were allowed no such luxuries as they drifted further behind Rangers, who threatened to make a mockery of the term 'Old Firm'. The strength of the new Rangers was nowhere better demonstrated than by the comparative lack of disruption that accompanied Souness's sudden departure from the club in April 1991. A few weeks later McNeill was sacked for the second time in his career with Celtic, and again the fury of the Celtic fans was directed against the board. Two unsuccessful replacements as manager failed to relieve the situation, while Rangers without Souness went on to even greater domestic success. It seemed as though they could do no wrong.

4. The Souness Legacy

Souness's departure from Ibrox was in the manner of his coming: sensational, but clinically pure in its execution. On 15 April 1991, just four games short of the end of the season and with a tense struggle with Aberdeen standing in the way of a third successive League Championship, he told David Murray officially that he had accepted the position of manager of Liverpool. Souness, who had been torn by the temptation of the Liverpool job since shortly after it became vacant with the resignation of his old club-mate, Kenny Dalglish, two months earlier, wanted to stay on to the end of the season. But Murray would have none of it and insisted that he pack his bags and depart forthwith. The man who had said Rangers was the biggest club in Britain and the only one he wanted to manage, a pledge he had renewed just a few weeks before in the official *Rangers News*, was returning to his old club Liverpool, which he now claimed to be even bigger than Rangers. In an interview with *Sportsweek* a few months after his arrival at Ibrox he had specifically stated that: 'Even going back to Liverpool would be a downward step.'[1]

At the press conference held on 16 April, after a curt introduction by Murray, a tense Souness read out a statement saying that he had left for two reasons: first and most important in order that he could be closer to his children who were living in the south of England; and second, because he felt he had gone as far as he would be *allowed* to go in Scotland, a veiled reference to what he saw as his bad treatment by the SFA and the media, and possibly, as it was later revealed, that his spending powers were being curtailed at Ibrox. Certainly, he was on a collision course with chairman Murray because of his abrasive attitude to anyone he disagreed with. There was speculation at the time that Souness could pocket a handy profit on the £600,000 worth of Rangers shares he had bought in November 1988, and now worth about £2.25 million on the open market, but in fact they had been bought under a special agreement with Murray's company that he could buy them back at a prearranged price.

Murray's insistence that his old friend depart immediately was echoed by press headlines that screamed 'Get Lost Souness!'[2] and 'Get Out Now!'[3] It was treatment Souness himself had dished out to players who had crossed him, but when the dust had settled, and while Murray was probably correct in saying that leaving Rangers was the biggest mistake Souness would ever make, the overall verdict of the Rangers fans was that he had been a good thing for the club: he had given them a team to be proud of and had taken them irrevocably beyond the parochial sectarianism that had blighted the club before he arrived.

McNeill's departure from Parkhead a few weeks later was another untidy affair, as the manager was kept wondering about his fate after another trophyless season. The board dithered before the one-time Celtic hero found out in a document leaked to *The Sun* outlining how the club could get rid of him with minimum embarrassment. Six years on and another Celtic hero would depart from Parkhead in acrimonious circumstances, and again for the same crime: failing to win trophies and beat Rangers.

At Ibrox, Walter Smith replaced Souness and led the team to unprecedented domestic success, while at Parkhead Celtic had no one in mind to replace McNeill. Souness went on to prove David Murray's warning correct in every way: after pulling Liverpool down to hitherto unheard of depths he went on to pass an undistinguished two years in Turkey, with Galatasaray, before returning to England in 1996, to all but oversee Southampton's relegation from the Premier League in 1997. In the summer of 1997 the rumour-mongers linked him with a return to Scotland – as manager of Celtic! A Rangers cast-off would hardly have enhanced the image of Celtic, and this particularly bizarre piece of gossip ended when Souness left to manage Italy's Torino, a team with a glorious and tragic past, but now in a lower division of the Italian League. There he lasted only six games before he was relieved of his duties and, after more speculation about a return to English football, finally settled for Benfica in Portugal. In the meantime, a more mellow Souness has discovered that there is more to life than managing winning football teams.

At Ibrox, however, despite the joy among some of the fans and their celebration that Ibrox was now a Souness-free zone, the final summary was positive. Souness was the man who had signed Walters and Johnston, brave decisions that would have been beyond anyone before him; he had brought top-class players from England and abroad, and although they were never given enough time to mould into a team with a style that their price tags warranted, Rangers won three League flags and four League Cups during his five seasons at Ibrox. Walter Smith wanted to give Souness the credit for the League flag won in a last game decider against Aberdeen in 1991: the Dons only had to draw to win the flag, but collapsed before an ever-improving Mark Hateley and an Ibrox crowd that surpassed itself in acting as a twelfth man that day. Murray was less generous than Smith about whether Rangers would have won the title without Souness, but he did recognise that Souness was the man who had 'turned the big ship round'.[4] On the eve of Souness's arrival, Ibrox had been noted for its mediocre players playing before sparse crowds who had come to tell them how awful they were. Included among the chants then was: 'Ally, Ally, get tae fuck.' Souness's unwillingness to play the same Super Ally had irritated the same Ibrox crowd who had come to love the irrepressible Coisty and no one had a wider grin than the star striker at the news of Souness's departure. He went on to a magnificent partnership with Mark Hateley, probably the best at Ibrox since Millar and Brand or, for those with memories of the cloth cap days, of Waddell and Thornton.

SOUNESS AND RANGERS

Souness brought the crowds back to Ibrox and he gave the club a new image. As had been said many times before 1986, Rangers would gain more supporters than they would lose by playing Catholics, and any who stayed away for that reason the club was well rid of. Under Souness this had been shown to be the case. Above all he brought success on the field. And yet his departure was never actually mourned by anyone – even David Murray claimed that Souness's abrasive manner was heading for a confrontation between him and the club: for Rangers it was a good move.

People who have met Souness and those who claim to know him will tell you that he is a most sophisticated man, an excellent dinner companion with a remarkable breadth of knowledge. There are also tales of his visits to sick children and of his bedside vigil talking back to a full recovery the son of a Sampdoria director who was seriously ill following a car accident.[5] But for the vast majority of us who have nothing to go by but his public pronouncements and his behaviour on the field, or his treatment of those in his employ, at least as transmitted through the media, it is another character altogether that emerges. Souness had never courted popularity, and said from the start that he would rather be respected than liked. But even respect is hard to find for a man whose winner mentality insisted that no one had the right to win but him. This was the Souness who earned three red cards in his first two seasons at Ibrox: one during his first game for a brutal attack on George McCluskey which put the Hibs player in hospital, the second in the game against Aberdeen that decided the Championship that year, and the third in the first Old Firm game of the 1987–88 season. A (now famous) tea lady at St Johnstone's MacDiarmid Park, television sets and dressing-room furniture felt his wrath after away setbacks, and a runners-up medal was thrown away in the dressing-room after Rangers lost to Celtic in the 1989 Cup final accompanied by an angry outburst that he did not collect these.

On the park the players followed his example, and even some Rangers supporters were alienated by the physical attacks on opposing players. The result was an inordinate number of red and yellow cards, while the atmosphere at the Barnum and Bailey Old Firm game at Ibrox in October 1987 when two Rangers players were sent off and one more booked after the game, was determined when Souness refused to let his team walk out onto the field at the same time as Celtic. He gave the press even more to think about when he astonished them by apologising for the behaviour of his players at another torrid Old Firm encounter, on St Patrick's Day 1991 that saw Celtic through to the semi-final of the Scottish Cup. Once more the guilty Rangers were Anglos: Terry Hurlock, Mark Walters and Mark Hateley, for a second bookable offence. Peter Grant of Celtic was expelled for accruing two yellow cards – in the space of seconds – and in total there were three red and six yellow cards flourished. Three more Rangers players were ordered off in the next four League games.

Inside Ibrox Souness brooked no dissent, and after a verbal exchange with Graham Roberts after a 0–1 home defeat against Aberdeen in April 1988 that almost ended in blows (according to popular myth it did), the Ibrox favourite was humiliated by being sent to third-team games around Scotland before leaving permanently for England. Terry Butcher, another Anglo whose whole-hearted commitment to the club in every sense won the hearts of the Ibrox crowd, was forced to leave in November 1990 following a dispute over being asked to play in a Skol Cup final against Celtic, the culmination to a period of friction over the captain's fitness. Like Roberts he left without being given the chance to say farewell to the fans, either on the pitch or in the *Rangers News*. Those with longer memories could recall Souness's treatment of Ted McMinn and Robert Fleck in the early Souness years, while Derek Ferguson suffered similar humiliation: but for many all this was surpassed by Souness's refusal to use McCoist in the starting line-up for most of the 1990–91 season.

Off the park, Souness allowed no one but Murray to challenge his authority. Alan Montgomery arrived at Ibrox to do for Rangers in the commercial field what Souness was doing on the playing field. Unfortunately he was one of those increasingly rare birds at Ibrox, a high executive who had been a fanatical fan in his youth. It appears that his anxiety to be part of the action with the players, turning up at their training camps, appearing in the dressing-room, annoying them by his presence on the team bus, and even offering his advice on who should or should not be playing, led to strained relations between the two powerful egos and a situation where either Souness or Montgomery would have to leave. The players made their opinion felt in what the Souness-friendly *Sun* called 'a multi-million-pound rebellion if Graeme Souness is forced out', headlining the article: 'If Souness Goes, We Go.'[6] It was no contest, and was resolved when David Murray returned from a brief holiday and transferred Montgomery to a less sensitive part of the Murray International empire.

Referees were not the least to feel the lash of Souness's tongue, on the field and even off it. At the end of a Celtic v Rangers game at Parkhead on 29 August 1987, when Celtic won 1–0 and Souness was sent off, he was in conversation near the exit when he was approached by the match referee, David Syme, whom he promptly told to: 'F*** off, you poof,' a remark that he allegedly repeated in front of the match linesman.[7] Three red cards and eight yellow cards saw Souness making several trips to the offices of the SFA, a body for which he had the utmost contempt. This was not helped when they imposed what he thought were tough penalties, and as a result Souness had to watch several games from the touchline even when he was not injured. Standing idle on the touchline often proved too much for him, and in February 1989 he was fined £1,000 and banned from the touchline until the end of the season for swearing at a linesman in a game against Dundee United at Tannadice. In April 1989 further abuse in a Scottish Cup semi-final at Celtic Park against St Johnstone earned him a £2,000 fine and banishment to the stand until the end of the following season. It was while under this second ban that Souness was picked up by the cameras of Scottish Television watching the game from the tunnel at Ibrox during a Hearts game in February 1990; this time he was fined £5,000 and banned from the touchline until the end of the 1991–92 season. Scottish football could indeed do with some redistribution of wealth, but this was hardly the way to go about it, and while Souness felt he was hard done by, at least linesmen at games where Rangers were playing could relax a little knowing that he was not breathing down their necks.

Souness vented his rage against the cameras that had picked him out breaking the touchline ban by refusing STV entry to Ibrox, and even when he was with Liverpool he decreed that comments made to the media were not to be used by STV. Referees, the SFA and the media were an unholy trinity that Souness thought were out to get him at every turn. Several print and television journalists were refused entry to Ibrox or to speak to Rangers players, and some newspapers were totally banned. At

Kiev Airport two reporters, from the *Daily Mail* and *The Scotsman*, were thrown off the transit passenger bus on the grounds that it was for Rangers players and officials only. James Traynor, then of the *Glasgow Herald*, was dismissed as a 'little socialist' for his criticism of Souness for what he saw as bad sportsmanship in a European game against Red Star Belgrade in 1990.

In the early days of the war with the press, the *Sunday Mail* had issued a two-page spread headlined 'Fortress Ibrox' with a mock-up picture of the main entrance to Ibrox with barbed wire and heaped sand bags around it. It was the *Sunday Mail* that had highlighted the story of Souness's admonition to David Syme to depart in the Celtic Park incident of a few weeks before and as a consequence it had been banned. But it was not alone; and only the Scottish-based *Sun*, to which certain Rangers players, including Souness, contributed for lucrative sums, seemed free from the wrath of the Ibrox officials.

The media had much to be grateful for in the Souness revolution, as his free-spending on players and the improvements to Ibrox supplied them with a constant stream of headlines and stories for their columns and sports reports. On a couple of occasions he had reason to be grateful to them, most notably, as Sandy Jamieson has shown, for the way they played down his attacks on St Johnstone tea lady Aggie Moffat, and ignored the near-physical confrontation he had at the same time with Geoff Brown, chairman of St Johnstone.[8] This was in the midst of Souness's turmoil over whether or not to accept the Liverpool position, but as he had shown long before this, he did not need private problems to provoke attacks by those who criticised him: Souness felt betrayed when the press commented on the negative aspects of his behaviour and criticised the team when it failed on the field. Never before had football so frequently occupied the front pages of not only the tabloid press, but even of papers like *The Herald* and *The Scotsman*. It was part of the increasing appeal of football to a wider social spectrum, part of a circulation war among the tabloids, and always an illustration of the way in which journalism was being reduced to blaring headlines and sensation rather than analysis.

New newspapers have always found it difficult to find a niche in the established market, and serious papers even more so. It is perhaps ironic, nevertheless, that David Murray's unsuccessful venture into newspaper ownership with the *Sunday Scot* in the early 1990s, one of his few business failures, was due in part to the lack of sports exclusives, many of which related to Rangers, with Murray himself apparently not even supplying titbits for his own paper. Not only did Murray reveal nothing of the impending departure of Souness, a matter which was decidedly delicate, but neither did he let it know that Walter Smith would be his successor. Other papers got these stories first.[9]

The most important aspect of Souness's contribution to Rangers came in a measured article from one of the more balanced contributors to *Follow, Follow* while Souness was still at Ibrox. In this article,[10] the writer calling himself 'MacDougall' challenged the almost pontifical position at Ibrox held by Bill Struth, the club's revered manager from 1920 until 1954, two years before he died, aged 81, on 21 September 1956. MacDougall claimed that Souness's legacy was much more important. Struth had certainly done more than anyone else in his 34 years in charge of Rangers to make the club what it was. In the post-war years, however, the methods that had served Struth in Rangers' period of sustained dominance were no longer suitable, as an ageing Struth seemed more intent on having his own way than bringing Rangers into line with more modern methods. As MacDougall reminded the Rangers fans, Struth had been involved in an unsavoury boardroom squabble in 1947 which had ended with the removal of the popular James Bowie because he had wanted a younger man to replace Struth. A few years later, at the end of 1953 when the club faced a slump, an unusual flurry of letters to the press advocated among other things the reinstatement of James Bowie, more spending on new and younger players (instead of floodlighting), while one even called for a boycott of the club if the directors did not brighten up their act. Struth, approaching 80, retired at the end of the season, but made sure he was replaced by someone of his own choosing, Scot Symon, who was guaranteed to carry on his policies. The great Rangers teams of the early 1960s took the pressure off the board for another few years, but failure in the face of Stein's Celtic resulted in an unusual fit of panic in the Rangers board in the late 1960s. Until Souness arrived, however, the club remained firmly anchored in the past created by Struth.

This is not the interpretation of the more traditional Rangers followers, who see Struth as a god-like figure, a spiritual presence still hovering over Ibrox into the 1990s, as he is depicted in the dramatised Rangers history, 'Follow, Follow'. The most recent Rangers history continues the deification of Struth, claiming that:

> [Struth] will surely be seen by history as one of the greatest of British football managers, surpassing perhaps even the achieve-ments of Jock Stein with Dunfermline and Celtic, Herbert Chapman with Huddersfield Town and Arsenal, and Matt Busby at Manchester United, all of them in differing [*sic*] eras.[11]

Struth can indeed be compared with Chapman. In the 1930s they were managers of the richest clubs in Britain and the glamour that attached to them. Arsenal were known as the Bank of England club and from 1933 the two teams played regular friendlies, most of which Rangers won. For both men, too, soccer was a secondary interest. It was said of Chapman that he had little commitment to the game itself, and was more concerned about packed grounds than the spectacle provided on the park. Unlike Struth, however, Chapman was a crafty tactician, albeit with an ultra-defensive outlook. He also had progressive ideas on the development of the game, from the use of floodlighting to the need for systematic coaching and regular contact with continental teams: for such reasons he has to be ranked with his two close friends, the Austrian Hugo Meisl and the Italian Vittorio Pozzo, as one of the three great figures of world football in the early 1930s.[12] Struth was hardly heard of outside Scotland and the best that can be said about his knowledge of the game is that he had the sense to admit his ignorance in this regard and to defer to the senior players.

As for later figures in British football, Matt Busby, Bill Shankly and Jock Stein, will always be on a different plane from Struth. These were men who lived and breathed the game for the game's sake, interested in it beyond their own club, men who knew what it was like to carve out a living working down the mines and who shared a sympathy with those who came from a tough background. They were disciplinarians who cared more about how the players conducted themselves on the park than whether they wore beards or ties or polished their boots before the game. But even in comparison with other Rangers managers, as MacDougall pointed out, Souness did more good for Rangers in five years, even considering the different eras from which they came, than Struth did in 34.

By the time Souness left Ibrox he was on much better terms all round than he had ever been, the worst complaints coming from his failure to play Ally McCoist in the starting line-up. Indeed, Rangers were on the verge of fulfilling most of the promise that had always been there. But they were still a long way from winning the prize that had been Rangers' main aim when Souness was brought to Ibrox, and the one thing that had justified all the expenditure: success in Europe as a preliminary to Rangers taking part in a new European Super League.

SUPER LEAGUES AND EUROPE

The logic of football since the earliest days has been for the best to play with the best: apart from ensuring attractive fixtures, this also ensured that the big clubs kept to themselves the money they generated. Once professionalism was established in England in 1885 the players had to be guaranteed regular fixtures to pay their wages. Friendlies and the hazards of cup games were not enough and so the Football League was founded by some clubs from the north of England in 1888. It was not called the English League precisely because it was hoped that Scottish clubs would join it. Its founder, the Scot William McGregor of Aston Villa, openly declared it to be a 'League of the Selfish'. Operating alongside but separate from the amateur Football Association, the aim of the Football League was to protect the interests of the professional clubs under its jurisdiction. A separate Scottish League followed in 1890, and professionalism was recognised three years later. The interests of the big clubs, however, despite the efforts of McLaughlin of Celtic and his Rangers counterpart, were restrained by a prevailing amateur ethos that frowned on trafficking in human flesh and which imposed restrictions that ensured that the weak clubs had as much say as the powerful. One hundred years on and the power structure of the Scottish game still prevailed, albeit with several readjustments of the league set-up, until the breakaway 'Premiership' of the top ten was ratified by the League in February 1998.

On the continent and South America there has seldom been much emphasis on the rich clubs helping the weak, and players were not bound by the conditions in Britain that tied players to their clubs in a virtual feudal relationship: or if they were they were well paid for it. It was one of the ironies of the English-speaking world, and that of the Scandinavian countries, where the Protestant work ethic prevailed, that the virtues of profit-making in commercial enterprises were seen as an evil in sport. In the Catholic countries, by and large, players were paid high wages and treated like stars without any twinges of conscience.

In the 1960s British clubs began to enter the brash new world of continental football, and in doing so adopted many continental practices that were often equated with Catholicism, in particular the desecration of the Sabbath. In England the abolition of the maximum wage in 1961 and the Eastham case of 1963 that ended the retain and transfer system paved the way for the open slather freedom of contract of later years. Scotland had not been bound by the wage ceiling, and the higher wages now on offer in England made playing there an added attraction, although it was the great teams of the 1950s, Hibs and Hearts and Aberdeen, who suffered most, as Rangers and Celtic had always been able to match the salaries paid in England. As well as which they had had the power of the jersey. From this point of view the Old Firm has been a good thing for Scottish football.

By the 1970s Celtic and Rangers had both been drawn into the

European football world, and for Rangers this meant compromising their stand as a Christian club that refused not only to play football on a Sunday, but which would not allow Ibrox to be used for commercial purposes on the Sabbath. Celtic, as a Catholic club, had less reservations about desecrating the Sabbath, but like Rangers before Souness they could still not accept paying continental wages, and like them relied on the services of home-grown players. All this would change: the last knell of the Christian ethos tolling when both clubs told the men of the cloth who had previously been admitted free to games at either stadium, that in future they would have to pay to get in. As one spokesman for the Catholic Church, Father Tom Connelly (reflecting the always ambivalent nature of 'progress') said when the gradual phasing out of clerical privileges at Celtic Park ended with their abolition in July 1996, 'The days of priests having no money and relying on hand-outs are long gone.'[13]

Football by the 1980s had become a truly global game, especially as television linked the entire world so that people in the most remote places could tune in and watch the giants of the world game. At the same time as football embraced the world, however, Europe took a stranglehold that concentrated the money being made from the game in that continent. South America still produced some of the world's greatest teams and players, but most of them were playing where the money was: in Europe. Out of Africa came young black stars, a trickle in the 1970s; but now few top-class teams in Europe are without a star African, or player of African origins. The loss of talented players to their homeland is part of the logic and history of the game: beginning with the Scots going south for the money on offer in England from the 1870s; the Argentines being tempted by open cheque books to play in Italy in the 1920s; the stars of the smaller countries of South America who went to Brazil, Uruguay or Argentina . . . Today there are football honey-pots in the Middle East and more recently in Japan, but money is not the only reason why these young men with talent in their feet leave their homelands: they also want to play with the best, and the best want to play with each other. And today, for good or ill, that is in Europe, where the European Cup, now called the European Champions League, is the world's most prized football competition outside the World Cup itself.

Entry to any European competition has to be through the domestic competition, and the peculiar set-up within the FIFA 'family' of the four 'nations' of the United Kingdom being allowed four representatives within the single political nation, has tied Rangers and Celtic to the Scottish game. Souness made it clear when questions were put to him in the wake of publicity after the publication of the centenary history of the

Old Firm in 1988 (*Glasgow's Giants*) that his ambitions lay outside Scotland – it was obvious that the vast Rangers expenditure was not to ensure victory against Raith Rovers or Dunfermline, let alone Celtic or Aberdeen. A British League was out of the question, as the English competition had little to gain from a merger with the top two or three Scottish teams, and such a move would play into the hands of those who would like to see the British nations reduced to a single entity. A British Cup was more feasible, or at least opening the FA Cup to the rest of the United Kingdom, as was the case until the SFA banned the participation of Scottish clubs in it in 1887. It would have been feasible, but unlikely as it has little attraction for the English teams, while the SFA would be concerned about the effect on its own cup competition.

Rangers' entry into Europe was guaranteed every year after Souness arrived, but they saw themselves as shackled by the domestic game and tried to blame this for their failures in Europe. Certainly the Scottish League system was in a state of disarray in 1991 and 1992, as it had been before and would continue to be afterwards, as the small clubs tried to survive in the top ranks and the richer tried to get rid of their influence. This has usually ended in compromise. When Rangers tried to break away from the Scottish League in May 1964 they were thwarted by the small clubs and Bob Kelly of Celtic, a constant champion of their rights. Rangers had then proposed that the League should be wound up and that whatever assets were left to the League after all its debts had been settled should be divided up among the clubs in the League at the time. This was clearly aimed at a breakaway by the bigger clubs, and the smaller clubs used their numbers to block the Rangers proposal. Throughout they were backed by Kelly.[14]

The Premier League was in part prompted by Jock Stein's frustration with the old Scottish League. At the height of his triumphs in the 1970s he had said: 'It is difficult to stay in an unhealthy house without catching some of the disease.' But he was calling for its reform, rather than expressing a wish to leave it, and the Premier League was the result. In 1986, David Hay said in exasperation at the refereeing after the Skol Cup final of 1986 that if he had had his way an application to join the Football League would be in the post at the earliest opportunity. In 1993 the most determined attempt until then to form a breakaway Super League was thwarted again by Celtic.

On 26 June 1992 five of Scotland's top teams announced the formation of a Scottish Super League (SSL). To comply with the League regulations, they declared their intention to resign from it so that they could start their new League in two years' time. The SSL was to be made up of eight teams, access to which would be available only to one approved club that beat the bottom team in the SSL in a play-off. In addition to the League, there would be a Super League Cup and a British Cup where the top 11 English clubs would be invited to join the top five in Scotland. Three points for a win would add an attacking flavour to the game and there would be a four-week winter shut-down. The five core clubs were Rangers, Celtic, Aberdeen, Dundee United and Hearts, to which would be added three more to make a SSL of eight clubs, based on the Premier League in England. It lacked, however, the wide range of top clubs down south, and one of the factors that made the FA's hijacking of the biggest clubs in the League so messy was that the top ten clubs in England in the late 1980s when the issue was being mooted were not the same as those in the 1970s – a decade when even Manchester United had been relegated. But an even greater impediment to the success of the SSL in Scotland, compared to the Premier League in England, was that the SSL was battling against both the SFA and the Scottish League, while it was the FA, reversing its traditional role in English football, that led the richest English clubs in their breakaway from the Football League.

Apart from the richest clubs ruling in their own interests, it is hard to see how the rest of Scottish football and its fans would have benefited. Hibs would have to have been added to the Super Five, but who made up the lucky two to complete the SSL was going to end up in a terrible bun fight – Motherwell, Kilmarnock, Dundee, Dunfermline, St Mirren and other clubs had often been within striking distance of the top. And to further confuse matters, one of the select five, Dundee United, managed to get themselves relegated from the Premier League in 1995. The breakaway was engineered by Rangers and Aberdeen, but it was Wallace Mercer of Hearts, fresh from trying to get rid of Hibs, who acted as spokesman for the SSL, claiming that the new streamlined competition was the way forward and all was for the best in the best of all possible football worlds. Murray's intentions were quite clear: he wanted Rangers to be freed from the tyranny of the wee clubs that made up the Scottish League. Above all the big two (or five or eight) would be free to keep more money to themselves instead of sharing it with those they regarded as little more than leeches. In the end it was Celtic, along with Partick Thistle, who scuttled the deal, by which time the proposed new League had been expanded to 12 teams.

Little was gained from it, but when Murray launched his next attack on the football authorities three years later, his plans were kept under wraps, the other nine teams in the Premier League were brought into the scheme from the beginning and the details were worked out by a private company before being released to the public, in part at least, in September 1997. Above all he then had Celtic's new owner as a firm ally. From the moment McCann arrived at Celtic Park in 1994 the Old Firm were back in business, ready to express their contempt for the underdogs of Scottish football. In the meantime both Rangers and Celtic continued to show that they were the underdogs in European football.

THE OLD FIRM IN EUROPE

There was a time in the decade from the mid-1960s when Rangers and Celtic could reasonably vie for the title of European champions – and that with home-grown players. In the early 1980s it was Aberdeen and Dundee United who most proudly carried the Scottish flag into Europe: Aberdeen beat Real Madrid in the European Cup-Winners' Cup in 1983 and went on to beat Hamburger SV in the Supercup over two legs; and a gallant Dundee United, who went so close to the final of the European Cup in 1984, lost in the final of the UEFA Cup in 1987. The glory days of European football now seem to be lost to Scotland, however, and neither Celtic nor the multi-million-pound Rangers, a few cherished games in 1993 notwithstanding, have been able to bring them back.

In 1984 both Celtic and Rangers were involved in torrid encounters in European competition, in one of which Celtic were cheated out of a hard-earned victory in the Cup-Winners Cup, and in the other Rangers were plunged into the Irish conflict in a UEFA Cup game in Dublin. Celtic had lost the away leg of their second-round UEFA Cup game against Rapid Vienna by 1–3, but in a night of passion at Parkhead on 7 November 1984 they had come back to win 3–0. Or at least they thought they had. Instead the victory was snatched from them thanks to weak refereeing, the antics of an Austrian player who claimed to have been felled by an object thrown by a spectator and whose wound was quickly bandaged up before anyone could see it, and worst of all by the complaisance of UEFA who decided that the game had to be replayed at a ground more than 100 miles from Glasgow. Desmond White decided to go ahead with the replay, confident of a win and assured of a monster gate, but the game played at Manchester turned out to be a nightmare as Celtic lost 0–1 and two fans, one wearing a Celtic jersey, attacked the Austrian goalkeeper and the Austrian scorer in separate incidents. This time UEFA's punishment was justified – lenient even – as they fined Celtic £17,000 and decreed that their next home match be played behind closed doors.

Celtic and Rangers played in Ireland as representatives of one or other of the religious communities there, so that when Celtic played in the south they were welcomed with all the symbols of Ireland and the fans of both clubs could join together in expressing their hatred of the British government. The Protestants of Belfast and Ulster regarded Rangers as their team, and happily followed them when they visited the island. Rangers had played in Dundalk in the Inter-Cities' Cup in November 1968, as the troubles in the North were brewing, without any problems, and in 1975 a Rangers visit to play Bohemians in the European Cup in Dublin passed without serious incident. But when the two teams were drawn to play each other in the first leg of a UEFA Cup first-round game in Dublin on 18 September 1984, the arrival of thousands of Ulster supporters of Rangers in Dublin resulted in a game that was played in virtual riot conditions. Buses coming down from Belfast had to run the gauntlet of missiles both to and from the game. Rangers lost 2–3 in Dublin, but won 2–0 at Ibrox, with both goals coming in the last six minutes, to go through to the next round where they lost to Inter Milan.

The story of Rangers and Celtic in Europe has, with a few exceptions, been a dismal one ever since. In the year before Souness arrived, Rangers were eliminated in the first round of the UEFA Cup by Spain's Osasuna. In Souness's first year Rangers advanced to the third round by beating Finland's Ilves Tampere and then Boavista of Portugal, with 2–1 at Ibrox and 1–0 away respectively. In the third round, however, which was also the quarter-final, they lost on the away goals rule to Borussia Mönchengladbach after two draws, 1–1 at Ibrox and 0–0 away. In his first taste of the European Cup with Rangers, Souness took them to the third round, defeating Dynamo Kiev and Poland's Gornik Zabrze before losing to Steaua Bucharest: they lost 0–2 in the away leg and gave away a first-minute goal at Ibrox to make their task impossible.

Back in the UEFA Cup for the 1988–89 season, Poland's Katowice were dismissed with a 5–2 aggregate, but a 1–1 draw against Cologne in the next round was not enough to overcome a 0–2 loss in the away leg. From then on it was all European Cups for Rangers, but Souness's last two in Scotland saw Rangers eliminated in the first round by Bayern Munich, and in his last European season the minnows of Malta, Valletta were crushed 10–0 over two legs, but Rangers then fell to Red Star Belgrade with a 0–3 away loss and a 1–1 draw at Ibrox. In the summer of 1991 Rangers sold Trevor Steven to Olympique de Marseille for a Scottish record of £5 million, and were bitterly accused in the press and by some of their fans of having given up any European ambition. Walter Smith's Rangers were duly eliminated in the first round of the new manager's first taste of European football as manager, but only on the away goal rule, at Ibrox, after Rangers had recovered from a 0–1 loss to Sparta Prague in the Czech Republic. Rangers took the Czech champions to extra time, and, when they scored twice seemed to be coasting to victory, only to give away a goal in a bizarre defensive mix-up that made the score 3–2, although it was 3–3 on aggregate. The following year, however, Smith was to enjoy his *annus mirabilis* with a clean sweep of the domestic trophies and a great run in Europe.

Rangers won the Scottish League Cup in October 1992 with a 2–1 victory over Aberdeen, and the following May they repeated the same score-line with another victory over the Dons in the Scottish Cup. In the League they coasted clear of Aberdeen to take their fifth successive League title, but it was in Europe that the real glory came, above all when they qualified for the new Champions League with home and away victories over Leeds United, 2–1 on both occasions. It was one of these few occasions when most of Scotland could enjoy a Rangers victory: beating the English is about the only time when some Celtic and Rangers fans can tolerate a victory by their rivals. Rangers in 1992, like Celtic in 1970, won in style, on the latter occasion McCoist and Hateley showing devastating form. Prior to disposing of Leeds, Rangers beat Denmark's Lyngby BK 2–0 at home and 1–0 away. In the Champions' League there were two sections of four teams and the winners of each would play each other in the final. In the league section Rangers never lost a game, beating Club Brugge and CSKA Moscow and drawing the other games; against Marseille, they drew twice, 2–2 at Ibrox and 1–1 in France. But it appears that there were other forces at work, as Marseille thrashed a supine CSKA and beat a Brugge team that seemed to have lost all interest in the competition, to pip Rangers for a place in the final when Rangers could manage only a draw with CSKA in the last game of the league section. If Celtic were cheated in their European game against Rapid Vienna, it is highly likely that Rangers were cheated out of reaching the final in 1993, as rumours of the way the French club had bought its way to victory that year became fact and eventually the club was punished when it was convicted of bribing players in the French League to ensure their title. As the investigations got under way there was talk of the final being replayed, with Rangers playing AC Milan, but it was not to be.

Rangers' success served only to heighten the depths into which Celtic had sunk, as they failed in the domestic competition and gave their fans little joy in Europe. In the year after the Rapid Vienna fiasco, Celtic drew 1–1 away to Atlético Madrid in the first round of the European Cup-Winners' Cup then lost 1–2 in the ghostly atmosphere of an empty Celtic Park, courtesy of UEFA's punishment for the excesses of the previous year. Shamrock Rovers were overcome in the first round of the European Cup in 1986, but Dynamo Kiev eliminated Celtic in the second round. They were never to advance further than the second round thereafter, and in the 1990–91 season Celtic failed to make it into Europe for the first time in 12 years. Celtic's return to Europe in Liam

Brady's first year in 1991–92 ended in Switzerland after a first-round UEFA Cup victory against Belgium's Germinal Ekeren: their 1–5 defeat at the hands of Neuchâtel Xamax in the next round was the worst in the club's European history, and gave the fans a new word for a thrashing: to be 'xamaxed'.

CELTIC AND THE SOUNESS CHALLENGE

By the time Celtic were being 'xamaxed' in Switzerland, Billy McNeill had left the club. The touch that had inspired Celtic in his first two seasons back in charge seems to have deserted him thereafter, and while he was given more money to spend on players than any previous manager, he was working from a much tighter budget than Souness. If Souness made any bad buys this was soon lost in the merry-go-round of players coming to and from Ibrox – nearly £16 million spent and just over £6 million on sales, but always the Rangers fans were left with the memory of those who had produced some scintillating moments: Trevor Francis, Ray Wilkins, Trevor Steven, Mark Hateley and Pieter Huistra.

McNeill's first buys were shrewd rather than spectacular: Chris Morris from Sheffield Wednesday for £115,000, Andy Walker from Motherwell for £375,000 and Billy Stark for a bargain £75,000 from Aberdeen. The £850,000 to bring Frank McAvennie from West Ham was a club record, and he was joined by a player of great promise in Joe Miller, who came from Aberdeen in November 1987 for £650,000. A cosmopolitan touch was added to the club in the summer of 1989 with the signing of London-born Paul Elliott from Pisa for £600,000 and Darius Dziekanowski from Poland for the same amount, while Mike Galloway was bought from Hearts for half a million pounds. Galloway was no success, Elliot had festering contractual disputes with the club, and the Pole 'Jacky' had some great moments but took too fondly to the Glasgow good life. In the following close season McNeill spent over £2 million on three players: £650,000 on Martin Hayes of Arsenal who was given a free transfer 18 months later; Charlie Nicholas, also from Arsenal, for £450,000, but the one-time Celtic hero was past his best and never reached full-match fitness; John Collins came from Hibs as Celtic's first million-pound transfer, had a patchy career and left the club for Monaco in 1996 on a free, thanks to the new Bosman ruling on players' contracts.

McNeill's later signings were often expensive failures, and of the £7 million he spent, only McAvennie, Elliot, Walker and Stark could have been said to be big successes. McNeill's purchase of Polish players was said to be because the money the board allocated allowed only bargain-basement buys. However that may be, McNeill was not given the money to match Souness's English signings – apart from anything else, too much was needed to staunch the haemorrhaging bank balance. McNeill's replacement, Liam Brady, was given more money to spend, but it often meant money wasted, especially when players were signed on weekly wages that chased away would-be buyers when they did not fit in. Brady bought Tony Cascarino from Aston Villa for £1.1 million in July 1991, with a £250,000 signing-on fee and a salary of £3,000 a week. As a result his four goals in 30 appearances over seven months works out at about £48,000 per appearance and £360,000 per goal (Celtic did recoup some of this in the shape of Tom Boyd when Cascarino was offloaded to Chelsea in a swap deal). It was all part of the insanity of contemporary financial orthodoxy as reflected on the football field: a frequently injured Gascoigne and a drug-bloated Maradona were costing their clubs on the continent even more for little return, while managers dismissed for lack of success could expect to walk away with a tidy sum in their bank balance. Still, it was no worse than in the business world at large, where directors of newly privatised companies could pay themselves six-figure salaries and directors in other companies rewarded themselves with massive dividends for doing little more than keeping their seat warm, or received massive pay-outs when they were shown to be incompetent.

McNeill had other problems. Like Jock Wallace he was a man brought up at a time when players were paid good but hardly startling wages, and who accepted the discipline of a manager who did not earn much more than they did. He had little time for agents, or players who spoke for themselves, and he lost some of their respect when he criticised them publicly. He was on bad terms with Celtic's chief executive, Terry Cassidy, as indeed everyone was, and resented his expectation that he should discuss team plans with the rest of the staff at Parkhead. But above all he had problems with the board.

McNeill was ultimately sacked for his lack of success, in which poor judgement in buying new players played its part, but if directors were to be sacked for their mistakes then there would have been a clear-out of the board at Celtic Park. The Celtic directors continued to close their eyes to the future, or if they saw it, did not like it and tried to turn their backs on it. They had rejected the offers of Fergus McCann and Paul Green because this would have involved them giving up some of their power. In turn the directors came up with a scheme at the beginning of 1990 in which they suggested that 30 of their wealthiest supporters give an interest-free loan of £1 million pounds to renovate Celtic Park. In return they would receive a few privileges involving wining and dining in the company of the board members, but without the slightest sniff of power-sharing. Perhaps the Celtic directors were even surprised when nobody came to the party, and so they had to come up with other ways of finding money to build a new stadium or have Celtic Park completely renovated. They also had to find more money to spend on players.

FACING UP TO THE FUTURE

Rangers during this time were not without their problems, but success on the field and a superb stadium served to silence the critics. Alan Montgomery, appointed as business manager to work alongside Souness, was quietly removed when Souness found that he could not work with him. When Terry Cassidy, in a similar position at Parkhead, fell foul of Liam Brady, the air remained poisoned for a long time before the unpopular Cassidy was finally removed. Even Murray's disagreements with Hugh Adam, manager of the Rangers Pools that had done so much to bring extra money to the club in its earlier days, and Jack Gillespie, whose share deal with Marlborough allowed the latter to take the club over in 1985, and who had also entered into an agreement with Murray regarding shares when he took over in 1988, were resolved with minimum adverse publicity. When Adam was removed from the board in late June 1992, he attacked Murray with a fulsome array of derogatory terms along the lines that Murray was little more than a 'football carpetbagger'.[15] Murray, however, had no jurisdiction over Adam's position as chairman of Rangers Development Fund and managing director of Rangers Pools, the most successful in the country. These were kept independent of the club in order that its contributions, given as 'donations', would not be subject to tax. According to Adam, Murray resented his independence, although he could not have been too enamoured, either, of Adam's contempt for his business sense; whatever, the two had been at loggerheads since Murray took over, although eventually Adam was restored to the board. Gillespie sorted out his problems with Murray in private a year later, but not before a few pounds had been spent in the courts. And compared to the controversy surrounding the slightest contretemps out Parkhead way at this time, it was all little more than a tiff in a tea-cup.

Rangers had a paper debt of £7 million when Murray took over in November 1988, and in 1992 he faced some financial stringency when the club and Murray International Holdings that largely owned it, was hit by the property slump and recorded a loss of £5 million. The income from attendances at home games at Ibrox in the early 1990s, at least half a million pounds, was still a major source of income, but increasingly, as with most big clubs throughout Britain, profits were coming from other sources: corporate hospitality, sponsorship, advertising and merchandising. Fans were encouraged to buy replica strips and parents forced to change them regularly as the clubs deliberately altered the design to ensure that they quickly went out of fashion, and so-called 'away' strips were often invented that had little to do with the traditions of the club – in this Celtic and Rangers were no better than other clubs. Fans were encouraged to ring special numbers to talk to their heroes, or at least listen to their recorded messages, giving them news about what was going on at the club. None of this was forced on the fans, but their commitment to the club was an increasing strain on their budget. When costs of entry to European games was raised to what some saw as extortionate levels the fans did see that there were limits, and crowds for some major European games at Ibrox were attended by anything up to 10,000 less than those who would come to an irrelevant League game. Now, as the money from sources outside attendance continues to multiply there is no reason why admission prices should not be reduced; already Berlusconi had said that in his aim of a mid-week TV league the fans could get in for nothing just to ensure the atmosphere.

However, Rangers still tried to keep in touch with their fans, to reach out beyond their 5,000 existing shareholders and 27,000 season-ticket-holders. This was the float by Murray, in August 1991, of 34,560,000 shares at 10p each – in effect existing shareholders found their shares, then selling at £70, increased by a factor of 100 but revalued at 70p. The intention was to increase the capital of the club by nearly £3.5 million and allow the less impecunious fans to buy a small share in the club. The move was passed at the September 1991 AGM and within a couple of years the value of these shares had increased by over 500 per cent.

While Rangers tried to involve their fans in the club, the Celtic board continued to keep them at bay, whether it was wealthy fans trying to buy into the board or others calling for it to be opened up to the public. In May 1990, however, the Celtic board made an inspired move that seemed to be setting the club in a more progressive direction when it appointed two new men to the board. A few months later it all turned to ashes when one of them was sacked and a club teetering on the brink was plunged into civil war.

The two new directors appointed to take Celtic into the new world of cash-driven football were Brian Dempsey and Michael Kelly. Dempsey was a wealthy, self-made property developer and builder, the son of a Labour MP for Airdrie and Coatbridge whose safe Labour seat had almost been lost in 1959 when he, a Catholic, was opposed by a candidate whose main claim to fame was that she was the sister of Rangers' Alan Morton. Dempsey was a Celtic man and chairman of two major building companies, earning enough to spend £350,000 on the club (although Celtic claimed when he withdrew his 'Skybox' in May

1991 that in the previous season he had spent only about a third of that)[16] in corporate entertainment, as well as £25,000 at Ibrox. He was a popular man and it was expected that his expertise would be used to establish a new home for Celtic.

The other was Michael Kelly, well known throughout Scotland, and a man whose name and well-publicised beliefs made him the ideal person to brighten the image of the club he had grown up with. With this appointment it seemed as though Celtic had secured a man of vision who had the name and the interests of the club at heart. It was Michael Kelly, after all, who had performed wonders while a Labour Lord Provost of Glasgow between 1980 and 1984, presiding over the transformation of the city under the slogan 'Glasgow's miles better'. He was criticised during this time for refusing to visit Ibrox, and made no secret of his sympathies for Celtic. He was also the grandson of the great James Kelly whose name went back to the origins of the club and nephew of his successor, Robert Kelly. But Kelly was also an academic, with a doctorate in economics, and perhaps not very comfortable with the idea of young men who expected to be treated like kings and rewarded with gifts beyond the dreams of Croesus for occasionally kicking a ball around.

The hopes aroused by the new blood on the board were crushed when Dempsey was sacked on 26 October 1990 when his name came up for what was expected to be the formality of his ratification. This roused the Celtic faithful to an even greater pitch of anger than that which would greet McNeill's dismissal a few months later – whatever the manner of McNeill's passing, he had had little success on the field. Dempsey's dismissal was a demonstration of the power that two men with the names and shares of Kelly and White could wield, and with that other name so long associated with the club, Grant, the 'families' set about ensuring that they remained in complete control of the club. Above all they refused to go public or accept money from outside sources that would threaten their power. Fans who could not earn in a year what some players were paying in tax increasingly vented their frustration on a board that tried hard to ignore them. With Rangers continuing to lead the way, from players and stadium to the collection of the fabled silverware, the board found itself assailed from all sides. Such was the wondrous power of success that Murray could even admit, without losing any popularity, that he wanted to set up a family dynasty at Ibrox, with his sons taking over when he left.[17] At Celtic Park the cries mounted for an end to the ruling dynasties, so much so that there were times when it seemed that the only support for the Celtic board came from joyous Bluenoses, as Rangers fans, in response to Celtic supporters' cries of 'Sack the board!', gleefully chanted 'Keep the board!'.

5. Uncivil War at Celtic Park

The optimism that greeted the appointments of businessman Brian Dempsey and public relations consultant Michael Kelly to the Celtic board in May 1990 was well warranted at the time. All it needed was for them to work together and the team to get back on the winning track and Celtic would be once more in pursuit of their great rivals. It all came crashing down at the AGM of that year, on 26 October, when Dempsey's ratification to the board was blocked, two days before Celtic were due to play Rangers in a crucial Skol League Cup final. The majority on the Celtic board wanted to ratify Dempsey's appointment, but this was opposed by Chris White and Michael Kelly, ostensibly because of Dempsey's determination to proceed with a new stadium project at Robroyston. The majority on the board was defeated by the votes wielded from the floor by Kelly and White, and greeted with dismay by the fans. The popular Dempsey made a dignified exit, but he had every reason to be seething, and while he did not show his anger, the fans did, especially when Celtic lost the final 2–1.

The defeat on the Sunday could not be directly attributed to the wrangling on the board, but squabbling among the directors did not make for a happy atmosphere at the club, and Celtic manager McNeill was probably being more diplomatic than honest when, in reply to a question by Michael Kelly before Dempsey's board ratification was blocked, he said that the players did not even know who the directors were. The fans did, and they were beginning to mobilise their discontent. Dempsey went home to nurse his wrath and had no difficulty in keeping it warm over the next three years. A young business consultant, David Low, wrote a letter to *The Herald* congratulating the board for getting rid of Dempsey, but soon he would become Dempsey's right-hand man in a scheme to buy up enough shares from small shareholders to bring about a revolution from within. Low, a business associate of Kelly before the two fell out, was the first to realise not only that Celtic shares were grossly undervalued, but that they were not invulnerable to outside interests, as the board believed, and this was the major factor in their ridiculously low valuation.

In Canada, Fergus McCann kept his eye on events with a calm and resolute detachment, increasingly determined that he would put up the money to see Celtic through its problems, so long as he got a controlling interest and part of the new funding came from the fans. Another millionaire who would come into the act, Gerald Weisfeld, had still not been converted by his stepson to become a Bhoy.

At Celtic Park the money to buy new players and renovate or relocate the stadium was not forthcoming, the players faltered on the field and the directors firmly averted their gaze from the future. In March 1992 a few of them committed themselves to each other in a self-preservation pact which, when it was made public, added more fuel to a fraternal bloodletting as bitter as all family quarrels, known when played out in the wider world by that grotesque misnomer, a 'civil war'. It all ended at Parkhead with the ousting of the old board in March 1994, to make way for a new regime under Fergus McCann.

SOME LESSONS FROM HISTORY

At the same time as the Celtic directors were retiring to their bunkers, two of the world's most odious regimes were opening up to the world at large: in the Soviet Union the reforms of Mikhail Gorbachev had led to the collapse of communism in Eastern Europe, while in South Africa apartheid was being dissolved without the anticipated bloodshed, thanks in large measure to Nelson Mandela, whose forgiveness of his former tormentors is without equivalent since the founding of Christianity. And it was nearly three decades since even the Catholic Church had brought itself into the modern age. None of this seems to have affected the Celtic board, who continued to live in another age, the traditional families clinging to power like the privileged élites of France at the time of Louis XVI. No more than the Bourbons before them were the offspring of the Kellys and the Whites and the Grants able to assure the worth of their descendants through some hereditary divine right passed on to their children and their children's children.

Of this offspring, clearly the most talented was Michael Kelly, but in his absorbing inside account of the events at Parkhead, *Paradise Lost: The Struggle for Celtic's Soul*,[1] he shows that the lessons of history are not read by all people in the same way. Kelly quotes appositely from Milton in his book, and criticises David Low for his use of 'one of the lesser' works of Niccolo Machiavelli, *The Prince*, as his bible in planning the destruction of the Celtic board. But he himself, if he was not to learn from some of the great individuals of his own time who were dealing with problems of power on a scale somewhat greater than that of the Celtic board, could have learned more from others who have written about the problems of coming to terms with inevitable change. Giuseppe di Lampedusa's *The Leopard*, for instance, where the wily old Sicilian aristocrat, faced by the intrusions of the money men in mid-nineteenth-century Italy, learned how to change to remain the same. Better might he have pondered over de Tocqueville and his analysis of the events that led up to the great French Revolution of 1789, where families intent on retaining their power and privileges, albeit in the name of God and His social order, refused to recognise the power of the moneyed and educated classes who would not submit to feudal subservience. The king, the prelates and the aristocrats, instead of losing some of their power and privileges, ended up by losing them all. Faced by opening up their ranks to the men with the money to build a new stadium, or a public issue that would have involved ordinary fans in running the club, the 'traditional families' of the Celtic board shut themselves up inside their own Bastille and waited until it was battered down by the force of public opinion. And financial reality.

In the final analysis, it is Kelly's book more than any other that shows just how effete the old board was, an indictment if ever one was needed, of the nonsense of nepotism and the futility of determining worth by birth rather than by merit. The sadness is that someone of Kelly's abilities should not only find himself embroiled with such narrow views, but become the leader of what he called 'the old guard who had run Celtic down remorselessly over the years . . .'[2] Kelly's is a tale of a board that was motivated by self-interest under the guise of 'family' or 'Celtic' tradition, of incompetence on a grand scale, and deviousness that Machiavelli would have criticised only for its amateurism.

THE DUMPING OF DEMPSEY

Dempsey's removal from the board was opposed by a majority of the board members: Kevin Kelly, Tom Grant, Jim Farrell and chairman Jack McGinn. However, on the basis of votes held by shareholders, White and Michael Kelly carried the motion, a shareholding power that they would use in subsequent meetings. The reasons given for Dempsey's removal was his insistence that the club should build a new ground at Robroyston, where Dempsey had several business interests. There were no doubt problems attached to Robroyston, in terms not only of planning approval but also of the emotional issue of taking Celtic fans away from the club's spiritual home. The concept of the new ground being part of a wider commercial, retail and leisure development was bold, but there were major questions about where the Celtic Football Club would stand in terms of the ownership of its own ground. Rumours surfaced about Dempsey standing to profit from the move to Robroyston, rumours that Michael Kelly still insists were well founded, but it was far from unusual and certainly not illegal for a football club director to benefit in his business from his position in the club.

The scale of Dempsey's proposals was huge, and consequently intimidating, but even more fear was held by some directors of his popularity with the fans: it was the insensitive way in which Dempsey was removed that most appalled the Celtic faithful. And its timing. The fans of 1990 were much more aware of what was going on behind the scenes than those of their father's generation, and less willing to put up with it. The players who went out to play Rangers two days later could well have been spared a controversy that was eventually to cost the board much more than the Skol Cup they lost that Sunday in October.

Celtic supporters have generally been more critical of their board than Rangers supporters, whose frustration about what happened on the field was more likely to be taken out on the players. In the 1980s fans were better educated than in the past – and better organised. With the changes in computer technology they were able to put out cheap publications to express their own opinions. On the broader front, and in reaction to the Heysel disaster and the debate on hooliganism that accompanied it, fans in England concerned about the game's image got together to defend it against those who would destroy it, be they the hooligans on the terracing or the vultures in the boardrooms. Out of this came the Football Supporters Association in 1986, bringing in the fans of clubs from all over Britain. Unlike the traditional supporters associations, in which Rangers and Celtic had been well to the fore over the years, which were essentially support bodies for the clubs in return for a few privileges in regard to season-tickets, travel to away games and the appearance at their socials of representatives from the club, the FSA was concerned about the future of the game and not just the welfare of a particular club.

At the same time fanzines started to appear, giving voice to those followers of the club who felt they were overlooked in the daily press and patronised in the bland club magazines. By 1990 what had started out as photocopied sheets held roughly together by hand-held staplers had become glossy publications showing all the expertise of the new desktop publishing. One of the best was Celtic's *Not the View*, an early arrival on the fanzine scene, in early November 1987, its name inspired by the club's official publication, the *Celtic View*. The first editorial in *Not the View* squarely set the board in its sights:

> We can all have a good laugh at the Huns as they go through the annual ritual of the shareholders meeting, which at times resembles the Nuremberg rallies with fat loonies in Rangers strips demanding that no 'Tim' ever be allowed to darken the doorstep of Ibrox. But at least they can make their views, however bigoted or stupid they may be, known to the directors face to face. The Rangers board must attend these meetings. Who are the Celtic directors accountable to?
>
> Celtic should go public and float a large number of shares. Not only would this provide a massive injection of cash, but with any luck we might end up with a chairman with a bit of style and charisma . . . at least they should be more accountable to the people who make the club what it is – you and me, the supporters. If we didn't go along every Saturday then these Mr Magoos wouldn't have a club to run.[3]

The new fanzine found favour with the fans, and was soon selling more than 10,000 copies, while its plans for modernising the club were taken up by a broader spectrum of Celtic supporters, whose hopes came to rest with a single director, vaguely echoed in that first editorial.

Among the other fanzines that started to proliferate, several devoted to Rangers and Celtic, was one that emerged directly out of the Dempsey sacking: *Once a Tim, Always a Tim*, founded by Matt McGlone. McGlone became one of the main leaders in organising fan discontent, not just through his fanzine, but through public meetings and well-organised publicity campaigns and demonstrations, ending with a successful boycott of a game at Celtic Park as the old board was in its death throes.[4]

Having lost Dempsey, the board decided to advertise for an Executive Director to make full commercial advantage of the club name. They chose Terry Cassidy, a man keenly supported by Michael Kelly, who saw in him 'a brilliant choice' but went on to make what was an error in English that perhaps revealed a more significant Freudian slip, when he wondered whether Cassidy understood the 'enormity' of the job.[5] 'Enormity', not to be confused with excessive size, has to do with outrageous or excessive wickedness – but this is perhaps going too far; Basil Fawlty and the Keystone Cops were images more appropriate to the board than Attila the Hun or any of the Renaissance popes.

Cassidy was duly appointed and wasted no time in making himself the most unpopular man at Parkhead, surpassing even the unpopularity of Hood at Ibrox because Cassidy upset not only the fans, but soon put the board off, chased away would-be sponsors, alienated himself from

McNeill and his successor, Liam Brady, and by a full and wholesome expression of his contempt for the media in all its forms, ensured that all of this would be picked up and amplified to his disadvantage. If managers get crucified for the mistakes they make in the players they buy, then directors can scarcely complain when the finger of incompetence is pointed at them for their dud appointments.

Cassidy was English, and while this is not something to boast about in Scotland, he was also happy to say that he was not a Celtic fan and thought Rangers were stupid for not employing him first.[6] He came with an impressive CV, but he never measured up to his own opinion of himself. And yet among his mind-boggling 'embarrassment of stupidities', the stupidity for which he is best remembered, his plan for the sacking of Billy McNeill, was in fact a reasonable attempt to set before the board a series of options, one of which included retaining the legendary 'Caesar'. The leaked document was manna to the press and *The Sun* made the most of it, especially when Cassidy claimed that there was no such document and challenged them to publish it. They did.

Cassidy's time at Parkhead was up when David Smith was appointed to the board in February 1992; thereafter his requests to be made a director were passed over and on 24 October 1992 he was duly sacked, with 14 months of his three-year contract, worth £60,000 per year, still to run. This led to a long and drawn-out legal case over the terms of his pay-out, in which claim and counter-claim were met in court before being settled in a private arrangement.

David Dallas Smith was a lifelong Celtic supporter, who lived in London but still made regular trips to Scotland to see his team play. Born in Brechin into a Celtic supporting family, he trained as an accountant in Glasgow and went on to make a name for himself in the field of liquidation and takeovers, most notably the £2.2 billion takeover of the Gateway supermarket chain by his own Isosceles company. He was a long-term friend of Chris White and he and Michael Kelly spent a great deal of effort trying to convince him to join the board. He was also a Protestant, which not surprisingly was mentioned in the press: indeed if there hadn't been so much else going on at the time it probably would have been a major splash – he was, after all, Celtic's first Protestant to be appointed to the board. His religion was irrelevant in the opposition by certain members of the board to his appointment, and as in the case of Dempsey's dismissal, Michael Kelly and White steam-rollered their choice through against the wishes of their recalcitrant colleagues. They were helped this time by the casting vote of chairman Kevin Kelly, who had replaced Jack McGinn in that position the previous October.

THE LEAGUE CHAMPIONSHIP.

LEFT: From the *Scottish Referee*, 3 February 1905 (and not entitled 'Apes and Aryans')

BELOW: The new divide: camel coats and cloth caps (courtesy Archie MacGregor and *The Absolute Game*)

Graeme Souness and David Murray at an Ibrox press conference, 1991, and (*below*)
announcing the Ibrox deal: (*back*) Souness, Marlborough and Gillespie;
(*front*) Murray and Holmes

MASS RALLY
Sack the Board
CELTIC PARK CAR PARK
at 2.00pm on SATURDAY
NOVEMBER 6th
CELTIC v. THISTLE
KELLY AND Co.
IT'S TIME TO GO
BANNER PROTEST

Malcontents at work: Celtic fans oppose the old board through meetings, placards and boycotts

New-look Paradise: fans become shareholders, the City arrives to give its blessing in the guise of Tommy Burns and Billy Stark, while McCann introduces the new chief trophy-hunters, manager Jock Brown and head coach Wim Jansen

The new voices of the fans: from works like these a new subculture grew

THE CELT

Mr. James Quinn.

NO. 1   AUG   1983   50 P.

THE RANGERS HISTORIAN

ISSUE No. 1   SEPTEMBER 1987

60p

N_{OT} THE VIEW

Issue No.1

Celtic Fanzine   **50p**

The shorts are too tight.

What do you think of the new strip?

Inside   Billy McNeill · Davie Hay · This Season's Squad
Dortmund · Old Firm Preview ·   And More

FOLLOW, FOLLOW

A RANGERS FANZINE   No.1   40p

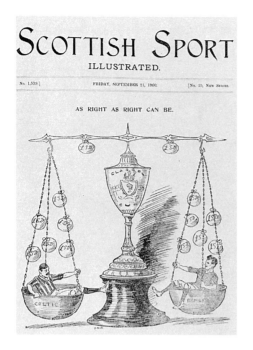

Still the same old story? Business before bigotry: *(clockwise from top left)* the *Scottish Sport*, 21 September 1900; the *Scottish Referee*, 10 February 1908; the *Mail on Sunday*, 26 January 1997; and the *Scottish Sport*, 24 August 1900

THE NON-APPEASEMENT PACT

It was Smith who concocted the 'shareholders' agreement' that brought some relief to a beleaguered board, but in the end it was to help destroy them. By this agreement, drawn up on the eve of an EGM called for 30 March 1992 (although the full details of its contents were not revealed to the public until June of that year) five of the directors agreed never to sell their shares without first offering them to the others. This was to bind the Kellys, White, Grant and David Smith together for the next ten years. By doing so they claimed to be achieving stability, safeguarding the soul of the club as Michael Kelly would have it, protecting it from the 'crusade of revenge'[7] being launched against it by Dempsey and his acolytes.

Before the pact was entered into, Kevin Kelly and Tom Grant had been in contact with the 'rebels' to come to some arrangement with them – but by agreeing to the pact they had thrown in their lot with the old regime. Grant was a troubled soul: shortly after his appointment to the board, Tom Grant had told *Celtic View* on 18 November 1987 of his fears about a public issue of shares, claiming that 'there are many for whom a public share offer would present an opportunity to destroy Celtic. We do not want to dilute what the club's founders envisaged.' By contacting the 'rebels' he showed his concern for the direction the club was taking, but by entering into the pact he demonstrated the dilemma he faced concerning what was best for the club and what was best for himself: a dilemma that would beset him for a long time to come. Smith, appointed to the board without any shareholding in the club, soon acquired the necessary shares to legalise his appointment. When the naked self-interest in the pact was revealed it was immediately denounced in a variety of images bestriding the world from Beijing (the 'Gang of Five') and Munich (the 'Non-aggression Pact' – Hugh Drake, a shareholder), to Hollywood (the 'rat-pact', Gerry McNee, the journalist).

Behind the pact was the knowledge that a group was at work buying shares in the club with the intention of challenging the board from within. In *Scotland on Sunday* on 19 January 1992, Kevin McCarra and Francis Shennan wrote an article entitled 'Secret bid to stir up Celtic' in which they revealed that a group of businessmen had got together to overhaul Celtic Football Club by bringing in £16 million to dilute the control of the White and Kelly families; this had involved meetings since the previous October in North America, Ireland and Scotland with the target of attaining a 51 per cent holding in Celtic shares. Low and Dempsey refused to confirm the story, and Low even denied it outright to the *Sunday Mail.* Shennan, a business journalist, had been in possession of the information for some time, and would go on, with Low, to write a book about it all,[8] but much of his information had come from privileged sources. McCarra on the other hand, one of Scotland's few journalists with an academic background, showed that this was no disadvantage as he ferreted out information through his own sources, so that the story had to break some time sooner rather than later.

One of those in on the secret was Matt McGlone. He met Low for the first time in November 1991 at a Glasgow University Celtic Supporters Club 20th Anniversary Night where he told the astonished schemer that he was about to reveal the story of his trafficking in Celtic shares in his fanzine. Low managed to persuade McGlone, with whom he was later to team up, to keep quiet. In the meantime Low continued his travels that took him, as the blurb to his book tells us, from 'secret meetings in luxury apartments in Montreal, Phoenix and the Caribbean to Belfast graveyards and Fermanagh cowsheds'. Low, financed by Dempsey, was playing on the feelings of a widely scattered family of Celtic shareholders who felt that they had been neglected by the club or did not like the direction it was taking. Some were even happy to accept the attractive price that they were being offered for the shares: as much as £350 for shares valued by the board at £3.

Under the articles of association all Celtic shares had to be ratified by the board, and so the sales were obtained with a proxy that allowed the would-be buyer to vote at the AGM. It needed 10 per cent of shareholders to call an EGM, and it was at such an EGM that the 'Rebels', as they came to be called and were happy to call themselves, hoped to topple the board. In a trip to North America in mid-November 1991, to secure Celtic shares from the Grant inheritance, Low went to Montreal in an attempt to win McCann over to his cause. McCann had returned to Scotland in 1990 to make a further offer to Celtic, similar to the previous ones, and was again repulsed. McCann also met Dempsey and Weisfeld on that trip, but neither then nor after his accession to power, could the three wealthy men get on with each other. Low failed to win McCann over to his scheme, and while McCann greeted him with typical bluntness, he congratulated him on his plan, but preferred to stick by his own scheme: to set up a public limited company, called Celtic's Future plc, into which he would put millions of his own money to gain a controlling interest and raise extra cash through a share issue to the public. McCann and the Low group, however, agreed on the need to remove the reigning board.

Low, who would later become a disciple of McCann, then flew to Toronto to meet Jim Doherty, a wealthy yacht broker and cousin of Tom Grant. Doherty was easily won over, as he, like the other shareholding

Canadians, felt he had been neglected by the board. It also helped that he had caught the soccer bug on a visit to Scotland earlier in the year, during which he saw the towsy Old Firm game of 17 March 1991. Doherty was unwilling to sell his shares, but acting as spokesman for his relatives in Canada he promised to give Low his full backing in the battle against the board. Doherty also helped blow their cover when he told Gerry McNee in a television interview on 13 February 1992 that the aim of the rebels was to get rid of White and Michael Kelly.

The rebels had been winning the public opinion war, but to strike a serious blow they needed to use their accumulated sales purchases to call an EGM and to use their voting strength to unseat the board. In fact the board acted first: in February 1992 they called for an EGM with the purpose of confirming Smith's co-option to the board. They also asked for the removal of Tom Grant and Jim Farrell who were deemed to have been openly disloyal to the board. The meeting was set for 30 March 1992 and like those before and those to come was preceded by deals: in this case that Grant's removal would be taken from the agenda if he joined the pact, and he in turn could vote for Farrell to have him retained on the board. This transpired and despite all going according to the plans of the pact, the rebels were declared to have won a great victory in saving Farrell and Grant. Their cause for celebration was that they were now out in the open and could be seen as a legitimate source of opposition to the board.

But it was clear that Grant had switched sides, and this led to suspicions about the secret deal. In the meantime the board had to show that they were worthy custodians of the Celtic soul; above all they had to come up with something concrete to convince the fans of their ambitions for the club.

BOARD AT BAY

And so it came to pass that the hitherto modest suburb of Cambuslang, a healthy jog up the road from Parkhead, became imbued with all the attributes of a modern Brigadoon. This was to be the chosen spot for a new stadium as part of a vast commercial centre which would trade off the club's name and take it, as the saying goes 'well into the twenty-first century'. The result of a feasibility study carried out over the previous year by a firm called Stadivarius, it was launched in April 1992 by Kevin Kelly. Revealed was a plan for a 52,000 all-seated stadium with what was described as a 'space-age roof', two railway stations, a 200-bed hotel, a Celtic heritage museum, cinemas and shops. There would also be a 30-lane bowling alley, fast-food restaurants and parking for 4,500 cars. It was along the same lines as Dempsey's plans for Robroyston, but as Michael Kelly insisted, this time the basic problems in regard to licences and funding for the £100–£120 million project were well under control.

In fact most of the projections were over-optimistic and even if things had worked according to plan, football would have brought in only a third of the stadium's income, with the rest having to come from American football, rugby, boxing, rock concerts and the like. Celtic would have only been a minority shareholder in the stadium, which would have been owned by a separate stadium company. Some might have wondered where the Celtic soul would have been in all this, and the public was sceptical, the media more so – even before stories surfaced of noxious gases that would have made the site impracticable. Worst of all there were no hard and fast offers of money to finance it all.

In the midst of this turmoil the team struggled on the park and Celtic finished another trophyless season in May 1993, third in the League behind Aberdeen and Rangers, who cleaned up with the treble. Since winning the League in 1988, Celtic had not even managed to come second behind Rangers, finishing fifth in 1990 and third in the next three years. After winning the Cup in 1989 Celtic failed to make it a treble of Cup victories in 1990 when they lost to Aberdeen in the final on penalties. They reached the semi-final in 1990, beating Rangers on the way, but fell to Motherwell after a drawn first game. In the following year they again reached the semi-final, but on 31 March 1992, on a rain-drenched Hampden pitch, they were unable to beat a Rangers team without Hateley and reduced to ten men from the sixth minute when David Robertson was sent off. McCoist scored Rangers' only goal, but Celtic were unable to equalise. Walter Smith claimed that his team came of age that Tuesday night with a dour struggle against the odds. Celtic thought they had no luck, what with hitting the woodwork three times and coming up against an in-form Andy Goram who was displaying the qualities that confirmed him as one of Rangers' best buys. Celtic were also denied a strong penalty claim in the last few minutes, which the conspiracy theorists will no doubt have engraved on their memories, while overlooking the offence that got Robertson sent off; Rangers fans and James Traynor of the *The Herald* thought the offence warranted a yellow rather than red card. It was a heart-breaking night for Brady's team, who had been playing some classy football in previous weeks.

Celtic failed miserably in the Cup in the following season, scrambling home to lowly Clyde over two games then falling 2–0 to Falkirk at Brockville. In the Skol Cup the story was no better: after losing to Rangers in the final in 1990, Celtic were eliminated on penalties by Airdrie in the quarter-final in 1991 and the following year lost to

Aberdeen in the semi-final. Brady and the divided spirits at Celtic Park had little to look forward to in the troubled summer of 1993. Meanwhile, Rangers celebrated their greatest season in recent memory.

Brady entered his third season at Celtic Park with little to show for the money he had spent, and after a poor start to the new season and a loss to St Johnstone in Perth, he offered his resignation on 6 October 1993. This was the signal for the rebels and the malcontents to regalvanise their forces.

In late June 1993 Michael Kelly and Fergus McCann had exchanged a fruitless series of faxes across the Atlantic, following which McCann issued a statement saying that he was finished with the negotiations. In fact Low was at work to bring him and Dempsey together again. Low also tried to get McCann and Weisfeld to work together, but no sooner had they met than they split up. On 24 September Dempsey, McCann and Dominic Keane told a packed press conference that they had come up with a package of £20 million to save Celtic, £12.5 million of which had been promised by McCann. They forced the calling of another EGM on 26 November 1993, joined this time by Weisfeld. Weisfeld, who with his Scottish wife had built up the immensely successful What Everyone Wants chain and had sold it for an estimated £40 million, was assisted by Willie Haughey and his stepson, Michael McDonald, who was a fanatical Celtic supporter. The pact used its power to reject the McCann proposals, but this time they were also met by an offer from Weisfeld through Haughey to buy up all of the directors' shares for £350 each, a total outlay of £3.6 million. This too was rejected, but it was an offer that set some of the pact members thinking about personal compensation should the unthinkable happen.

In the meantime, the rebels retired once more, again with some bitterness, but the fans were infuriated that the board had once more turned down an injection of funds, and were determined to do something about it. A couple of months after the Dempsey sacking, on 25 February 1991, Willie Wilson, an ordinary supporter from Clydebank, had invited 300 Celtic fans to a meeting at Shettleston Town Hall where a group calling themselves Save Our Celts was formed. The meeting was chaired by the prominent Glasgow lawyer, Joe Beltrami, and attended by Brian Dempsey, as well as Celtic directors Grant and Farrell. Christopher White turned down the invitation saying that the meeting could only serve to embarrass the club. George Delaney of the official Celtic Supporters Club went even further and dismissed it as 'a nonsense'. Lisbon Lion Jim Craig was there, the one who gave away the penalty on that day in 1967, as Michael Kelly reminds us. He was also the son-in-law of Jim Farrell, the longest-serving member of the Celtic board, but a director at odds with 'the families'. He spoke passionately, and a few days after the meeting was dismissed from his job as a commentator at Radio Scotland. No freemasons to blame for that one!

Save Our Celts had a few more rallies, but there were always problems in maintaining a rage against the object of your affection, and it was difficult, if not impossible, to clearly distinguish attacks on the board from attacks on the club. The board liked to attribute the anger of the fans to conspiracies by their enemies, a standard fall-back for bankrupt regimes, and dismissed the fans as 'malcontents' fed by the lies of their enemies and subsidised by the finances of the unscrupulous. In fact the opposition to the board came from fans at all levels, including the sponsors of the executive boxes. One of these was Harry Hynds of Harry Hynds Travel, and in April 1991 in response to a gibe by Cassidy, he had formed with other sponsors a Celtic Fair Weather Supporters club. They spent £2,000 to sponsor a match at Dunfermline, where Celtic were the visitors, so that as well as sharing the corporate facilities with the visiting Celtic directors, they listened in amusement as the tannoy, to the confusion of the fans and the embarrassment of the Celtic directors, announced several times that the game that day was being sponsored by the Celtic Fair Weather Supporters. Cassidy replied by ending Celtic's relations with Harry Hynds Travel, a company in which Dempsey had a 75 per cent stake.[9]

The disillusion among Celtic fans was spread right through the ranks, from the Jungle – finally closed down to install seating in the summer of 1993 – all the way to the executive boxes. Even *The Celt*, a precursor to the fanzines, but more a mild-mannered recorder of the club's affairs than an uninhibited critic, gave new words to the 'Celtic Song':

> *They are Celtic directors,*
> *Useless through and through*
> *Always and always*
> *They haven't got a clue*[10]

The departure of Brady sparked renewed activity by Celtic fans, leading to the formation of 'Celts For Change' in October 1993. Brendan Sweeney and Matt McGlone were the instigators, helped by Dempsey and Low, but ultimately inspired by the energy and contribution of fans who had had enough of the old board. A first general meeting, advertised in the press to be held in Glasgow's City Hall in the Candleriggs, was attended by 30 people in a room that held 50. But then came the board rejection of the rebels' offer of cash injections and the next meeting, held on 2 December 1993, had to be shifted to a much larger room to hold the 450 who crushed inside, leaving another 500 outside. A week later 850 people attended a meeting in the Govan Town Hall.

Out of this came a campaign of advertising, banner-waving, picketing of the Celtic shops and even the Bank of Scotland, Celtic's bankers – with the ultimate weapon, a boycott of games at Parkhead, held as a last resort. The board, naturally enough, refused to allow the banners and other signs of organised protest inside the ground, but the ingenuity in overcoming this resulted in the CFC's most spectacular success. This came when various individuals went to the home game against Hibernian on 18 December 1993 dressed in jeans and white T-Shirts which sported a single, innocent letter. They had arranged that an area around the Jungle be kept free of spectators and it was there that those sporting the T-shirts lined up in prearranged order to spell out in perfect view of the assembled fans, the photographers and the television cameras, the words: 'BACK THE TEAM; SACK THE BOARD'. The official Celtic Supporters Association had refused to back the 'malcontents', but many of their members were sympathetic, and they formed an Independent Celtic Supporters Association. Then the official Celtic Supporters Association turned on the board: on 3 October 1993 they passed a vote of no confidence in it, and at another meeting on 30 January 1994 a delegates' meeting representing 150 clubs demanded that the directors quit immediately.

The pressure was telling on the board, but the main pressure came from its own internal contradictions. No stadium was emerging, the team was still falling behind on the field, and the overdraft at the Bank of Scotland was growing beyond that which any self-respecting business could allow. Income was declining because of the poor attendances and the drop in commercial dealings within the club. On all fronts the prospects were getting more dismal by the day, and on 1 March 1994 the Celts For Change group finally went ahead with its threat of a boycott. It was another success, as little more than 10,000 (according to the group's independently contracted invigilators) turned up for a home game against Kilmarnock, including a fox that mysteriously streaked across the pitch and offered the only moment of light relief when the fans there took up the chant: 'There's only one Michael Kelly!'

THE END OF THE OLD REGIME

The 'Gang of Five' began to crumble, and members of the board were forced to admit that outside money was needed to save the club. But before that they played their last desperate card with the presentation to a packed media conference of their latest plans for the new stadium at

Cambuslang. The plan proposed by David Smith on 25 February 1994 was indeed a thing of wonder, a magnificent vision of the future along the lines set out so optimistically by Kevin Kelly two years before. The sceptical journalists were no more impressed this time than they had been before by this 'Field of Dreams' (mark II), a sarcastic reference to the 20-carat corn of the American movie of that name, but thought by the Celtic directors to be an apt allusion.

The meeting was told that a Swiss company called Gefinor had put up cornerstone funding of £20 million, and this time the board allowed provision for public funding. The final blow to the board's ambition to keep themselves in power was delivered by Allan Caldwell, a freelance journalist whose articles for the *Evening Times* had brought the board many times to curse the existence of a free press (and who in turn would also write a book about the affair, entitled *Sack the Board*). Working away with terrier-like tenacity he discovered that Gefinor knew little about the deal, and had hardly even heard of the Celtic Football Club.

Now the board fell apart as Kevin Kelly made overtures to the rebels and Tom Grant appeared to side with the coming strength. Even Michael Kelly seemed to be cutting his losses as he stood out for a decent return on his shares, defending at the same time the families whose interests he was protecting. On offer was the £350 per share from Weisfeld that was still on the table, and Weisfeld was so confident of taking over that he went on a holiday to Australia – a fatal mistake so far as his own ambitions were concerned. Dempsey and McCann prepared to move in for the kill as the Bank of Scotland put pressure on Celtic to decrease its overdraft or come up with increased security, terrifying the directors by saying that they would have to pledge their personal property. Weisfeld, who several times thought that his offer to buy the club out had been successful, returned from Australia to push his claims, but in the end it was the unprepossessing figure of Fergus McCann who strode through the doors of Celtic Park on 4 March 1994 as the new owner.

Much has been made of the dramatic last hours, with newspaper headlines screaming that the club had been saved with only eight minutes to spare. It is doubtful if millions of pounds are going to be rejected because they come in late – this was not a student essay coming in after the deadline after all. And if McCann and company had been real sharks instead of individuals concerned about the club they would have done better to let it go into receivership and to pick up the pieces at a much reduced price later. But despite what everyone says, football is not a business, especially not where Celtic – and Rangers – are concerned, and this was recognised by the bank. Indeed banks throughout Britain have recognised this, dealing with football clubs on different terms from normal business companies. The nature of a football club was also at the heart of all the discussions concerning the rival groups. The families of the old board, however, believed that they alone should hold the key of succession in unbroken line, that they alone could interpret and speak on behalf of Celtic traditions, that they were the keepers of the Celtic soul. By the 1990s, however, infallibility was a long discredited doctrine.

It is a characteristic of revolutions that those who gain power soon start to squabble among themselves. The conditions that create revolutions and the character of the men needed to carry them out mean that life for the new regime will not be easy: they often end up in dictatorship. McCann, however, helped by the retreat, once more, of Dempsey, soon established a firm authority over the new board. Of the old board, Michael Kelly, Chris White and David Smith retired to their private affairs, but Kevin Kelly, Grant and McGinn held on until they resigned in the autumn of 1994. James Farrell fought to stay on the new board, but he was removed at an EGM in September 1994. McGinn and Kevin Kelly were given titular appointments: McGinn as legislative adviser, Kelly as chairman emeritus and president of the boys club. Tom Grant was offered a position as stadium manager, but this became a rather empty title and when he had to report to Celtic's capital projects manager, Charles Martin, and became derisively known as the 'janitor', he resigned in July 1996. The last link with the old board was effectively gone, as Kevin Kelly and McGinn were seldom to be seen in the official corridors of Celtic Park.

McCann would have preferred to have made a clean sweep of the old board and to have carried out his pledge not to give any of them 'a thin dime'. In retaining the services of four of the old board, McCann recognised the role they had played in bringing him to power, while he had no choice but to pay out on the shares of the departing directors. He was then involved in claims for compensation by Superstadia for their work on the Cambuslang project and faced another problem in the form of manager Lou Macari, a bizarre appointment of the old regime to succeed Brady. He was sacked in June 1994, leading to a bitter court fight that was still unresolved in the summer of 1997. Macari claimed £431,000 for wrongful dismissal, McCann counter-claimed for breach of contract and compensation of £250,000. Macari was forced to resign from Stoke City, the club he managed when he left Celtic, at the end of the 1996–97 season, in order to fight his case.

On to the new board McCann brought Eric Riley as financial director, Patrick Ferrell as marketing director, and three men who had played a role in the ousting of the old board: Willie Haughey, John Keane, the Edinburgh builder, and Gerald Weisfeld's stepson, Michael McDonald.

It was not the new board that would be controlling the club, however, and a couple of years down the track McCann started to emerge as a new Napoleon. He created a public liability company, with men of proven reputations in the business world and prepared to sink some of their own money into the club. McCann was the first Celtic official to invest a substantial sum of his own money in the club, and with Celtic plc he brought in three other major investors: Patrick Sheehy, a former BAT chief; Brian Quinn, formerly of the Bank of England; and Dermot Desmond, a property investor said to be one of Ireland's leading stock-brokers, who was also a close friend of the Irish Prime Minister Charles Haughey. And all were men with names that chimed in tunefully with the Irish image of the club, even if only one of them was actually Irish. Above all they were businessmen with a knowledge of finance, held in respect by the new mystical god of the football world: 'the City'.

In Fergus McCann, David Murray at Ibrox now had a man closer to his own mettle at Celtic Park, but the gap between the two clubs was still enormous. On the field Celtic came to the end of the 1993–94 season without any joy on the field. Off the field they were faced with a huge debt, a crumbling stadium, a disappearing business reputation and a dwindling number of season-ticket-holders, now as low as 7,100. Under McCann, however, there was to be a resurrection on all but one front (unhappily the most important) with a new manager, a magnificent new stadium and a response to the share issue from the Celtic supporters that surpassed all expectation. The Old Firm was back in business, even if it might have been more appropriate to call it the 'New Corporation'. There were some who feared that the Old Firm was now under a 'New Firm' of two men whose interests were not so much in upholding a tradition or safeguarding a soul, as in capitalising on the products they had bought in order to maximise their profits. This was a foreign language to most of the Tims and Bears who followed the two clubs. According to the jargon of the day, fans did not watch football, follow it or get involved with it, but consumed it, while the clubs were not so much objects of their devotion, outlets for their passion, but commodities at the disposal of those with their hearts in their hip pockets. In the eyes of the business world, the loyalty of countless thousands of Celtic and Rangers fans had nothing to do with the hopes and dreams of whole communities, but were brand names whose loyalty could be milked for millions. This was the language emerging out of the moral chaos of the postmodern world, but behind it lurked a reality that was in some ways as ugly as the bigotry of bygone days. McCann and Murray had no time for bigotry, but there were fears harboured by some as to whether they could save their clubs from the corporate raiders.

6. A New Firm: Murray and McCann

As McCann started going through the accounts at Celtic Park to find out just how big a hole he had been left, Rangers proceeded to complete the 1993–94 season with their sixth League Championship in a row. Earlier in the season Smith's team had wrapped up the Skol Cup with a 2–1 victory over Hibs in the final, but had lost 0–1 to Dundee United in the final of the Scottish Cup. Celtic's interest in the Cup ended on 29 January when they were eliminated by Motherwell by the only goal of the game, and staggered on to finish fourth in the League. Under the new regime, however, high hopes were held for the coming season, as Celtic fans waited over the summer break to see what plans the new manager had.

The close season break was the time for fans to take off for their various holiday retreats, now spread well beyond Saltcoats and Troon to take in the delights of the Mediterranean and points closer to the sun. For Rangers fans the summer break was also the time to wait and wonder in eager anticipation about which new foreign stars would arrive in Scotland to don the once light blue jersey, but now a regularly changing combination of colours and design to please the marketing men, the only constant being the name of the brewers who had paid to have their name emblazoned across it. In Smith's first year in charge he had to cope with the 'three foreigners' rule that meant he had to sign Scottish talent. Two of these were in fact born in England: Andy Goram who signed on from Hibs and after some spectacular blunders went on to make enough saves to break the hearts of many team managers, and Stuart McCall from Everton. Also signed that year was David Robertson from Aberdeen. Among the more exotic imports was the Ukrainian Alexei Mikhailichenko who joined from Sampdoria. But it was with established players, the Friesian Pieter Huistra and the partnership of McCoist and Hateley that Rangers surged ahead. The summer of 1993 saw the arrival at Ibrox of another home-based talent, the tall striker from Dundee United, Duncan Ferguson, for a record Scottish fee of £4 million. Ferguson had a stormy time before moving south to Everton, at first on loan, then permanently, while he became the first professional Scottish player to be jailed for an incident on the field, when he was convicted of head-butting John

McStay of Raith Rovers during a League match at Ibrox in April 1994.

In the summer of 1994 Rangers signed Basile Boli from Marseille for £2.7 million, an African-born French national who was a republican and a Catholic, but worse, an outspoken critic of Rangers' training methods and the abilities of their manager, so that when he left a year later it had nothing to do with his politics and religion. Signed along with Boli in the summer of 1994 was the man who became revered as the 'Prince of Denmark', Brian Laudrup from Italy's Fiorentina, and he was joined the following summer by the English wonder-boy Paul Gascoigne, from Lazio in Rome. Contrasting characters off the field, the Dane and the Geordie shared a range of skills on it that elevated them to a class above most of those with whom and against whom they played. Between them, but above all Gascoigne in his first season, they accounted for Rangers' eighth League flag in a row and set the club up for its tumultuous struggle for the much coveted ninth.

McCann's summer of 1994 saw the return to Celtic, as manager, of Tommy Burns, a former Celtic player of great skill and popularity whose private life fulfilled the most demanding code of the most traditional followers of the club. However, his lifetime devotion to Celtic, as a supporter, a player and then as manager, was to prove of no avail when he failed to build a team that could halt the Rangers juggernaut. To get him Celtic engaged in practices that did not meet the approval of Kilmarnock FC to whom Burns was contracted, and in addition to the bitterness this caused, the SFA upheld Kilmarnock's grievances and hit Celtic with a whopping £100,000 fine. It was the first of several incidents that set McCann against the SFA, in the course of which he found an ally in David Murray. Whatever differences the two millionaire club owners had, they could agree on the need to do something about the pettiness of the Lilliputians in Scottish football trying to tie down the giants who should have been ruling the game.

FROM GAPS TO GULFS

Celtic would never quite catch up with the expensive signings of Rangers, but they did begin to attract players of international class. Pierre van Hooijdonk came from the modest Dutch club NAC Breda for £1.25 million in January 1995, and it was with Celtic that he blossomed into a star striker. This caused some problems when his enhanced status encouraged him to try to renegotiate his contract and force more money out of the club, especially when later arrivals were on conditions much better than his. On the issue of payment to players, Celtic still had echoes from the past coming to haunt them as several players were linked with the club but for one reason or another did not sign, with hints that they did not like the financial terms. McCann himself expressed a few pertinent remarks about over-paid players, which, however justified, could hardly have helped the situation. Shortly before winning the Scottish Cup in May 1995, Burns made the acid comment that while his vision for the club consisted of 'hopes and dreams', the managing director saw only 'profit and loss'. Burns was forced to back down, but the two continued to be at odds over expenditure on players, leading almost to an explosion with the negotiations over the signing of Andreas Thom from Bayern Leverkusen in August 1995.

This was a problem at the heart of the contemporary game. Burns was angry at McCann's reluctance to spend the money to buy the players he wanted, but McCann had every reason to baulk at Thom's financial demands on top of his transfer fee of £2.2 million. Celtic fans, however, had seen too many star foreigners unsuccessfully associated with the club and the effect on their overwrought emotions of having to bear more taunts from their rivals about failed transfers finally decided the issue. The personal terms thus won by Thom provided fuel for future dressing-room squabbles when other players earning less, but performing better, reacted jealously to what Thom was being paid.

Of the foreigners Celtic had failed to sign, the most notable were David Ginola from Paris Saint-Germain, Marc Degryse from Ander-lecht, and the Russian, Dimitri Radchenko. Worst of all they had Gordan Petric of Dundee United stolen from under their noses by Rangers, attracted by the higher wages on offer. Celtic's failure to sign these players was not always their fault: Degryse never really sounded serious about coming to Scotland, while Ginola allegedly used the club to negotiate a better deal from Barcelona, although it was Newcastle who signed him in the end. When he was abused by Celtic fans at a pre-season friendly, however, Ginola claimed his interest had been genuine, but that he had been advised not to go to Celtic by his compatriot, Basile Boli – prompting one sardonic Bear to declare that this was the only good thing Boli ever did for Rangers.

Another delayed transfer had nothing to do with McCann, and had the Celtic owner fuming: this was over the Portuguese striker Jorge Cadete from Sporting Lisbon towards the end of the 1995–96 season. McCann accused the SFA of deliberately holding up the transfer, which meant that for five crucial weeks, three of which were taken up by Cadete arranging to buy out his own contract with his club (or getting Celtic to buy it out) Celtic were without a player who could have made all the difference as they chased Rangers to the penultimate game of Rangers' eighth successive League flag.

Celtic's frustration in regard to signing big-name players was afforded little sympathy in some sections of the press, and in February 1997, Ian McGarry of the *Evening Times* claimed, on the strength of one Italian agent, that Celtic were regarded by some as a joke in Europe, making offers but never concluding any deals.[1] McGarry was referring to the hold-up in the signing of the defender Enrico Annoni from Roma. Despite McGarry's allegations, Celtic went on to sign the Italian. He joined the other foreigners who had come to grace the Parkhead turf – Thom, van Hooijdonk and Cadete, and the forward Paolo di Canio who had come from AC Milan in the summer of 1996 and was an immediate hit. Di Canio became a close friend of Burns and adapted wholeheartedly to the atmosphere at Celtic Park, adding his voice to the chorus that cried out bias against Celtic. He broke the long run of Rangers players winning the Scottish Players' Player of the Year award when he won that honour in 1997. Perhaps less fortuitously, Celtic paid a record £5.5 million to bring Alan Stubbs from Bolton on a five-year contract. With players of the calibre of Cadete and di Canio, Celtic were well and truly into the big time, but despite this, Rangers with Gascoigne and Laudrup were just that extra class ahead.

With the fortune spent on bringing in these foreign players, Rangers and Celtic left the rest of the Scottish League clubs in the rear, and the climactic 1996–97 season had all the features of a two-team shoot-out. The gulf between the two Old Firm teams and the rest of Scottish football was further emphasised as an impressive new oval-shaped stadium arose at Celtic Park on the site of the old, financed as McCann had promised by some of his own money and a share float among the fans.

McCann wasted no time in tackling the stadium issue shortly after he arrived at Parkhead, opting for what some had always seen as the natural one: building a new stadium at Paradise. This he did by injecting several millions of his own funds and then putting the club on the open market. The Celtic fans responded eagerly, and soon 10,000 of them were in possession of shares sold at £60 each and which would soon reach a market value of £300 and going as high as £425 at the beginning of 1997. It was the most successful share offer in British football, and no other club had such a wide fan involvement. At the end of McCann's second season with the club, Celtic had 37,000 season-ticket-holders, as against Rangers' 36,000, and the stadium was well on its way to completion with a projected capacity of 60,000, all seated. McCann turned a loss of £180,000 into a profit of £2.74 million for the financial year ending 1995, on a turnover that increased from £10 million to £16 million. Average crowds were up to more than double what they had been in the last season of the old regime, from over 25,000 in 1994–95 to over 34,000 the following year. With the increased seating capacity for the 1996–97 season, the average at over 48,000 was as good as the attendances at Ibrox.

With the biscuit tin a distant memory, Celtic embarked on a series of commercial developments that fully exploited a brand name that could be bettered for customer loyalty only by Manchester United, Liverpool and Rangers in Britain. A new mail order scheme doubled Celtic's income from merchandising for the 1996 Christmas period over that of 1995. The array of goods on offer from the Celtic Merchandise mail order scheme could be pored over in the colourful brochure itself on sale for £1. Set out in this catalogue is a range of goods in green and white from children's wear to adult leisure wear and full dress tartan for the special night out: clothes for all occasions, from the cradle to the Celtic Ceilidh or the Caledonian Ball. On offer are beer and wine, specially coloured to suit the Celtic palate with matching containers to drink from; trinkets of various shapes and sizes, and wallets and pennants and key-rings, all with the club's logo or colours. There is even the odd book or video on football, to remind you of what it is all supposed to be about. And for any Celtic fan concerned about the prices, there was the consolation of knowing that the profits would go towards bringing some millionaire to Glasgow and helping him to get by on his £10,000 a week for wearing the green and white hoops (or whatever other colour or design then in fashion).

Over at Ibrox it was all much the same, with only the colours being changed to protect the sensitivities of the buyer: red, white and blue instead of green and white, and a tartan of a more distinctly blue shading. And lots more of it! In 1996 Rangers added to their shops sprinkled around the city with a new superstore at the ground itself, crammed on match days with a procession of people adding to their stock of ways in which they could be associated with the club (and none of them in any way concerned that the foundation date that dominates the decor outside is one year out). And if some of the eager buyers had to make economies in the domestic budget to subsidise their loyalty, at least they knew Walter Smith was going to have even more money to bring even richer players on even bigger weekly salaries than those being paid at Celtic Park.

The bulk of the income of football teams throughout Britain at this time was now coming from sources other than admissions to the grounds. By 1997, the commercial side of Rangers' income, made up of corporate hospitality, sponsorship, advertising and merchandising, was claimed to account for 43p in every pound.[2] Since 'turnstile' admission accounted for about 35p in every pound, this left 22p from other sources, mainly television. For the rich clubs, television and merchandising seemed to offer ever-expanding pots of gold. Rangers did have some anxious moments in 1992, but they soon recovered from them and by January 1995 they had returned a net profit for the first time in three years.[3] Despite this, the club still felt it necessary to ask its fans to dig deeper into their financial resources to help realise the club's vision of a 'blue heaven'.

By this scheme, called 'Ready for the Future' and launched in mid-April 1995, Rangers fans were asked to fork out £399 to buy the right to season-tickets for the next 25 years. This was expected to bring in £5 million, and would help pay for the £4 million to fill in the corners at Ibrox and bring the capacity of the ground up to 51,000. At the same time the club took the opportunity to paint all its seats blue, removing the anomaly of having brightly coloured seats spanning the entire spectrum with the solitary omission of green. In return the purchaser had the right to his name on the seat, transferable to family members, and a 10 per cent discount on Rangers goods, as well as a free weekend ticket to Rangers' pre-season international tournament.

While the ordinary fan pondered the £400 outlay, selected wealthier fans were asked to pay an estimated £1 million to achieve the honorary title of associate director, a means of raising money that had been popular with French monarchs feeling the financial pinch in the years before the Revolution, by creating positions at court that could be bought complete with a title to go with it, and a bit extra to make it heritable. Rangers, of course, were not plugging a hole to prevent a deluge, but were building for the future set just a few years off, in this case the year 2000.

Murray still resisted floating the club on the open market, and claimed to be comfortable with his 82 per cent holding. His April 1991 share-issue had aimed at involving a wider range of fans in the club, but it was clear that the gulf between the club and its fans was getting wider. In *Follow, Follow*, the faithful showed their alarm at the way they were being treated like dollar signs and were incensed at what they called the 'extortion racket' in prices for European Cup games, while unflattering comparisons were made with Manchester United in the way they treated their fans. Always, however, there was the consolation of the victories against the Tims and the pleasure of being part of the cathedral that was Ibrox. And at least until January 1997 it all seemed to stay inside the family.

KEEPING IT IN THE FAMILY?

Money has been part of football since its earliest days, when *Scottish Umpire*, *Scottish Sport* and the *Scottish Referee* constantly denounced its commercial aspects, in editorials, outraged articles and pungent cartoons – it was indeed disgust at such involvement that led to Rangers and Celtic being called the 'Old Firm'. In more recent times, however, football seems to have been engulfed by talk of deals and profits and the effect on the stock market of failing to make it into Europe or a defeat there after qualifying. There have always been individuals ready to use football for their own personal gain, but most directors, however fatuous or incompetent, have usually had a basic love of the game: until recently most of the people involved in the financial deals also had an involvement with the club. David Murray was bereft of Rangers credentials before he became a high-class Bear, but since then he has directed all his energies into the club, taking no salary or fees and ploughing profits on shares back into it. Fergus McCann was an avid Bhoy in his youth, a social convener for the Croy Celtic Supporters Association and he never missed a game in the 1962–63 season, the one before he left for Canada.

Nevertheless, when McCann and Murray leave football, they will depart with a massive profit on their investment, a shining example of the new age in which those with millions can walk off with even more millions. There was a time, not so long ago, when the involvement of the rich in football was a way to pay back rather than cash in on the passion of a misspent youth: among the football lovers prepared to plunge their personal fortune into a club was Elton John at Watford, while Jack Hayward at Wolves, Jack Walker at Blackburn and John Hall at Newcastle are millionaires for whom money expended on a mere hobby was to prove immensely profitable in the 1990s. Alan Sugar at Spurs had no interest in football nor indeed, it would appear, in anything that had no obvious profit outcome, until he saw the dollar signs flashing in English football with the imminent arrival of a Super League;[4] David Dein, football lover as a kid, had a foot in both camps, while Robert Maxwell had a finger in several clubs, none of which suffered for the criminal activities for which others among his employees have had to pay. Probably no one has made more out of sport than Rupert Murdoch, although unlike his one-time compatriot, Kerry Packer, the Australian by birth but American by commercial choice is not renowned for any particular interest in many things beyond making money, which has not prevented this scion of good Presbyterian stock being awarded a papal knighthood in 1998, like all such dubious awards a reflection on the giver as much as the receiver. Martin Edwards inherited his role as director and chairman of the legendary Manchester United, a legend which many followers of the club with memories of Matt Busby, the Babes and a time when the club was concerned above all about football, believe has long been betrayed.

The Celtic board before 1994 tried to keep at bay millionaires wanting to invest in Celtic, but despite their expressed fears, all of these millionaires, even Weisfeld, had an interest in the club beyond profit. Now Rangers have allowed a certain Joe Lewis to stake a massive £40 million in the club, a man who is neither Scottish nor has any great interest in football, although he is said to love the sports more traditionally associated with men of money – tennis, golf, horse-racing and sailing. It is just possible that he could be the first man to join the club with the explicit intention of making money from it. As the *Daily Mail* reported: 'It is understood Mr Lewis sees the deal purely as a money-making scheme to make a big profit when Rangers is eventually floated on the Stock Market.'[5] Since then he has investigated the money-making potential of other football clubs.

Towards the end of 1996 David Murray had let it be known that he was considering diluting his holding at Rangers by issuing new shares that would still give him a majority holding, but reduced to about 61 per cent. After a few whispers as to who this might be, the headline news on 23 January 1997 was a variation on the theme of the 'Mystery Midas' or 'Bahamas Billionaire'.[6] Lewis was reported to be a recluse, who refused to give interviews or to be photographed, but all agreed that he was one of the wealthiest individuals in Britain, a man who had made his billions by various theme ventures, including investment in the immensely successful Hard Rock cafés and Planet Hollywood restaurants, and even a chain of banqueting suites 'often used by freemasons'.[7] Above all, however, his profits had come from speculation on the international money market.[8] He became a tax exile in 1979. A neighbour of Sean Connery in the Bahamas, it was thought to be through the former Agent 007 and one-time Celtic supporter, who had once been linked to a take-over of the club, that Lewis came to offer Murray the £40 million that gave him a 25.1 per cent stake in Rangers. Then again he was a friend of Dermot Desmond, the non-executive director of Celtic who had invested £4 million in Celtic shares in 1995, and it could have been he who had told him about the money that was there for the making. Whatever it is, there is no talk of him entering the club in any custodial capacity. As reported by *The Scotsman*, the deal was made by Albany Inc, a holding company set up by Lewis's English National Investment Company (ENIC).[9] Some of Murray's money was invested in ENIC and two of the English company's employees were appointed to the Ibrox board, one of whom, Daniel Levy, declared that football was merely a financial concern for the company. The proportion of the small shareholders in Rangers fell as a result of the deal, from 19 per cent to 14 per cent.

In the meantime Daniel Levy, using the Rangers brand name to help gain entry, has bought into three long-established European teams: close to 30 per cent in Italy's Vicenza for £2.4 million with an option to buy a controlling interest for £2.6 million; a controlling interest in Slavia Prague, former great of Central European football, now fallen on hard times; and AEK of Athens. With these teams and Rangers, Levy and ENIC could run a European mini-league of their own teams.[10] Levy, like Lewis, makes no pretence about having any interest in football: it is to be hoped that UEFA and FIFA, who surely do, keep a close eye on those intent on using the game purely for their own interests.

Half of Lewis's money was said to be immediately put aside to buy more players, while the rest would be used towards the building of a 150-bed hotel at Ibrox and a nearby multi-purpose leisure centre. Murray told the Rangers supporters to go and enjoy themselves over a few beers, but for the more thoughtful Bears there was little to cheer about. Rangers might have further distanced themselves from Celtic, but even further were they distancing themselves from their own natural fans. Shortly after the Lewis share deal was completed, more sober columns in the press passed on the news that the company that had started the Rangers revolution, John Lawrence (Glasgow) Ltd, had gone into receivership.

At the same time as Lewis sought to advance his millions by speculating on Rangers shares, Brian Dempsey reappeared on the Celtic scene like a blast from Celtic's past – not so much the recent past, the memorable moment when he had stood outside Celtic Park on 4 March 1994 and announced that 'The rebels have won', but rather to the days before John H. McLaughlin and company took over almost exactly a century before, when the club had been run by enthusiastic volunteers. There can be little doubt about his sincerity, and his emphasis on youthful players to eliminate the need for an influx of foreign players has much to recommend it. Above all it would be reassuring to have football finance in the hands of people who love the game, as he would like to see it: but it seems impossible in the present financial climate for anyone to keep shares in Celtic out of corporate hands, as Dempsey says he would like to, by gaining control so that he could then 'give the club back to the people who support it by selling them shares at a price they could afford'.[11]

In December 1997 Fergus McCann confirmed that he would adhere to the promise made in 1994 that his commitment to the club would be for five years, and that as from the summer of 1999 he would return to what will no doubt be a life less stressful than kicking against the pricks of petty authority and having to justify himself before fans who thought they owned the club he had bought. The charms of bringing up a young family and relaxing with a few rounds of golf bears no comparison with suffering fools less than gladly and putting up with the abuse and ungratefulness of outraged football fans. In line with his commitment to the club as a custodian of its essential values, he has promised that he will try to ensure that his shareholding be made available to the Celtic faithful.

Unlike Murray, McCann seems more willing to involve Celtic fans in a broad ownership in the club, which has not prevented Murray criticising Rangers fans for having had it too easy, never having to put their hands in their own pockets to finance all the wonders he has achieved at Ibrox. McCann, more than Murray, seems to have a better understanding of what it is like to be a fan, with all the irrational devotion this involves. Both men, however, have dedicated their life to commercial success and see football through the eyes of businessmen, and in the amoral commercial climate of the new football, as in the wider world of the economic so-called rationalists, there is no place for those who cannot defend or look after themselves, be it football teams that cannot attract supporters and the sponsors' dollars, or children in Asia working on slave wages to supply leisurewear for the world's rich and footballs for the giants of the world game. If football was ruled from the heart and not the marketplace, Partick Thistle would not be fighting for their very life, yet football in Glasgow without the Jags is unthinkable, and not just from the standpoint of the masochists and the light relief of those who do not follow the Old Firm. That said, and there must always be a place for the wee teams of Scotland, rich in their own particular histories, the future of the game now lies beyond the borders of Scotland, where only Rangers and Celtic have a realistic chance of competing at the highest levels.

A LEAGUE OF THEIR OWN

Celtic and Rangers have been called the giants of Scottish football, but they have now virtually outgrown it. Effectively they are in another league compared to the other teams – and literally wish that they were. In the now lopsided Scottish game there will still be upsets in Cup games and the odd league reversal, but it is hard to see how even Aberdeen or the Edinburgh teams can match the spending of the big two. Rangers still tower above Celtic in this regard, but since the McCann takeover the Parkhead club has managed to stay within the financial orbit of its main rival.

As Rangers and Celtic outdistanced the other clubs in Scottish football, so they increasingly came to treat with contempt its ruling bodies,

unfortunately often with good reason. Rangers fans even found themselves, by their accusations of bias against their club in the media and by
the men who ruled the game, joining in harmonious counterpoint with
the paranoia chorus of their rivals. At the highest levels the two clubs
came ever closer together, and as the two teams fought it out on the park,
Murray and McCann, in the spirit that gave the Old Firm its name in
the first place, joined forces to ensure that the power and wealth they
represented was reflected in the running of the game in Scotland.

McCann showed no reticence in pointing out what was rotten in the
running of Scottish football, beginning with the SFA and the League
itself: in his estimation both were overstaffed and overpaid, Hampden
was a white elephant as far as football was concerned, 30 clubs needed to
be wiped off the League's playing-fields, and clubs that loaned players for
national duty had to be paid for this service. Such sentiments would have
sounded as music to Murray's ears, and so it was little surprise when the
Ibrox supremo sympathised with McCann in his battles with the
authorities.

McCann's first confrontation with the SFA and the League was over
the fine he received for poaching Burns, followed by a tribunal order to
pay Kilmarnock £200,000 for inducing the manager and his assistant
Billy Stark away from the club. Appeals proved fruitless as the League
and the SFA backed each other up, ignoring that the fine against Celtic
was so much greater than for any previous similar offence, namely the
£5,000 Rangers had been fined for poaching Ferguson from Dundee
United. Certainly payments to players were rocketing at an astronomical
rate, but this fine still seemed excessive. Above all, Celtic had no recourse
to legal opinion outside the football authorities, and this brought
Rangers to their side.

At the SFA's AGM in May 1995 Celtic moved, seconded by Rangers,
that clubs in the League have recourse to law should they disagree with
the rulings of the SFA. The motion was clearly defeated: there had been
occasions enough in the past when Rangers in particular had been
angered at 'outside' interference in the game, as after the notorious Old
Firm game of 1987 or the prosecution of Duncan Ferguson, but this was
different. The small clubs were telling them what to do, and since they
had recourse neither to the laws of the land nor entry to another football
league, Rangers and Celtic would have to remould the game in Scotland
so that it more accurately reflected their interests.

Murray had been involved in a few battles with the old Celtic board,
most notably when he banned Celtic fans from Ibrox after the Parkhead
club refused to pay for damage to seats in the Broomloan Stand following
an Old Firm game in October 1993. He claimed £7,800 compensation

for this, although up to £20,000 damage had allegedly been done at previous games. Murray was equally upset that Celtic supporters did not buy the club's programme or sample the fine Bluenose catering on offer: a Broomloan stand full of Bears was obviously a much more profitable concern. Michael Kelly had little time for Murray and his ways, and McCann and Murray are hardly bosom buddies, but they are business-men and they shared a disdain for those who made the laws and carried them out, McCann with the added suspicion that the SFA and the League looked on Celtic with a malevolence that had its origins deep in Scotland's past. A series of what appeared to be bad refereeing decisions fuelled Celtic's anger, and in January 1997 rumours circulated about the club's plans to buy English Premiership club Wimbledon as a means of entering the English Premier League. Wimbledon had themselves thought of relocating to Dublin, but no one seems to have asked them, at a time when they were still in line for a UEFA Cup place and doing well in the two English cup competitions, what they thought of going out of existence in Scotland. The issue was given serious treatment in the *Evening Times*,[12] which 'revealed' the story, but most serious com-mentators treated it as pie in the sky. McCann was no doubt serious about his earlier idea of bringing a Dublin team into the Scottish League, but talk of Celtic joining the England Premiership had to be seen as little more than a broadside at the Scottish football authorities.

Murray was equally contemptuous of the Scottish league system, controlled as it was by 40 clubs, many of which he could have bought with his pocket money and thrown away – if League rules had permitted it. Yet these were the teams whose numbers could frustrate the ambitions of the bigger clubs, and whose instincts for survival refused to recognise the need for rationalisation, a favourite buzz-word of those ruled by the economic imperative. Murray saw the small-team mentality reflected in the SFA and the League, and in this he could have found many to agree with him – and outside the Old Firm. The SFA's Think Tank, dreamed up at the beginning of the 1996–97 season to set out guidelines for the future of Scottish football, was seen as a joke by some observers, especially when Murray and McCann were not invited to be part of it.

The two men called their own summit meetings instead, the first of which took place over a private lunch at Celtic Park on 13 November 1996. As was later revealed, part of the discussion at that meeting was over the fate of young players and how to introduce a standardised youth training scheme, a particular concern following the Bosman judgement laid down earlier that year, which gave players freedom of contract and, in the case of a youth player, the right to walk away from a club that might have invested a great deal of money and time in his development.

Out of this discussion, carried on between Smith and Burns, it was suggested that the reserve leagues be scrapped and that young players instead be 'farmed out' to first-division clubs. A similar scheme had once existed in Scotland with 'Junior' teams acting as the nursery club, and in Germany, Italy and Spain it was common practice. The proposed scheme would allow the big clubs to reduce expenditure on youth training, while the lower-division clubs would have the use of an up-and-coming youngster at no expense. There were obvious difficulties to be overcome, one of which would be convincing the League that this scheme was in the best interests of Scottish football and not just of Celtic and Rangers.

The next meeting of the two tycoons in mid-December resulted in an open avowal of their intentions to go it alone if need be. In mid-December Murray made the peculiar declaration that the other teams in the league had lived off the big two for long enough and it was time for the Old Firm to patch up their differences: 'In the past Scottish football has lived off the split between Rangers and Celtic. That will not happen any longer. Fergus and I have a mutual respect for each other and we want to work together for the good of the game.'[13]

The Scottish authorities were unimpressed, but still seemed intent on driving them closer together. In addition to the League refusing to allow Rangers to postpone a game against Hibs despite having medical certificates for 28(!) players, the chief executive of the SFA, Jim Farry, made remarks that deeply irritated both McCann and Murray. On 7 January Farry allegedly told *The Herald* that there were too many foreigners in the Scottish game, and less than two weeks later he was reported to have said in *Scotland on Sunday* that there were too many entrepreneurs in the game. He specifically referred to McCann as one of those whose investment in Scottish football had been to its 'detriment'. Armed with these accusations, to which he added his continuing resentment over the delayed Cadete signing, McCann 'went to war' against the SFA with a letter of 27 January for discussion at its Executive Committee meeting of the following day.[14] He demanded that Farry be called to account for his behaviour and demanded an explanation for the delay in the Cadete signing and compensation for two weeks of the player's salary.

At the same time as McCann battled with the SFA, Clydebank chairman Jack Steedman called a meeting of all the First Division clubs and five from the Premier League to seek approval for a reorganisation of the four leagues of ten teams into three of 16 in the top division and 12 in each of the two lower ones. When the plan was put to a League meeting in April, it was rejected. It was then that the plans for an élite breakaway league of ten teams, an idea that had been mooted throughout the season, was brought into the open. On 9 April 1997 a meeting of the chairmen of the ten Premier League clubs announced that they had taken steps for the creation of a new league system, run by themselves, and that as a consequence they would be retiring from the Scottish League. Aware of the mistake he had made in 1992 by telegraphing his intentions, Murray, who had never dropped the idea of a Super League, kept a low profile while consultation went on with the other Premier League chairmen. In the outcome they agreed to hire an independent professional adviser to prepare plans for a new league to be in place by the beginning of the 1998–99 season. This would be an autonomous body, independent of the League, and so it would be able to work out the most lucrative television contracts and keep the revenue to themselves: a copy, more or less, of the English Premiership, albeit without the support of the game's ruling body, and a microcosm in comparison. For Rangers and Celtic it would be their preparation for the European Super League.

Some details of the plan being cooked up by the existing ten Premier League clubs (plus Raith Rovers) were revealed to the public in September 1997. Among its ironies was that the top ten clubs already hogged so much of the wealth in Scottish football (85 per cent) that it would cost very little to compensate the 30 other clubs in the League. More than money was at stake, however, and the more ambitious of the excluded clubs were not at first prepared to let the breakaway Premiership ten (plus one, later two) have it all their own way, insisting that they have more information before they approved the plans and allowed the others to retire and set up the new league before the statutory two-year period. They were particularly concerned about access to the new league and whether it was worth their while investing in ground improvements, such as all-seated stadiums for a minimum number of spectators. The main aim of the top ten (plus whoever else hoped to be part of it) was to run their own affairs in their own interests, but they also claimed that they were acting in the best interests of the game, since they would attract more money to Scottish football than the SFA and the Scottish League had done. They tried to back this up by making the always spurious comparison with the English Premiership, and offered inducements to those they would exclude from their private league, smaller slices of what would be a much larger cake, enough to keep the noses at the windows of the rich clubs' banquet harmlessly on the outside. The would-be benefactors of Scottish football also made the obligatory comments about being concerned about youth development in the Scottish game, although this never excited the same enthusiasm as the dollars expected to come rolling in to pay for the wages and other expenses of the élite clubs.

As the debate dragged on, the exclusiveness of the new league was breeched to suggest that 12 and then even 16 teams might be included. By December 1997, faced by the ungratefulness of the sulky malcontents who refused to accept the offerings from the rich clubs' table, Murray took out the big stick and warned them that if they did not accept what was on offer they would get nothing and the deserving rich would go their own way in any case. In all the claims and counter-claims it was hard for the ordinary fans to see how their enjoyment of the game was going to improve, and there was very little talk of money going back to what had once been the bedrock of the Scottish game: the schools, churches and other grassroots competitions, now struggling to survive in the dog-eat-dog world of municipal competition and savage cutbacks. The proponents of the new league were concerned about the game only at the élite level, and from this point of view it is true that in a country with a population as small as Scotland's, 40 professional clubs claiming equal access to power is unrealistic. These clubs all have their place in Scottish football, albeit for some of them perhaps in a regional league, but they also have the right, however unrealistic such an ambition may seem, to aim for promotion to the top ranks, whether it be a single Premiership of 10 or 12 or 16 clubs, or a two-division league of 10, 12 or 14 in whatever combination. Whichever way it finally works out, Rangers and Celtic will still be calling the shots.

THE OLD FIRM, SCOTLAND AND THE WORLD

The imbalance in Scottish football has been with the game for most of this century. Rangers and Celtic have consistently attracted crowds for home and away games that no other club could match: even in the early 1980s when Aberdeen and Dundee United were playing the best football in Scotland, the crowds who came to see them were small in comparison with those who turned up to see the Glasgow clubs. And when either Celtic or Rangers were playing poorly and fewer fans came to their games, witness the resurgence after Souness at Ibrox and at Celtic Park after the civil war, it would appear that these fans occupied their Old Firm-free time in pursuits other than watching football in Scotland. It was a sad fact, but a fact nevertheless, that the Celtic and Rangers fans coming from all over Scotland and Northern Ireland every other week in the season had at best only a secondary interest in their local team. Whether or not this has been good or bad for Scottish football is a perennial matter of debate.

For some, Rangers and Celtic have kept Scottish football alive in the way they have provided a gravy train, a milch cow or whatever metaphor you wish to choose to picture the weak living off the strong, the poor surviving on the hand-outs of the rich. Others might compare the Old Firm to the legendary Upas Tree that was believed to have the power to destroy other growth within a radius of 15 miles, an image used in the title of a history of Glasgow that saw its heavy industries as having a detrimental domination of the city's economy and society.[15] However that may be, the Old Firm and the Scottish League have been stuck with each other, knowing that a breakaway needed the approval of the SFA, who could call on support from UEFA and ultimately FIFA to back them against recalcitrant clubs. And the world body has never lost a battle with nations that have bucked its authority, whether it was Colombia in the early 1950s or Australia a few years later. But that was all in the past; above all it was pre-Bosman.

There is little doubt that if Rangers and Celtic were playing regularly in a competition such as the English Premier League they could hold their own and would soon be challenging for the top spot. But a British League or an expanded Premier League to include them is a pipe-dream – the only way the Old Firm could be brought into a British League would be if the greed of the richest clubs in England encouraged them to break away from the merely wealthy clubs to form a smaller league which included the two Glasgow clubs. This reduced league programme would allow them at the same time to take part in a European league. This would also require the approval of UEFA and FIFA, but as the Bosman judgement has shown, there is an appeal beyond the courts of the gods who run the world game: a Bosman-type appeal on behalf of the rich clubs could smash all the existing rules and allow them to play in whatever league they wanted. More likely, FIFA would intervene and give its approval: either way it would be in the logic of the game's history: a Super League of the world's best teams.

In the meantime, Murray and McCann, with their eyes on Europe and the Scottish game merely an entry point for the more lucrative leagues to come, are in a contradictory situation. The more successful Rangers (and, to a similar degree, Celtic) are in Europe, the more money they earn and so the further they find themselves adrift of the other Scottish teams. And yet without a strong competition in Scotland they have inadequate preparation for their European encounters. And the more unattractive the Scottish league becomes, the more difficult it is to persuade top international stars to play there: Rangers and now Celtic have the money to spend on these players, and the stadiums and facilities that go with them, but there is little attraction for a Vialli or a Zola playing against Aberdeen, Hearts or Dundee United four times a year, let alone Dunfermline or Kilmarnock, all teams that once held their heads high in Europe. According to Fernando Couto when he rejected a Rangers offer,

Scottish football was 'rubbish'. Ronaldo was much more polite when he rejected what must surely have been the most attractive offer ever made to any footballer. Rangers' offer to the brilliant Brazilian – one which the cynics say was made because they knew it would not be accepted, or was made after he had signed for Inter Milan, but which was in any case a mere publicity stunt – was mindboggling not just in its payments to the player (a salary of more than £4.2 million and a percentage of his transfer fee if he left before the end of his four-year contract), but in Ronaldo's right to choose the games he wanted to play in, thus excusing him from having to go through the motions against the majority of the Scottish teams Rangers had to play against each week. All this in addition to the £20 million transfer fee to be paid to his club, Barcelona.

For many in Scotland, above all the fans of the Old Firm, primeval passions were centred more on home turf than the baubles to be gained on foreign soil, and for them as the 1996–97 season got under way and the bitter memories of early departures from Europe were pushed into the background, there was only one question that bore serious considera-tion: whether or not the resurgent Celtic could stop Smith's Rangers from equalling the record set by Jock Stein's team back in 1974, a record that several commentators said at the time, and for well over a decade later, would never be beaten.

7. Nine Down, One to Go

Rangers, despite a shaky start, won their seventh consecutive League flag in 1995 at a canter, with Celtic finishing in fourth place. Standing between a revitalised Celtic and Rangers' eighth successive League flag were Gascoigne and Laudrup, above all the former, as Celtic fought their main rivals to a finish only to come in second, four points behind the winners. With the magic nine-in-a-row approaching, the other trophies seemed inconsequential to Rangers. They fell to Hearts 2–4 in the fourth round of the Scottish Cup in 1995, but had their revenge in the final the following year with a 5–1 hammering of the Edinburgh club. In the League Cup Rangers were beaten by Falkirk (1–2) in the third round of the 1994–95 season and by Aberdeen (1–2) in the semi-final the next year. By then the momentum begun by McCann off the field at Parkhead was showing results on the field, as Celtic dramatically cut the gap between the two clubs.

In McCann's first year at Celtic Park, Burns's team got off to a sparkling start to the season, taking Rangers apart in a 2–0 victory at Ibrox on 27 August 1994. To add to their natural joy at triumphing over the Huns, the Celtic fans could also take a perverse pleasure in seeing Rangers supporters turn on Walter Smith and the team as Rangers' crushing defeat came just three days after their elimination from the preliminary rounds of the European Cup by AEK Athens; then on the last day of August Rangers were beaten 2–1 in the League Cup by Falkirk, their third successive defeat at home, and all in key games. But the gods must have been teasing the men from Paradise, as Rangers soon found form and outstripped their rivals. Celtic reached the final of the League Cup that season, but lost to Raith Rovers in a penalty shoot-out, leaving the good folk of Raith to dance in the streets while the Bhoys tore their hair out in anguish. In May 1995 Celtic won the Scottish Cup, but even this first touch of silverware in any form since 1989 was greeted more with relief than celebration. It was a lacklustre victory, 1–0 against Airdrie, but it was a trophy nevertheless.

In McCann's second full year, Celtic won nothing, and yet there was an air of expectation, even euphoria, at the club, as the fans were buoyed with dreams of what lay ahead. This, they hoped, would be the year they stopped Rangers matching the Stein record. It was a year as tense as the pundits predicted, with controversies on and off the field, but with a climax that proved to be more of a whimper than a bang.

SHOWDOWN SEASON

Rangers won the first trophy of the 1996–97 season with a 4–3 victory over Hearts in the League Cup final after Celtic had been eliminated by the Edinburgh side (1–0) in the quarter-finals. Celtic made up for this in the Scottish Cup, where they went through to the semi-final on a wave of delirium after eliminating Rangers with a classy 2-0 quarter-final victory on 6 March. Again the promised joy turned to torment as they were brought down to earth with a thud by lower-division Falkirk, who beat them 1–0 in a replay after a 1–1 draw and went on to lose to Kilmarnock in the final. Celtic's defeat was more devastating than the League Cup loss to Raith Rovers, as this time they were beaten without recourse to penalties and in a replay, which would normally have been a formality for either of the Old Firm teams when held by a minnow in the first game. Disaster in the league chase also cut short the optimism that accompanied the elimination of Rangers from the Cup.

That Cup victory over Rangers on 6 March 1997 had ended a long drought in Old Firm encounters going back ten games to 6 May 1995, but hopes of a turn-around in Old Firm fortunes ended in a crunch league game just over a week later, on 16 March, when the championship was all but decided after Rangers beat Celtic 1-0 at Celtic Park. At one stage in the league race towards the end of October, with 11 games played, Celtic were at the top of the table on goal difference; two games later they were five points behind. One of these games was against Rangers, who won 1–0 at Ibrox, the second of Rangers' four Old Firm league victories in the only season when one team whitewashed the other in Premier League games. Rangers charged ahead in the league after the Ibrox victory, but a win for Celtic in the Ne'erday game at home would have kept them in the race. Instead, Rangers won a controversial encounter with a 3–1 scoreline that flattered the visitors, who benefited from a disputed refereeing decision when a late goal by Cadete, which would have equalised the score at 2–2, was disallowed. At that stage Celtic were applying all the pressure, having regained the initiative after the daftest of defensive errors had cost them their second goal. Eric Bo Anderson sealed it for Rangers in the last minute. The Ibrox side were now 14 points ahead, although Celtic had two games in hand. Celtic then won five games in succession, and Rangers, suffering from a string of injuries which had plagued them for much of the season, including a broken ankle for Gascoigne in a pointless tournament in Amsterdam, meant that they dropped some vital points. Celtic somehow managed to do the same, but by the time the two clubs met for their last league game against each other, Celtic had cut the gap to five points.

Played on 16 March 1997, the last Old Firm game of the showdown season turned out to be a spiteful encounter. Mark Hateley, temporarily back with the club he had left against his own wishes, was sent off for a gentle head-butt on Stewart Kerr, while Malky Mackay of Celtic was also red-carded. Paolo di Canio and Ian Ferguson carried on their own personal feud, but boiling point came at the end of the game when Rangers, having won 1–0, celebrated with a mockery of the Celtic huddle. This was a ritual that Celtic had introduced into the game, usually before matches, but in the recent Cup game they had used it to celebrate victory. Throughout the tensions, the supporters kept their cool, showing a discipline that they certainly had not learned from the players or even the manager. Burns denounced the manner of the Rangers victory, prompting Walter Smith to speak out in defence of his players when he returned from a scouting trip to Italy. He pointed out how Rangers had congratulated Celtic after their defeat in the Cup game, which his players had accepted without recriminations. The signs were there that tensions were building up at Paradise and it all burst into the open when Celtic were knocked out of the Cup by Falkirk.

In the meantime Rangers tormented their fans as they failed to kill off the league race in the style they craved. It all seemed to be falling into place on 15 April when they thrashed Raith Rovers 6–0 at Kirkcaldy and were all but mathematical certainties to win the flag. They could even have won it without playing another game after that, but Celtic delayed the popping of the champagne corks with two victories, against Aberdeen and Hibernian, while Rangers themselves held up the celebrations when they failed to beat Motherwell in a Monday game at Ibrox on 5 May. The giant party planned for Ibrox on the Monday night, including a 20,000-fan congo line all the way to George Square, had to be postponed. Celebrations took place two nights later, on the east coast, or in pubs and private homes and public places throughout the country as Rangers duly wrapped up their ninth consecutive flag when they went to Tannadice and Brian Laudrup scored the game's only goal. As if to give a special touch to the magic he had been producing all season, it was Laudrup's first-ever headed goal for the club.

Rangers fans were even deprived of a proper celebration at their final game, against Hearts. They lost 3–1 at Tynecastle, with 30,000 fans at Ibrox that day decked out in party gear to watch the last match of the historic season relayed direct from Edinburgh and projected on the new giant television screens. However disappointed by the result that day, Celtic's record had been equalled and there was every chance that the chant of 'Ten-on-the-Trot' would become a reality the following season – especially when Celtic appeared to be disintegrating as the hectic season came to an end and Rangers went in for ever more fantastic buying sprees over the summer.

SUMMER OF HOPE AND HEARTBREAK

When Motherwell beat Rangers that Monday, some of the more optimistic Celtic fans were still hoping for a miracle, that Dundee United might repeat Motherwell's feat on the Wednesday. It all became irrelevant when, that same night, Celtic could only draw 0–0 against Kilmarnock, so that Rangers did not even have to take a point at Dundee to win the trophy. Celtic by then were managerless, Burns having left the club a few days before. In reality, Celtic's season and Burns's career as the club's manager ended after the Falkirk defeat. After another long, drawn-out saga about his future, during which Burns is said to have demanded that McCann back him or sack him, the chairman ended the speculation when he refused to renew the manager's contract and effectively forced Burns to resign on 2 May 1997 by offering him a new position at Celtic Park as head of youth development, an offer Burns was not expected to accept.

It had been a stormy partnership from the outset, and there was speculation that Burns had not even been McCann's first choice as manager. Ivan Golac of Dundee United and Bobby Robson, then in charge of Porto, had been linked with the position. And Kenny Dalglish. But if Dalglish were to come back to Glasgow, it seemed more likely that it would have been not to his former club, but rather to the team he had supported as a boy. Dalglish's 1996 autobiography reads in places like an application for a job at Ibrox,[1] and indeed he looked all set to go there on an outrageous salary as some sort of roaming ambassador and public-relations man for David Murray's other leisure concerns, when Newcastle United intervened and Dalglish joined the Geordies instead, replacing Kevin Keegan as manager.

Over the summer of 1997, with Burns off to contemplate his future and find some way to let the world know of the wrongs that had been done to him at Celtic Park, Keegan and Robson were back among the names being touted as the club's new manager, while the *Daily Record*, which seemed to be running a campaign on behalf of Bobby Robson, announced in an exclusive that the former England coach would definitely be joining Celtic. McCann refused to show any sign of being

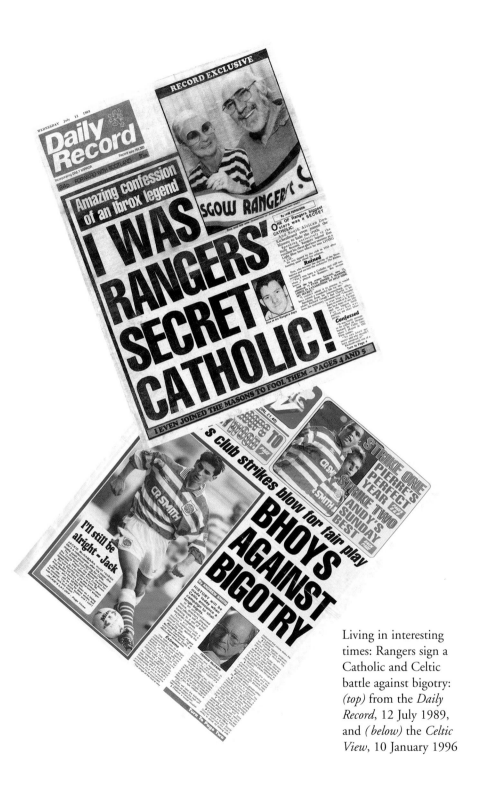

Living in interesting times: Rangers sign a Catholic and Celtic battle against bigotry: *(top)* from the *Daily Record*, 12 July 1989, and *(below)* the *Celtic View*, 10 January 1996

Playing the game: Paolo di Canio (*above*) and Jorge Cadete (*below*) failed to stop the Rangers juggernaut or revise their contracts, so they moved on

Rangers continue to collect the trophies: (*above*) with the Scottish Cup, and (*below*)
Basile Boli and Brian Laudrup celebrate another goal by Ian Durrant

Souness shows off his multicultural Rangers: Johnston, Hateley, Gough, Ginzberg and Walters, and (*below*) Maurice Johnston, centre of the storm in July 1989, in a more familiar pose in pursuit of the ball

Three to go: Paul McStay, Pierre van Hooijdonk and John Collins look forward to the new season but injury, a contract dispute and a free transfer highlighted some of the problems that beset Celtic at this time, and (*below*) Simon Donnelly, young Celtic star and an increasingly rare bird in Old Firm encounters today – a native-born Scot

Happy days: Walter Smith with the treble trophies in 1992–93 and (*below*) Rangers stalwarts McCoist and Durrant with the League Cup in 1993

Paul Gascoigne, the Geordie genius, shows his jubilation and dejection

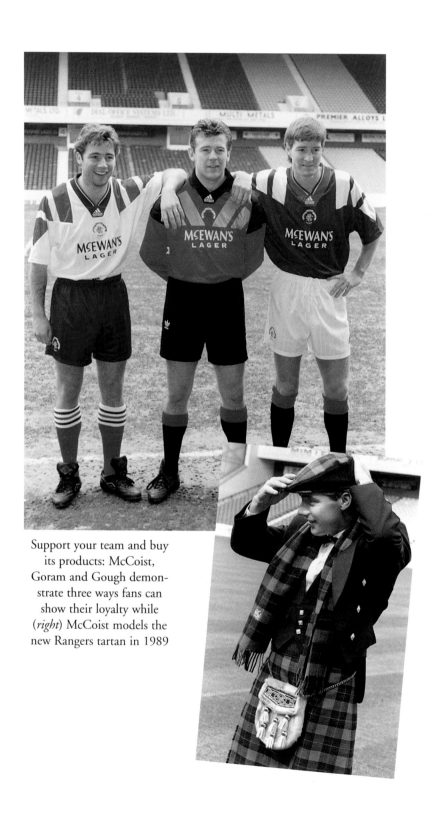

Support your team and buy its products: McCoist, Goram and Gough demonstrate three ways fans can show their loyalty while (*right*) McCoist models the new Rangers tartan in 1989

rattled by the rumour-mongers as he embarked on his plan to restructure the club around the model of that of the best of such continental teams as Ajax and Juventus, with a head coach and a general manager to run the team and its business affairs. It took an agonisingly long time before McCann, ignoring the clamour in the press to accept one of their candidates, finally, in July, settled on the Dutchman Wim Jansen as coach. Jansen, whose only previous connection with Celtic was as a player in the Feyenoord team which beat the Glasgow side in the European Cup in 1970, was not the big-name signing the fans had hoped for. The new man, six months out of work after a spell coaching in Japan, was signed on a three-year contract to work with the general manager, who would deal with the legal and administrative affairs of the team. If Celtic's choice of coach caused some dismay, the appointment of Jock Brown as general manager on 20 June had provoked a few agonised protests, and not for the reputation for arrogance that he brought with him from his previous job, and which would allegedly lead to serious conflict with the head coach. Of more concern to some Celtic supporters, including a spokesman for the Celtic Supporters Association, spouting a religious purity so recently the preserve of the Protestants, the club was in danger of betraying its origins. Such suspicions were reinforced with the departures under a cloud of Burns and later Davie Hay, the latter muttering darkly about Celtic straying too far from their traditional roots, while Burns warned McCann that 'Celtic have to be wary of mixing up bigotry and tradition'.[2] In an amazing response, and without naming the two former managers, McCann denounced the accusations of people he branded 'Catholic bigots'.

Brown was the son of a Hamilton Accies man; his brother Craig, the Scotland coach, had once played for Rangers; and another brother was a Church of Scotland minister in Aberdeen. And while Brown was a fully qualified lawyer, he was best known as a football commentator and was widely thought to be a Rangers supporter. The new man spared the public protestations about how his life-long ambition had been to manage Celtic, but with his signature came his commitment and a reminder that two of Celtic's greatest ever signings, Jock Stein and Kenny Dalglish, came from non-Catholic backgrounds.

It was his skills as a lawyer which had brought Brown to the attention of the Celtic board, but it would have needed more than a genius from Philadelphia to sort out the sea of troubles that faced the new manager. Above all there was the running sore of Celtic's two outstanding players, Cadete and di Canio, who openly expressed their dislike of McCann, their love of the Celtic fans and a desire to play elsewhere. When eventually they left the club – Cadete following his wife back to Portugal and di Canio heading to Sheffield Wednesday – the two former idols, like Van Hooijdonk before them, had used up the last ounce of goodwill that the fans had so bounteously lavished on them. There was a time, before the retain-and-transfer system was abolished, when players were often treated abominably; now the boot seems to be on the other foot, and players on what some would describe as obscene wages are not even prepared to stick by the contract they signed of their own (and their agent's) free will. But these were not the only problems facing Brown.

In the week before Burns left Celtic, Willie Haughey, one of the front-runners when McCann won his battle with the old board, left the club in acrimonious circumstances, to be followed a few days later by Dominic Keane, apparently out of sympathy with Haughey. In the game against Hibs, shortly after Burns's resignation, Paolo di Canio, professing anger at what had happened, threw his jersey into the crowd and told the press that he had lost faith in McCann. Burns had been Celtic's fourth manager in six years. As a player he had often lost his temper and even with his millionaire employer he could not keep his tongue or his feelings in check, at times seeming to be deliberately provocative. McCann was not a man easily provoked, more and more a Napoleonic figure as he restored order after the civil war and revolution, but in danger, like Napoleon, of alienating his support by too authoritarian an approach.

The departure of Haughey and Keane, prominent in the unseating of the old board, and the re-emergence of Brian Dempsey with his plans to save the club from corporate control and return it to the fans, had all the makings of a challenge to McCann. There were rumblings of a new civil war, with some of the same faces in similar roles but with changed allegiances. This time McCann had complete control through his share-holding, but also the support of the bulk of the fans among whom the general feeling was that if Burns had done his job as well as McCann had done his, Celtic would not have trailed Rangers in the climactic season.

All this faced Brown when he took on the job at Parkhead, and no magic wand came with the job description. In contrast to the star players, it is unlikely that Brown is being overpaid, but if he can sort out the problems at Celtic Park, and if Jansen can create on the field what his more fancied predecessors failed to do, then some faith might be restored that gods other than Mammon are at work in the football firmament.

Over at Ibrox the only news during the summer of 1997, give or take the odd bid to secure the world's best footballer, or the signing of a new coach, Tommy Moller Nielsen, to relieve Walter Smith and prepare for his move upstairs, was on those days when Rangers were not linked with the transfer of some multi-million-pound foreign star. At the end of June Murray's expenditure on players since he arrived at the club passed the

£45 million mark. Several of the new players are Italian, presumably Catholic, and with those Catholics already at the club they could eventually make up the majority of the first team.

Despite the excitement surrounding the new arrivals at Ibrox, it was the retention of the two reigning stars, Gascoigne and Laudrup, that most cheered the Rangers faithful. Not that the newcomers were not looked upon with some wonderment: above all, the four Italians – the youngster Gennaro (Rino) Gattuso, secured on freedom of contract from Perugia; Marco Negri, also from Perugia, a striker who would set up an amazing goalscoring streak in his first dozen games, for £3.7 million; Sergio Porrini from Juventus (£3.2 million); and Lorenzo Amoruso from Fiorentina (£4 million). Amoruso, like Sebastian Rozental, has proven to be an expensive buy, living the life of a millionaire footballer on the dole, unlike Rozental not even having kicked a ball in serious competition. He arrived with an injury that was not properly diagnosed by the club doctor and so cost the club (and the fans) a fortune while he underwent expensive surgery. In addition to the Italians there was the Swede Jonas Thern, the Norwegian Stale Stensaas, and some other more minor signings, including the Australian Tony Vidmar, out of contract with NAC Breda. Their arrival was waited with cautious optimism, but the re-signing of Gascoigne was greeted with delight tempered with foreboding, while the retention of Laudrup when he seemed set to leave the club was received with unalloyed joy.

Gascoigne, even by his own standards, had had a troubled time both on and off the field in the last half of the 1996–97 season, and although Smith allowed his inner thoughts to be transformed into press headlines about the nightmares the player had caused him, he still put his paternal trust in the troubled Geordie, and Murray persuaded him to stay with the club. Brilliant displays for England brought Gazza back to the attention of English clubs, and Glenn Hoddle caused a stir when he said that Gazza needed the keener competition in England to bring out his best. But, to the surprise of some and at a substantial financial cost to the club, Gazza chose to stay in Scotland. He was also repaying a debt, to Walter Smith for his understanding and to the club in general for all it did to help him overcome his demons by occupying his mind when not playing football, engaging him in commercial deals and any other work that kept him from wandering along the empty corridors of his mind.

One player who had openly expressed his disgust for Gascoigne's behaviour was Brian Laudrup, and in the summer of 1997 it looked as though he was set to leave Rangers, to join his brother Michael at Ajax, with one year of his contract still to run. Murray seems to have been at first prepared to cash in on his prime asset, but a stream of abusive phone calls and faxes that blocked the daily routine of Murray International Holdings is said to have persuaded him otherwise. Murray flew the unsettled Dane by private jet to his holiday home in Jersey, and in addition to outlining his plans for the future and showing him the long list of players he intended to buy, introduced Laudrup, a wine connoisseur, to his collection of fine wines. As the story goes, Laudrup fully appreciated the tasting, while Murray, for whom the wine was more an investment than a complement to fine eating, enthusiastically agreed with Laudrup's judgements of the bottles on offer. Retaining Laudrup might have cost Murray a few bottles from his cellar, but he was also giving up the minimum £4 million the club would have earned from his transfer. It would all be money well spent, however, if Rangers finally laid to rest the ghost of European ignominy and secured the success on the continent that had eluded them until then.

FOREIGN FIELDS

Before the start of the showdown season, the performances of the two Old Firm teams in Europe had been embarrassingly poor. Despite a cheque-book that allowed Rangers to compete with the richest clubs in Europe, they failed to come anywhere near the *annus mirabilis* of 1992–93. They did not even make it to the European Champions' League the following year, being eliminated in the preliminary round by Levski-Sofia, whose two away goals in a 3–2 defeat at Ibrox saw them through when they won 2–1 in the Bulgarian capital. Worse followed the next season when AEK Athens knocked them out at the same stage, winning 2–0 at home and 1–0 at Ibrox. Rangers did qualify for the league section in 1995, but only by the odd goal after 180 minutes of football against Cyprus's Anorthosis Famagusta. In the league section they failed to win a game in six matches against Juventus, Steaua Bucharest and Borussia Dortmund, although they did manage three draws. Despite Laudrup, who seemed unable to lord it over opponents in Europe as he did in Scotland, and Gascoigne, who did not enjoy the favour of the referees on the continent as he did in Scotland, Rangers were outclassed. In their games with Juventus (minus Laudrup in both games and Gascoigne for the home game), they lost 4–1 in Italy and 4–0 at home.

It was to be the same story the following year. Rangers went through to the league section after magnificent wins both home and away to Alania Vladikavkaz of Georgia, but then the promise disappeared. Gascoigne once more let his teammates down by being sent off: in his first season he was red-carded against Borussia Dortmund, and in 1996 he was dismissed for a petulant foul on Winston Bogarde of Ajax. Beaten in their first game against Grasshopper of Switzerland, Rangers then lost to Auxerre, the team from a town in France which, with a population of 40,000, is not much bigger than Largs. Rangers' only victory came when it no longer mattered, a 2–1 win over Grasshopper at Ibrox. Rangers had an inordinate number of injured players in these games, but as suggested elsewhere, a few injuries can be bad luck, a whole coach-load smacks of more than carelessness.

Celtic were equally unable to revive their glory days of European competition. In the 1992–93 season they did well to recover from a 2–0 defeat against Cologne in Germany by winning 3–0 in Glasgow, but then went down home and away to Borussia Dortmund in the UEFA Cup. In Lou Macari's only taste of European football as a manager (1993–94), Celtic beat BSC Young Boys of Switzerland with a 1–0 aggregate, but in the next round took a one-goal home lead to Portugal, only to be eliminated on a 2–1 aggregate by Sporting Lisbon. They failed to qualify the following year, but then Burns led his team into the 1995–96 Cup-winners' Cup, losing both legs to Paris Saint-Germain after beating Dynamo Batumi of Georgia in the first round, 7–2 on aggregate. In Paris the score was 1–0, at Parkhead it was 3–0, the visitors leaving the field to a standing ovation. In the qualifying round for the UEFA Cup in 1996–97, Celtic survived the first round with a 1–0 aggregate against FC Kosice of Slovakia, Cadete scoring the only goal in the first leg in Glasgow in the 88th minute. Against Hamburg, though, Celtic were easily eliminated, 2–0 in both legs.

Freed from the tyranny of 'nine-in-a-row' and filled with hope by Walter Smith's summer spending, Rangers fans had every right to look forward to their club's progress in the European competition of the 1997–98 season. There was the small matter of qualifying for the league section. GI Gotu of the Faroe Islands were eliminated 11–0 on aggregate in the first qualifying round, but beating their second-round opponents proved a more difficult proposition. Rangers found themselves 3–0 down against IFK Gothenberg and with a mammoth task to face in the return leg. It turned out to be too much, and the Swedish minnows went through instead of the Glasgow giants after a 1–1 draw at Ibrox. Having been knocked out of the Champions' League, Rangers were allowed into the UEFA Cup which, if it did not have the prestige of the European Cup, was still a major competition and promised a compensatory financial bonanza. They were drawn against Strasbourg, struggling at the wrong end of the French first division, but no more than against the Swedish part-timers were the millionaires of Rangers able to assert any supremacy, falling 2–1 both home and away.

It was a disaster in no way mitigated by Celtic's elimination in the same competition; worse, in fact, in that Celtic at least departed from Europe with some honour. In the early rounds, they dismissed Cable-Tel of the Welsh League, 8–0 over the two legs. They came back from Austria having been beaten 2–1 by FC Tyrol and, despite losing three goals in an amazing game at Celtic Park in the return leg, scored six to win 7–5 on aggregate. The reward was another Battle of Britain encounter, Celtic against Liverpool. The Merseyside club may no longer have been the great Liverpool team of the days before Souness became their manager, but they were a side bristling with individual talent nevertheless. Memories of Leeds in 1970 (or even 1992) were fresh in many minds, but it was the defeat of 1966 that was repeated, the result hanging on a brilliant Steve McManaman last-minute equaliser at Celtic Park to make the score 2–2, and a Simon Donnelly miss at Anfield that failed to break the 0–0 deadlock. Liverpool went through on the away-goals rule.

LOST ILLUSIONS

The two Old Firm teams were back to domestic competition, and the Rangers fans had to face up to the reality that the millions spent on players had been wasted: nine-in-a-row salved the souls of the narrower spirits, but the real goal was as far off as ever. Walter Smith realised this and, at the AGM on 28 October 1997, said he would resign at the end of the season. His dignified recognition of reality was not met with the same detachment among the contributors to *Follow, Follow*, who, angered by the European disasters, launched into vitriolic attacks on those running the club. The Govanhill Gub denounced, and on the face of it not without some justification, the 'shoddy work practices, poor coaching, non-existent shambolic medical care and financial incompetence on a horrendous scale'; his solution was for Murray to go, taking 'the manager, assistant manager, Mutton Chops [Donald Findlay], Mr SFA Ogilvie, Hood and the rest of the hangers-on Rangers entourage with him'.[3]

Shortly after the defeats by Strasbourg, Murray further annoyed the Rangers fans in an interview he gave to Graham Spiers in *Scotland on Sunday* of 21 September 1997, where he expressed his dislike of some of the citizens of Glasgow whom he characterised as 'very loud and vociferous' with 'an awful lot to say'; more specifically, he castigated the 'incredible arrogance about some Rangers fans', whom he chided for not even knowing how to spell some of their favourite swear words. Murray's sin was compounded by giving the interview to what *Follow, Follow* saw as the Edinburgh-based enemy of the club, especially its Rangers-hating chief sports columnist, known in some quarters for his neutrality as the 'Fenian baptist'.

As if to prove Murray's assertions about the citizens of Glasgow correct, *Follow, Follow* savaged the dictatorship of Mr Mint and made at least three references to Bill Struth 'turning in his grave' at the direction the club was taking. Not for the first time, John Greig was lambasted for his failure as public-relations officer to present the club in a better light, although this, coming from a fanzine that gives every impression of regarding PR as a dirty word, sounds particularly rich – or more appropriately in this case, rancid.

Among the Celtic faithful, there was little in the appointments of Jock Brown and Wim Jansen to get terribly excited about, but the Dutchman soon assembled a team with international talent which he moulded into a skilful unit. None of his imports could match Gascoigne or Laudrup, or the goalscoring feats of Negri, but they had impressive credentials – or, as has happened in the past with Celtic, promised to emerge from comparative mediocrity to star status: to foreigners like the Dutch star Regi Blinker, the Swedish striker Henrik Larsson, the Dane Marc Rieper, the Frenchman Stéphane Mahe and, later, the Norwegian Harald Brattbakk, Jansen added Scottish internationals Craig Burley, Paul Lambert and Darren Jackson. They joined the Dane Morten Wieghorst and the Italian Enrico Annoni who had been signed by Burns. Jansen's team, after a faltering start, put together a string of victories, but the real test was delayed until November when the Old Firm faced each other for the first time.

The first Old Firm game of the 1997–98 season was to have been played on the Monday evening of 1 September 1997. Events in Paris, namely the tragic death in a car accident of Diana, Princess of Wales, the previous day, determined that it be postponed until a future date. Games were played in England that night, but to have allowed the Old Firm game to proceed would have been to invite trouble. Among the Celtic support would have been the handful of cretins prepared to express their contempt for royalty, and enough outraged royalists among the Rangers support to see the need to exact honourable retribution.

There were no Premier League games in Scotland the following Saturday because of the Scotland–Belarus World Cup qualifier, and none in England because Princess Diana's funeral was taking place that day. Jim Farry of the SFA, showing a not unusual insensitivity to public feeling, gave every sign of going ahead with the Scotland–Belarus game, but it was left to three Rangers players in the squad, McCoist, Goram and Gordon Durie, to protest and let him know that they would not play on that day. For this they were warmly applauded, but for those who could not overlook the fact that Diana's death had been caused in part by a drunken driver, the moral stance of two of these players lost some of its impact.

As a result of this, there were two Old Firm games in November. Rangers won 1–0 at Ibrox, thanks to two crucial saves from Goram and a goal from the newly returned Richard Gough, who slotted home an inch-perfect Laudrup pass, to ensure justice for their superiority on the day. In the game at Celtic Park it was the home side who dominated, but until the 90th minute Rangers had the only goal, Negri scoring in the 71st minute. Rangers played with ten men for most of the second half after Gascoigne was finally red-carded in a domestic game. It was Stubbs who came to his side's rescue with a last-gasp header, saving Celtic not only from falling a further three points behind Rangers, but also from a psychological blow that would have been difficult to survive.

At the end of the year Celtic were in a better position than at the same time in 1996. Rangers were knocked out of the League Cup by Dundee United, who in turn lost to Celtic in the final, to give Jansen his first trophy. For a while Hearts looked as though they might have rewritten the script to upset the 'ten-in-a-row' season, but a 5–2 thrashing by Rangers at Ibrox, followed by a 1–0 defeat by Celtic the following week, seemed to betoken an end to their hopes. Celtic, however, managed to lose games while Rangers dropped points in draws, so that if Hearts had beaten Hibs at the derby game on New Year's day, instead of drawing 2–2, they would have begun 1998 at the top of the table. Celtic won the Ne'erday derby at home 2–0 after a brilliant spell in an otherwise scrappy affair, so that the title race remained wide open. The result was almost overshadowed by the political fall-out (discussed later), Gascoigne's flute gesture to the Celtic fans and Goram's black armband, claimed by some against the protestations of Goram himself, to be worn out of respect for murdered Protestant terrorist, Billy Wright, in the Maze prison.

As Rangers and Celtic continued into 1998, fighting to gain or frustrate ten-on-the-trot, the battle did not have the same desperation as equalling the Stein record. The defeats in Europe at the start of the season had brought a sense of reality to most Rangers fans, where only a fanatical minority could convince themselves that there was something of global significance in ten successive league flags. In the Scottish situation the importance of the pursuit by Rangers of Celtic's nine successive titles was understandable, just as a tenth successive flag would be the justifiable excuse for further rejoicing by Rangers fans, or, if thwarted, a cause for celebrations by Celtic fans if their team win the League, relief if Hearts do: but to claim that this has any relevance outside Scotland is ludicrous. To try and place such a domestic success on a world scale is an embarrassment rather than something to be proud of. The health of a sporting competition is not in the stranglehold of its two top teams, but in the competition as a whole, as can be seen in the contrasting examples of the English league with its multitude of contenders for top honours and the now thankfully defunct East German league and its domination by Dynamo Berlin.

THE WAY TO THE FUTURE

Television technology has dominated the finances of football in the last decade and more, and for the first time the game seems to be coming second to outside interests. Since the first ball was kicked in serious competition over a hundred years ago, the media have established a symbiotic relationship with football: first the press, then the radio, which grew with the game and helped promote it without ever threatening to take it over, although this is not how the football authorities saw it in the early days. The fears with regard to television seemed more rationally based, and through to the 1980s football clubs imposed restrictions on live coverage of matches, afraid that spectators would prefer the comfort of an armchair to the real thing. In the last decade or so, television technology has leapt ahead and there is more to be gained by the richest clubs from television exposure than there is from live spectators.

In the days before TV coverage, a shirt logo or an advertisement on a perimeter fence meant little when the only people who saw them were at the ground. Now the original black-and-white television with limited viewpoints has been replaced by colour, instant-replays and multiple camera angles so that every aspect of the game can be analysed in the minutest detail; from a commercial point of view the smallest detail on a player's shirt, shorts or socks, as well his boots and the ball, can now be blown up and flashed instantaneously throughout a world united around a single television set. It is brand exposure undreamt of even a couple of decades ago, with all the riches that this conjures up.

Cable and satellite television, and the break-up of the state monopolies in favour of privatised television channels, were behind the revolution in the organisation of the European game in the late 1980s, Silvio Berlusconi in Italy leading the way by buying up television channels and AC Milan (along with a few supermarket chains and multifarious other enterprises) so that he could have it all to himself. His main aim, apart from becoming prime minister of Italy – however briefly – has always been a midweek televised European League, run through his TV station. Neither Murray nor McCann is likely to buy an entire television company, but they could buy interests in one, or present their own programmes, such as the weekly shows on the recently formed satellite/cable company, Sky Scottish: *The Ibrox Club Hour* and *The Celtic Park Hour*.

With the development of digital television viewing, club owners will be able to claim a monopoly of any game in which their team appears, with the right to charge individual homes on a pay-per-view basis. Instead of watching a game at the stadium, or trekking to a pub to watch it on the big screen, or buying a subscription to one of the pay TV channels who decide which games to televise, payment is through a smart card which allows you to watch the team of your choice at home on your own television set. What Rangers and Celtic are looking for is the market of fanatics outside Scotland: in the rest of the UK and Ireland, North America, South Africa, Australia and New Zealand. For those on the other side of the world, given the trouble and expense many of these expatriates endure to tune in to games played by their favourites, it would be a joy to perform the equivalent of putting some money in the meter and see the match in your own home – especially when it is being played in the middle of the night. For the big clubs, not only is their revenue multiplied by an astronomical factor, but their beady-eyed owners can rest assured that no one is watching the team for nothing or the price of a few bevvies. No longer need David Murray worry as he watches £30 million pounds of his players perform in his £60 million stadium that 'the general public [can] just switch on for nothing'.[4] No longer being ripped off by the non-paying public, the club will have even more cash to spend on players and luxury facilities. And so it goes, greed without end. At least for the foreseeable future.

Those who claim to hold the key to reality will tell you how there is no alternative to paying ever more money to preserve the lifestyles of ever more extravagant football stars. As well as managers walking off with a fortune after being sacked for incompetence, the testimonials for millionaire players is an echo of the vacuous values of today's economic irrationalists. In the old days a testimonial was a just reward for a player who had devoted his career to a club which paid him a modest salary. Now players on thousands of pounds a week still expect the windfall of a game paid for by fans who have helped to make them millionaires, even in the case of Ally McCoist in one of his less humorous moments showing them an empty wallet as a symbol of the need to give to the deserving rich. Or Richard Gough, who admitted that if the Bosman ruling had come in earlier he might have left Ibrox for a better deal instead of staying on for the nine-in-a-row. Despite the money raining in on the rich clubs from sources other than spectators at the game, admittance charges continue to rise. The fans are told to put up with it, otherwise they cannot expect all these foreign stars to come to Glasgow to entertain them. Yet who would seriously suggest that any Rangers team since Souness has given the supporters more pleasure than Greig's European triumph in 1972 or the team he played for as a youngster in the early 1960s, or that any Celtic team since McCann has given supporters more pleasure than the Celtic teams of the Stein years. Certainly Brian Laudrup has brought an unprecedented class both on and off the field to the Ibrox club, while Gascoigne for Rangers and di Canio for Celtic, whatever their inanities off the park, have produced magic with the ball: but even these exceptional talents have not been able to surpass the spectacle provided by Jim Baxter or Jimmy Johnstone at the height of their careers – and at a fraction of the cost.

And now success in Europe seems further off than ever, although that must change soon. But while Europe remains the main goal, it is the games between the big two in Scotland and the big names in England that hold the greatest interest: perhaps only Manchester United and Liverpool and the major Italian clubs have such a devoted following outside their own country – even Barcelona in Spain with their massive home following do not have the Rangers and Celtic interest abroad. Games between the Old Firm and the best in England are top priorities for television viewers, and the financial backing and fanatical support of the Glasgow teams is of more importance to the commercial backers of a new league than their performances on the park. The big question when Celtic and Rangers enter Europe on a regular basis is the role they will continue to play in the domestic Scottish game. Where a league without the two would leave the rest of the country's clubs is a doleful thought. It might also answer in an even more depressing way the question about the importance of the Old Firm to the health of the Scottish game. Most likely they will continue to play in Scotland, and games with each other will continue to be first in the Old Firm fan's sporting priorities.

The peculiar ferocity of the Old Firm clashes is something that foreigners will never be able to understand, especially now that the antagonisms are based more than ever on bygone days of yore than present realities. As Rangers set out to surpass the Stein record it could be with a team boasting no Scots and a majority of Catholics; no longer are its true-blue stalwarts regulars in the first team. At the start of the 1997–98 season, while the more thoughtful fans might have mused under the influence of the (English) bard: 'O brave new team that has such players in it!' Hearts fans greeted their visitors from Glasgow with the jeering refrain: 'More Tims than Celtic! They've got more Tims than

Celtic!' The reaction of the Rangers fans to these changes is the real test of the claim that it is the jersey and not the men who wear it that gives a club its identity. The era begun by Souness is now at a watershed: whether it is at an end is another matter.

8. Bhoys, Bears and Bigotry

Fergus McCann is first and foremost a businessman, but he looked on the club he had loved as a young man as a source of pride rather than a means of lining his pocket. So it was that he sought to enhance the meaning of the club in the community by launching his 'Bhoys against Bigotry' campaign at the beginning of January 1996. He was perhaps a bit put out when the idea was not taken up wholeheartedly by the Scottish public, while Rangers did not feel prompted to embark on a parallel 'Bears against Bigotry', or even a joint 'Bhoys and Bears against Bigotry' campaign. Perhaps Murray thought that through Alistair Hood and his hard-man tactics he had crushed the problem, and since the club now openly signed and played Catholics, bigotry was no longer Rangers' problem. Just as likely he had no wish to see Rangers tagging along behind an initiative begun by Celtic. For the Rangers fans the whole thing was purely cosmetic, an attempt to create a brighter commercial image. They could perhaps even see in it a concealed barb against Rangers in the Celtic claims that their campaign reaffirmed 'Celtic's pride in its joint Scottish and Irish identity and its charitable and non-sectarian history'. Celtic may have been well aware of Rangers' history with regard to sectarianism, but they were more cloudy on their own origins.

IF YOU KNOW YOUR HISTORY

The 'Mission Statement' that launched the campaign called on history to claim that Celtic had been founded to feed the poor and help integrate young Catholics into Scottish society: specifically that a 'new football club would be a vehicle to bring the communities together . . .' In fact, Celtic were founded, as mentioned earlier and discussed in more detail below, to keep young Catholics in the faith, free from the dangers of Protestant soup kitchens and mixing with Protestants in their leisure time. The aims of Brother Walfrid and such stalwarts as John Glass were soon thwarted when John McLaughlin and the businessmen took over. They realised that a professional football club run on purely Catholic lines was not a good commercial proposition since an all-Catholic team might have had difficulties succeeding on the park. Hence the refusal to limit the club to playing only three Protestants, as was proposed in 1895. But while McLaughlin and company set out to provide the sound commercial basis necessary for the success of any professional football club, the entire ethos of the club remained steeped in its Irish and Catholic origins, attracting the best Catholic players in Scotland and Ireland, and retaining its identity with the Catholic Church through its exclusively Catholic directors until the brief reign of David Dallas Smith in the 1990s.

By the time the businessmen had taken over at Celtic Park, Walfrid had left Glasgow, and although he might have had some concerns about the departures from the club's charitable foundations, he need not have worried about it being a continuing source of inspiration for young Catholics. Keeping young men in the faith had always been one of his principal concerns, and before he conceived the idea of Celtic he had organised a 'literary society' and other football clubs for boys who had just left school and who were at the most dangerous time, as he saw it, of falling into apostasy. This was brought out in a 'Sketch of Brother Walfrid' presented in the *Glasgow Observer* of 24 November 1900 in the form of a conversation between two characters speaking in thick Irish accents. One of them comments on how Walfrid did not want to see young lads who had just left school:

> . . . stragglin' away an' forgettin' their religious juties; because, as he said, 'twas the most dangerous time for the young fellos, jest afther they had left school, and begun t'mix up wid Prodestand boys in the places where they wor workin'. [And later in the conversation, how he was spurred into action in regard to the cheap dinners because] . . . there was a hole lot av soup kitchens got up thro' the town by the Prodestands, because av the grate amount av sufferin' there was in the town; an' 'twas afeerd Bro Walfrid was that some av his little wans wud be snared away, an' get a 'thract for kitchen wid every plate av soup, the same as they used to do in Ireland long ago'.[1]

Had Brother Walfrid seriously tried to *integrate* Catholics into Scottish society, he would soon have been sent on his way, and the Archbishop's appeal for subscriptions of January 1888 is concerned only about 'Catholics', with no thoughts of mixing with Protestants: it specifically refers to the membership of 'several of the leading Catholic footballers of the West of Scotland', of a team that would 'do credit to the Catholics of the West of Scotland as the Hibernians have been doing in the East', and that the recreation ground set up would be for 'our Catholic young men . . . to enjoy . . . various sports'. That a Catholic football club was set up for the benefit of Catholics will come as no surprise to those familiar with the history of the early years of football. Church groups were at the forefront in founding football teams in the early years of the game, and several of those in the top ranks of English football today were founded in this way: in the days of Muscular Christianity there was nothing unusual in Catholics adopting the methods of other branches of Christianity to take advantage of the passions of the young. Nor will Catholic fears of apostasy surprise those familiar with the history of the Church, which, through to the reforms of Vatican II, rigorously condemned under pain of condign retribution any compromise with the Truth and insisted that education and marriage had to be within the One True Catholic and Apostolic Church.

This historical detail, even for a club proud 'to know its history', should not detract from what McCann and Celtic set out to do: on the contrary, the club should recognise the way in which it has changed over the years and is now to the forefront in combating bigotry in Scottish society. Certainly, some aspects of the campaign left it open to the barbs of the sceptics: proclaiming that you are in favour of the 'Universal Declaration of Human Rights' is a bit like saying you should love your mother; charity envelopes at Celtic Park for fans already making sacrifices to help pay the wages of the wealthy wearing the hoops has aspects of the widow's mite; and there is something distinctly demeaning in the spectacle of Celtic manager Tommy Burns going out to feed the hungry – a sorry reflection of contemporary society, although it is hardly Celtic's fault if Scotland seems to be heading back to the indignities of the 1890s when all the poor had to rely on was charity. It was good that Celtic players went out to many of Glasgow's schools with their message, but nowhere was it suggested that the very separation of these schools into Catholic and Protestant, so that the one would not become contaminated with the ideas of the other, is in itself a potential source of bigotry.

All that aside, there was more to be praised than criticised in the campaign, and this was recognised when the club was awarded the European Commission Scottish Equality Award one year after its launch. In May 1997 both Murray and McCann were offered an anti-bigotry award by the Glasgow City Council. Murray refused on the grounds that he was interested only in sport, although he may well have come to the sensible conclusion that in 1997 employing Catholics to play for his football team was hardly something to warrant a medal. Michael Kelly, quoting Aristotle and aware of a long history of Celtic and Rangers being treated equally even when Rangers had a manifestly bigoted policy, referred to the injustice of treating unequals equally, for even in the post-Souness era, he claimed, Rangers still flaunted the blue and orange, had a director who 'incorporated an Orange Walk around his house as part of the New Year celebrations' and still did not have a Catholic on the board.[2] He also had a few shots at the Celtic supporters, but congratulated McCann as being a worthy recipient of the award.

BHOYS WITHOUT BEARS AGAINST BIGOTRY

McCann had every reason to be proud of what the club had done since issuing the 'Mission Statement'. It offered tickets and hospitality at Celtic Park to vendors of the *Big Issue*, the journal of the city's homeless, and the Celtic Charity Fund set aside £47,000 for donations to local projects to help different groups in the community. It also recruited ex-addicts to warn young people about the dangers of hard drugs. In addition the club continued to support the Northern Ireland Children's Holiday scheme aimed at bringing Catholic and Protestant children together. All very much to be applauded. Celtic cannot solve the problems of feeding the hungry, housing the homeless or healing the sick: only the government, through professionals paid by a taxation system where the rich pay a fair share, can properly deal with this. But they can help ease the pain. Moreover, there are areas that the state cannot reach, and this is where football clubs like Celtic, with their hold over so many of Scotland's young folk, are in a unique position to influence their lives for the better. Celtic have openly recognised this by working with others in the community and through the education authorities, offering alternative leisure pursuits to vandalism and gang violence, helping to give some meaning to otherwise empty lives that lead to drugs and despair – that is to say, meaningless despair as opposed to the despair of following a football team that never quite makes it.

At the time of the Dunblane tragedy, Celtic players and the club did what they could to bring some joy into shattered lives. So too did Rangers, although at the request of the folks of Dunblane this was not given prominent coverage in the media, highlighting perhaps a difference in approach of the two clubs. Defenders of Rangers' refusal to act along with McCann will claim that the Ibrox club do their good work by stealth, eschewing the blowing of trumpets, and certainly under Murray Rangers have contributed to the local community in a way that was unknown before he arrived. Above all, the club sends out coaching staff to more than four hundred primary schools in the Govan area, as part of their Community Coaching Programme, reaching out to more than two thousand boys and girls, regardless of their religious denomination.

There are areas where the good works of the two clubs should be trumpeted, however, so that the message can get through to those who need to hear it: above all it is incumbent on Rangers and Celtic to act together in areas involving the bigotry with which for a host of historical reasons they have become associated. If Rangers and Celtic sent joint delegations to Northern Ireland or other areas where sectarianism is rife, they would show in no uncertain terms that the two clubs have no truck with that aspect of their past. McCann and Murray have shown that they can work together in their own commercial interests; it would be an immense step forward if Murray was to join McCann in showing their followers that whatever their differences on the field of play, they can work together on that part of the Celtic Social Charter committed to 'projects that develop and promote religious and ethnic harmony'.

It seems, however, that Murray has never been comfortable with what he sees as moral posturing by McCann, and this came into the open in January 1998 when he criticised McCann in the *Rangers News* over a letter he had written to the SFA complaining about what was claimed to be a sectarian gesture by Paul Gascoigne at the Old Firm game of 2 January 1998. The letter was also said to contain other examples of a sectarian nature involving Rangers, and this, coming on top of various other incidents that had got under Murray's skin, nettled him into making an unprecedented attack on McCann in which he accused the Celtic chairman of meddling in what should have been a private matter, adding that he wondered 'why Fergus does certain things. Sometimes it's as though there is another agenda'. In the press, some saw McCann's action as being more provocative than Gascoigne's, and there were references to him being a clype, a tell-tale, a dobber, or whatever phrase one chooses to describe the sneak who tries to get his classmates in trouble.

McCann himself was acting in regard to an incident that took place at Celtic Park and the letter was sent at the request of the SFA. Moreover, Rangers had appeared to be brushing the matter under the carpet, using their time-honoured excuse of dealing with their own problems in their own way. Whatever the outcome, and there has been much worse pro-vocation in the past, all that has changed is a rise in the temperature of the moral heat: it is apparent that the commercial closeness of the Old Firm bosses is not reciprocated at the moral level.

Undeterred by the cynics and the absence of reciprocal gestures from Ibrox, McCann has gone his own way in the battle against bigotry. At Celtic Park he has pursued with unremitting zeal his campaign to make the new Paradise a bigot-free zone. Inside the stadium the club made regular attacks on those supporters who insisted on singing IRA songs, and asked that the decent supporters drown them out with non-political songs. The Irish tricolour flying above the stadium is no longer the source of irritation it once was, and there is little the club can do about away supporters who add IRA messages to the tricolour banners they wave in support of Celtic. The most notorious incident of this nature came in Germany where Celtic supporters at the away leg of the UEFA Cup in Hamburg, on 24 September 1996, added 'Provos on Tour' to the Irish flag they waved in support of the club. It is also to be applauded in this multicultural age that the club takes pride in its Irish and Catholic origins. To give its endorsement to 'The Fields of Athenry', however, is surely misguided. No song about the Hungry '40s in Ireland, the darkest decade in Anglo-Irish relations, can avoid political overtones. This was a time when millions were forced to leave Ireland or starve to death because of a famine which, if it was not actually caused by the British government, was due in part to its policies and was embittered by the contempt with which the native Irish were treated. The effects of the potato blight were disastrous, but it was all exacerbated by a government committed to economic policies that, over a century later, would be called 'Thatcherism'. Charles Edward Trevelyan, the supervisor in charge of famine relief, was prepared to bring in the corn referred to in the song (unfortunately it was an iron-hard Indian maize which the Irish could not convert into flour) to distribute among those who could prove that they were deserving and so long as this did not interfere with the profits of the merchants. He religiously refused to interfere with the workings of the market, so that in the midst of the starvation caused by the potato blight, boats loaded with other foodstuffs sailed to markets abroad.

When Dublin man Pete St John wrote the song in 1979 he might have seen it as a simple love song, but whatever his intentions the dirge is about an Irish patriot, a hero languishing, as the opening lines of the song tell us, by 'a lonely prison wall', 'cut down' in his prime because he rebelled against 'the famine and the crown' by stealing corn to feed his wife and child. Now she is left to care for the two of them alone, while he waits for a prison ship to take him to Botany Bay, final destination of a host of political prisoners before him. The pro-IRA fanzine *Tiocfaidh Ar La* was 'heartened' by the 'famine ballad', provided its readers with chorus and all the verses, while 'Mick Derrig' discoursed effusively on how British atrocities of the 1840s were comparable to the Holocaust of the Second World War.[3] The British had 'starved Ireland for profit' and now the IRA was fighting back with 'mortars raining in . . . on their nice buildings in London and their poor soldiers'. And also, presumably, bombing pubs in Guildford, discos in Birmingham and other places of innocent assembly. If it was the club's Irish connections Celtic wanted to celebrate – and there is nothing wrong with that – then there are many themes of a less political nature that could have been chosen, as Glen Daly showed when he brought out 'The Celtic Song' in 1961.[4]

Before McCann the club's associations with Irish republicanism were an occasional source of embarrassment, one of which was when the editor of the *Celtic View* was trapped into admitting support for the IRA. This was in August 1989 when Kevin McKenna allegedly told Mark Dingwall at a freebie dinner to discuss the Old Firm, of his sympathies for IRA terrorism, including the recent killing of 11 innocents at Enniskillen.[5] Some people found Dingwall's use of a secret tape-recorder at an off-the-record social evening reprehensible, although this was how Matt McGlone helped bring down the old board at Parkhead when he taped an attempt by Michael Kelly to get him to write a spoof against the press for *Celtic View*. Others criticised Dingwall for taking advantage of McKenna being the worse for drink: the more cynical were reminded of the well-known Glasgow expression about the effect on the tongue when you have had a few bevvies too many: *in vino veritas*. McKenna was sacked when his indiscretions were revealed to the tabloids, although this has not affected his subsequent rise, despite what many Celtic supporters claim is an anti-Catholic media, to become sports editor for one of Scotland's best newspapers.

The club is always at pains to distinguish what it would see as the culture of Ireland and the politics of terrorism. From this point of view it is happy enough to be seen, as one prominent Catholic in Ireland put it, as 'almost a proxy for Irish football in the European Cup'.[6] The Rangers fanzines might see something sinister in this, as *Follow, Follow* is free in its accusations of Celtic being 'the athletic wing of the IRA' and that its supporters are 'Provo-loving Republican scum'. It is unlikely that the Celtic board, old or new, would take anything the fanzines say seriously, but every now and then it gives them something to feed from.

The old board committed a *faux pas* in late 1990 when it allowed the stadium to be given over to the Irish political folk band, the Wolfe Tones, to make a video advertising their concert and they took the opportunity to express a few sentiments in praise of the IRA. The original Wolfe Tone, of course, was a Protestant and one of the first to take up arms in favour of a united and independent Ireland, but he was defeated ultimately because of the lukewarm nature of the support from the Catholic Church. The group assured the club that they were not sectarian, and in choosing the name of the Protestant hero they could be said to be emphasising this, but in the present climate any support for a united Ireland, to which the Wolfe Tones are committed, has political overtones that can be construed as showing a sympathy for the IRA. A few months later the Pogues, whose song on behalf of the wrongfully jailed Birmingham Six was banned by the British government, were guests of the club. Again anyone with a sense of justice would be outraged by the way the Birmingham Six were framed and fitted up, but the interpretation in terms of more general Irish oppression is open to debate. Since McCann, the club has been more wary of being caught by such groups, and in a 'voice against bigotry' policy, has banned any advertising in the official *Celtic View* that could be construed as sectarian.

BEARS ON SONG

At Ibrox Rangers continued until recently to play over the tannoy a sanitised version of 'Hello! Hello! We are the Billy Boys!' substituting references to the gang of the inter-war period with 'Rangers Boys' and removing references to being up to one's knees in Fenian blood. The fans continued to sing along in the original – or at least the Rangers original, as the tune goes back to the American Civil War and the soldiers' song 'Marching through Georgia'. There have been calls for the club to be more positive in putting out acceptable lyrics for the fans to sing, but as one Celtic fan delicately put it with regard to McCann trying to eliminate IRA chants, this is 'pissing in the wind'. Football is not a game for the faint-hearted, although at Ibrox the clamp-down seems to have been so successful that some games take place as though you were in a morgue, with the greatest activity among the spectators coming from the constant coming and going of fans taking off to buy bluenose burgers or whatever else is on sale below the stands.

To attract sponsors and enter international competition both Rangers and Celtic have had to project an appropriate image. A sectarian Rangers could never have entered the world of multinational business, and since the signing of Mo Johnston they have gone a long way to eliminating the last traces of their anti-Catholic past. But while the excesses of the fans have been crushed or driven out of the stadium, others closely associated with the club have caused it some embarrassment with their over-enthusiastic singing of sectarian songs, allowing the club's detractors to claim that below the surface nothing has changed at Ibrox. Souness saw the Mo Johnston signing as one of his greatest triumphs, but he was well aware that a simple signature would not eliminate the remnants of bigotry at the club. This was one of the reasons he left Rangers in 1991. In an article on Souness that appeared in *The Independent* of 14 October 1996, Ian Stafford reported Souness's complaints about the obstacles that had been placed in his path at Ibrox. When pushed by Stafford to explain, he said: 'Well, I'll never be comfortable with bigotry, and it will always be at Rangers.' Just over a year later, Stafford interviewed Souness again, this time for *The Scotsman* (1 December 1997), when Souness was manager of Benfica. Whether Stafford got his notes mixed up, or Souness remembered exactly what he had said the previous year, his opinions about his hassles at Rangers were repeated almost word for word, with the difference that the reference to bigotry always being at Ibrox was omitted.

It is clear, too, that Souness was not referring to the bigotry of the fans. There was a time when they were the only ones blamed for the bigotry, and even James Handley, in his otherwise engaging history of Celtic published in 1960, was guilty of talking tripe on the matter: and snobbish tripe at that. In his short discussion of the trouble between the two clubs he claimed that:

> until a Catholic centre-forward in a Rangers blue jersey scores a goal against a Celtic team the tension will persist. If that should ever come to pass then the rabble would be bewildered and all its fire extinguished. The notion that the mob can be ultimately educated to see the folly of its way is a hollow one, for the creatures who compose it are ineducable.[7]

A Catholic player has now scored that historic goal, the 'mob' and the 'rabble' have shown themselves to be more educable than Handley gave them credit for, but the tensions persist. Clearly today as in the past the problem is not just on the terracing.

When Gascoigne performed his famous flute impersonation to celebrate his first goal for the club in July 1995, it was obvious that someone among the players had put him up to it. In 1994 a player was reported to have been seen celebrating the championship of that year wearing a 'Hang IRA Murderers' T-shirt. For new arrivals at the club there has always been someone to teach them about the club's traditions, usually a player who was a supporter in his youth and whose commitment to the club was due to its Protestantism. Among the newcomers who have taken it all very seriously is Andy Goram. Goram was born in England, but part of his bonding with the Rangers supporters has been by letting them know that he is a proud Protestant. In his autobiography, *My Life*, and in other ways, he has made no secret of his sympathies for the Protestant cause in Ulster. Soon after arriving at Ibrox he was keen to learn about the history of the club and what it stood for, and he made more trips to Belfast than any other player. In 1995 he and McCoist went to the Shankill Road in Belfast to switch on the Christmas lights and mix with the community; as he told Roddy Forsyth, 'I suppose it's my way of giving them something back.'[8]

For such reasons it is not surprising that when Goram wore a black armband at the Old Firm game of 2 January 1998, five days after the murder in the Maze prison, near Belfast, of Loyalist terrorist Billy Wright, few people believed his claim that he wore it out of respect for an aunt who had died back in October, an aunt for whom Goram's mother did not remember her son having any overwhelming affection. A sort of delayed shock it would appear, or perhaps Goram, with all his other off-field problems, hadn't been able to find a suitable armband until then. Blarney about this being the first appropriate time to display his familial affection fooled no one, although Rangers chose to believe him. Goram has been arguably the best goalkeeper Rangers (or Scotland) have ever had, and no doubt it was this rather than his role as a paragon of Protestant virtue that saved him from punishment for an action that would have provoked a storm if a Celtic player had dared wear a black armband out of respect for a murdered IRA terrorist.

Goram's black armband display was overshadowed by the controversy that surrounded Gascoigne's flute performance as he warmed up before taking the field at the same game, a fleeting gesture which would have been missed by all but a few but for it being caught on television. It was just one more incident in a litany of musical performances that accompanied the club on its trips around the football grounds of Scotland, as the walls of wherever Rangers players were celebrating reverberated with the songs and chants of the terracing.

When Rangers beat Dundee United at Tannadice on 21 April 1990 to win the Championship, television cameras allowed into the dressing-rooms recorded the vociferous renditions of what were called 'sectarian songs' with 'obscene references to the Pope'.[9] Homes throughout Scotland were thus, according to their persuasions, able to join in with the players, or ring up in protest. We can never know how many sang along, but the BBC is said to have been inundated with calls of protest.

What the cameras were doing in the dressing-room is a question some might want to ask, and others could plead that adults have the right to do what they like in the privacy of their own dressing-room, but at Celtic Park on 24 November 1996, following a Coca-Cola Cup final victory over Hearts, the full-volume renditions of 'The Sash' were so enthusiastic that the police had to be called in to ask that the volume be turned down – apart from annoying any Celtic people in the vicinity, the celebrations threatened to drown out the post-match player interviews. Some of the Rangers top brass were reported to be with the players, but their role in the choir was not specified. One thing that seemed to be quite clear was that being at Celtic Park added a special lustiness to the rendition of the choruses. It was also said that a framed portrait of the Queen was hung up in the dressing-room, although this was apparently a not uncommon practice at away games.[10]

One Rangers player even got into trouble when he was caught in happy harmony with some friends on a day when he was injured and had come along as a spectator. It was the all-seeing eye of the TV cameras at the Ne'erday game of 1996 at Celtic Park that caught the unsuspecting Stuart McCall in this compromising situation, upsetting the Celtic supporters who were near him, and leading to calls for his removal. The police TV monitors picked him out singing some Ibrox favourites with those around him, but the police did not take action at the time, as they did not want to provoke any trouble. The incident was reported to Rangers after the game and McCall was asked to make sure that on any similar occasions in the future he follow the more accepted practice of sitting closer to the directors' box.

Some of the foreign players found it all a bit hard to take in. Most bemused of all was Basile Boli, who arrived from Marseille in the summer of 1994 without a firm grasp of English. He had been born in the Ivory Coast, but came to France aged 13, where his father had been a bodyguard for General de Gaulle. He was also a Catholic and as such used to the adoration of female images, but he could not understand why there were pictures of the Queen all over Ibrox; coming after Souness, however, he was spared the former manager's exhortations to the players in his pre-match build-up to 'think of the Queen'.[11] His nickname, King Boli, the humour of which can be enjoyed only with an appreciation of the Glasgow pronunciation of the French, showed that he was welcomed by the fans, some of whom changed the intonation of their favourite song to 'Hello! Hello! We are the Boli Boys!' The Rangers players did their best to make the newcomer feel at home, Laudrup and Gough in particular going out of their way to welcome him, but their efforts were rebuffed. On the field where it counts, however, Boli was played out of position and had trouble adjusting to the more frivolous approach to the game in Scotland. Reports in French newspapers of him criticising not only the omnipresent images of Her Majesty around Ibrox, but also the Rangers manager himself, led to him being censured. This was a standard response, and not only at Ibrox, to criticism, but Boli was taking things a bit too far when, having expressed his lack of approval for two Ibrox favourites, he went on to declare his admiration for the Pope. Despite this, he left with the best wishes of the fans and suffered neither for his religion nor his colour while he was with Rangers.

Boli had also been annoyed at being told not to cross himself in front of the Ibrox faithful, and this was a warning given to all subsequent Catholic imports. Jörg Albertz, who came to Rangers from SV Hamburg in the summer of 1996, was well aware of this and had no troubles settling in. He claimed in the *Frankfurter Rundschau* that the Glasgow supporters were more disciplined than those in Germany and fought each other only with battle hymns.[12] The young Chilean star, Sebastian Rozental, followed Albertz at the beginning of 1997. His Jewish name would never have been a problem at Ibrox, but there was a time when the very name of his club, Universidad Catolica (Catholic University), would have kept any Rangers scout at a distance. Although Jewish, he had adopted his club-mates' practice of crossing himself before the start of the game; but, like Albertz, he was told to touch his religious parts in private.

Making the sign of the cross, in Scotland at any rate, is not always an innocent gesture: in some situations it can have the same effect as a two-fingered salute or spitting, and it was closer to this spirit that Mo Johnston made his famous departure from Hampden in the Skol Cup final of 1986. Such was clearly not the situation when Partick Thistle's coloured Catholic player from Liverpool, Rod McDonald, was given a yellow card for crossing himself as he left the field in a game against Rangers at Firhill on 3 February 1996. McDonald was reported to the police by two Rangers fans in the main stand, sensitive souls like their equivalents at Celtic Park a year later who reported Gascoigne, who claim to have been offended when he made strange gestures that they interpreted as religious, but which in fact were imaginary pistol shots being fired into the air to celebrate his equaliser. He then did, as was his custom, cross himself as he left the field, and this was reported to the referee by a linesman. The caution was given in the dressing-room during the half-time interval and, unaware that he had been booked, the unfortunate McDonald was astonished when he was ordered off for a tackle on John Brown that earned a second yellow card.

The referee in that particular game, Jim McGilvray, provoked the anger of all neutral observers, above all for his lenient treatment of Gascoigne who was cautioned in the first half for running beyond the advertising boards to celebrate his goal, but went on to commit more serious offences in the second-half that went unpunished. McGilvray did not help his credibility when he retired as a referee soon after, claiming that he felt like a robot obeying SFA instructions for the Gascoigne booking, and unburdening himself to *The Sun* in the 'sports exclusive of the decade'.[13] McGilvray admitted that Gascoigne should have been given a second yellow card, but he did not do so for fear of provoking the Rangers fans into a riot.

For Walter Smith of Rangers it was part of a witch-hunt against their star player. For Celtic supporters it was just one more proof of the way in which referees helped Rangers on their way to nine-in-a-row. For agnostics it was another example of the religious nonsense that made Scotland a laughing stock beyond its borders.

One of the most insidious examples of Rangers pandering to the prejudices of the Prods was largely passed over by the press. This was at the finals of the Scottish Schools Cup played at Ibrox on 28 April 1996, a seven-a-side competition in front of 50,000 people at half-time in the crunch Rangers–Aberdeen League decider where Gascoigne scored a hat-trick. The winning team was Christ the King Primary School from Holytown, but they did not play under their own name, being called 'the red team' instead; even references to where they came from were fudged, with Motherwell being preferred to Holytown. The decision to label the teams by colour rather than by their real names was taken when the finalists became known: in addition to the winning team, the losing semi-finalists were St Bridget's of Baillieston and St Flannan's of Kirkin-tilloch. In explanation, it was pointed out that the organisers wanted the boys to enjoy themselves without a section of the crowd turning against them.[14]

Ten years on since Mo Johnston was signed and the time has surely come for Rangers to lift the ban on Catholic players blessing themselves on the field of play. Jörg Albertz has all the appearance of a blond, blue-eyed Nordic god, and it is ridiculous that he cannot express himself harmlessly in his own religious way. Marco Negri is closer to the Rangers image of a Latin, and so Catholic, but forbidden from crossing himself on scoring goals he opted for a surly lack of enthusiasm – annoying some fans who sarcastically call him 'Smiler'. If Rangers can ban their players from crossing themselves, they can also ban them from playing the flute to incite the opposition, as Gascoigne did while warming up in the Ne'erday Old Firm game of 1998; unlike his début before an all-Bear audience at his first rendition, this reprise was in front of nearly 50,000 baying Bhoys. Rangers claimed this was a private matter, and smacked his wrist with a belated fine of a week's wages and a dictated apology. Nor did they take any public action against Goram's black armband display at the same game, although in both these cases such actions could be seen as provocation that flew in the face of any battle against bigotry.

Opinions vary on these issues, as they always have, the one saying it is all trivia and should not upset rational human beings, the others claim-ing that it is an incitement to riot. And both are right. It is a trivial matter and in a sane world this is how mimicking a flute would be seen, especially when the player concerned is responding to taunts, however accurate, of him being a wife-beater. But even in 1998, sanity is still not the norm at Old Firm games. Unlike Gazza's flute impersonation, which does have a comic touch, wearing a black armband allegedly out of respect for a convicted terrorist is sinister. There is nothing Rangers can do to prevent a player making an ill-advised gesture, but they have complete control over what their players wear on the field of play. And there can be no two opinions on the right of schoolboys playing at half-time in the big games to do so under the name of their school and not a colour, even if this means references to Lourdes, the Blessed Virgin, the Bleeding Heart or other images that are seen as offensive by some Rangers supporters. This is a challenge the club must force them to face – or go back to the old days and stop playing Catholics.

MASONS IN BLACK

Celtic supporters have been obsessed throughout their history by the idea that the SFA and its referees are biased against them. Many have had the famous Quinn/Craig case from early in the century passed down to them from father to son as an example of the suffering the sons of Erin have had to bear from the sons of William. As shown in *The Old Firm*, however, the Quinn/Craig incident is one that has become seriously confused in the minds of those who pass it on, and indeed it reflects very poorly on Celtic. In the wider world, Catholics in Scotland have claimed to suffer from the machinations of the freemasons, and barely an issue of the Catholic press in the days before the Second World War would appear without further examples of their sinister influence. The two have been easily conflated and in the desperation of the last couple of years in particular some Celtic supporters have blamed what they see as their unjust treatment at the hands of referees on a masonic plot.

Some Celtic fans were said to have set a private detective at work to compile a dossier on a particular referee, Jim McCluskey, after the Skol Cup final of 1990, while another has engaged in historical research to prove that there is a conspiracy against Celtic. According to Father Peter Burns, a Jesuit based in Los Angeles in the US, his study of Old Firm games as reported in the *Glasgow Herald* between 1945 and 1996 'clearly' reveals that over the 51 years covered by his investigation Celtic have been denied as many clear penalties as Rangers have been given dodgy ones.[15] Such 'research' obviously raises more questions than it answers, and it is interesting that in the newspaper chosen for the 'study' one of the main sports writers was Cyril Horne, who conducted a virtual one-man campaign against Rangers throughout the 1950s. Horne was a brave reporter, and his employers even had to assign a minder to protect him on his way home from the newspaper office, but any attempt to judge the worth of penalty claims would have to be based on a variety of sources and not just those sympathetic to Celtic, as Burns has admitted.

Celtic have even found support for their suspicions in an article published in the Catholic journal, *Flourish*,[16] where the eminent professor of English at Glasgow University, Patrick Reilly, showing that the spirit of Man in the Know is still alive and well in certain Catholic circles, claimed that religious bigotry was behind the series of decisions that went against Celtic, and anyone who thought otherwise was as blind or blinkered as the Holocaust deniers or believers in a flat earth. His article was framed by one on the great truth of the risen Jesus and another on the duties of Catholics as Lent approached, including the fight against 'the astronomical abortion toll'. Never before can a disquisition on disputed goals at a football match have found itself in such exalted company.

More credible evidence of Celtic being on the wrong end of a series of bad decisions came from an article in the Aberdeen *Evening Express* on 26 November 1996, on the eve of a visit of Rangers to Pittodrie. Much of it was based on the hearsay of an anonymous referee and one former player, who claimed to have been hounded out of the Scottish game by referees who kept sending him off, something that would not have happened, the ex-Don said, if he had been a Rangers player. But the article also revealed statistics that suggested 'a pro-Ibrox bias among our top referees – and a strong link with the masons'. The links with the masons are tenuous to say the least: it is highly likely that many Scottish referees are masons, but this is irrelevant to their conduct of the game, and even if they have Rangers sympathies this is no proof that they will give them favours. A tally of red and yellow cards distributed to clubs in the Premier Division makes much more interesting reading. According to this, Rangers was the only club where no player had been ordered off in the current or previous season, and more telling, that in this same time they had received 90 yellow cards. This could show that Rangers players had the sense to behave themselves once they had been warned, but that begs the question of why they could not exhibit the same discipline in European games: there Rangers players had accumulated four red cards in less than a dozen games. As for the masons in black, and given the number of red cards to Rangers in the Souness years, one has to ask whether there has been a sudden influx of masons among the whistlers in the past few years.

Football would cease to be a game if all elements of luck and refereeing error were eliminated. This is what keeps discussion alive in the space between games, and is the last resort of the disappointed fan who bewails in time-honoured fashion: 'We wuz robbed!' In the New Year game at Ibrox on 2 January 1997 Celtic were deprived of a goal by Jorge Cadete that would have made the score 2–2. In the entire stadium and the viewing audience at home or in pubs around the world, it appears that only the linesman saw an infringement by Cadete, who did not himself protest in case he earned another expulsion.[17]

Reports soon followed claiming that this particular linesman was a well-known Rangers supporter and, inevitably, a freemason. It would seriously deplete the pool if referees who were freemasons were banned from officiating at Rangers games, but perhaps in this particular case the SFA could have exercised more caution: an individual who flaunts his sympathies, as this one is said to have done, is different from one who keeps them to himself. The furore that erupted was not helped by the policy of silence that prevents referees from explaining their decisions after the game. Or even during it, as is the case in American football, and indeed as is done by the best referees, by clear hand signals, in British football.

There does seem to be one factor that has influenced recent events, however: Paul Gascoigne. Despite Gascoigne's claim that he was picked on by referees in Scotland so that they could boast to their pals about booking him, it would appear that he has received preferential treatment from Scottish referees. Given the number of games he has won for Rangers almost single-handedly, this could have had a substantial effect on the outcome of key matches. But rather than any sinister influence, it is more likely that he was treated in much the same way as John McEnroe whom umpires were never willing to throw out of the many tennis tournaments where he metaphorically spat in their faces. (Given the money he brought to the game it is the umpire who would have suffered for taking such action.) However that may be, and whatever concessions to genius were made by some referees, however unconsciously, Gascoigne's misdemeanours on the park frequently escaped the severity they deserved.

There have doubtless been several occasions in the past two years in particular where Celtic fans have had reason to cry out in despair at the bad luck – and perhaps worse – that has gone against them, but when bad luck seems to keep on cropping up it ceases to be an excuse. Rangers supporters could give a list of the decisions that helped Celtic on their way to nine-in-a-row in the 1970s – and like Celtic supporters they would on many occasions have been justified. But, unlike Celtic fans, Rangers fans don't have the masons to blame it on.

SECTARIANISM IN RETREAT

There is little the 'Bhoys against Bigotry' campaign can do to calm the darkest thoughts of those who would believe in a satanic plot against the club, and Murray at Ibrox has done as much as he can to erase the club's anti-Catholic image. In addition to Boli and Albertz mentioned above, as well as many other Catholics since, Rangers have tried to sign the Italian Gianluca Vialli, the Argentine Gabriel Batistuta, the Portuguese Fernando Couto and the Brazilian Jardel . . . through to Ronaldo and the recent arrival of a small invasion of Italians who are probably Catholics. For Murray the question of signing Catholics is no longer an issue. In that Rangers is a business committed to maximising its commercial potential by winning football matches, Murray need not go any further than this, but for those with a broader view of the club's responsibilities this is not good enough. Above all, Gerry McNee has conducted a long campaign against both Old Firm chairmen, ultimately provoking the normally unflappable Murray into a stinging personal attack on the credentials of 'The Voice of Football' and his motives in criticising Rangers, and to a slightly lesser degree Celtic. This was in January 1998 when McNee wrote in the *News of the World* that Rangers were 'rotten to their sectarian core'. Over a year before, McNee had claimed that 'sectarianism is getting worse not better and both clubs are still guilty of encouraging it'.[18] McNee accused Rangers of not signing a local Catholic, but whether or not this is Rangers' fault is another matter, as any young Catholic star is still likely to prefer Celtic, and despite the changes at Ibrox since Souness, there is still an atmosphere there that could make some Catholics feel uncomfortable: especially if they can understand the language or can make sense of the accents enough to know what the songs and chants around the ground and in the dressing-room are all about. Paul McStay and Paul Elliott were mentioned as Rangers transfer targets in the summer of 1992,[19] and a year later John Collins claimed that Murray tried to sign him, saying that he 'would have paid me almost anything to sign for Rangers'. This forced Celtic to 'up their own offer for him'.[20] Michael Kelly's criticism of Rangers for not having a Catholic on their board is perhaps misplaced, but the situation has improved from the time when a director (David Hope) was blocked from becoming chairman because he had married a Catholic 30 years before. As much a matter for criticism has been the absence of Protestants on the Celtic board, given the much larger percentage of Protestants in Scotland. Both clubs have their Protestant and Catholic diehards, but this is more a hangover from the past than a matter of policy.

The sectarian situation has been around in Scotland for so long that it

157

is easy to attach the label to any mindless incident. When Duncan Ferguson committed his act of thuggery against John McStay of Raith Rovers, one of the subsequent headlines and stories of the player's life concerned the tears of his girlfriend who knew that he was no longer the 'boy she'd fallen for' when 'Duncan stood on a table and sang "The Sash"'.[21] Rangers seem to have had more success in crushing the overt expression of sectarian outbursts among their fans than they have in curbing the excesses of some of their players. And as a club that has long claimed to be proud of the image it presents to the public, it has on many recent occasions been let down by the behaviour of its players, off the field as much as on it.

The most spectacular 'sectarian' incident came at the summer international tournament at Ibrox in July 1995 when Paul Gascoigne made his first appearance for the club. The new player, who had to be reminded that he had signed for Rangers and not Glasgow, showed that he was a quick learner in other ways. When he scored his first goal he demonstrated his delight with a flute-playing mime that was splashed in colour on the pages of the tabloids and beyond. The game was a friendly against Steaua Bucharest, and as such before an audience of Bears who loved the performance. The match was not televised, but the BBC bought the videotape and when they showed the flute incident they were banned by the club. Gazza was treated more lightly, as he would be in the future, although in this instance he was merely engaging in a bit of in-house fun.

Marx said that history repeats itself: the first time as tragedy; the second time as farce. But in Scottish football history farce seems to follow farce. At Ibrox some of the English imports in particular seem to have been intent on giving some historical continuity to the matches where they had distinguished themselves. First there was Gazza following in the footsteps of Graham Roberts, then there were 'The Ibrox Four' of November 1995 following 'The Ibrox Four' of October 1987. This time it was Gascoigne, John Brown and Alan McLaren (with Billy Dodds of Aberdeen) following in the footsteps of Butcher, Woods and Roberts (with Frank McAvennie of Celtic). This came out of an ill-tempered match at Ibrox against Aberdeen on 11 November 1995. As a result the four players were summoned to appear before the SFA disciplinary committee. The case against McLaren and Dodds was deferred, while John Brown and Paul Gascoigne, whose offences were missed by the match official, but reported by the referee's supervisor, each received a one-match suspension. The incidents involved an alleged head-butt by Gascoigne on a Dons player that resulted in him needing stitches in his face; and, according to some sources, another four bookable offences.

Duncan Ferguson, then with Everton but out of jail and appealing against his 12-match ban by the SFA, might have looked on rather cynically, although his head-butting incident came at a time when he was already on probation for two previous offences. For Dumbarton, whose goalkeeper, Ian McFarlane, received a five-match ban for 'exceptional misconduct' at the same time, it smacked of one law for the rich and another for the poor. For Rangers, their criticism was not of anything their players had done, but of the powers given to someone acting in effect as a second referee. But they accepted the punishment: before it was handed down they had been preparing a legal defence should Gascoigne have received a lengthy penalty. There would be other times when Rangers' attempts to protect their expensive but temperamental import would show where the club's priorities lay with respect to breaches of common morality off the field and winning matches on it.

At the same time as Gascoigne was amusing the fans in his first game at Ibrox, Celtic fans, or some of their supporters in England, were involved in 'ugly scenes' during a friendly against Birmingham. Offensive flags were confiscated by none other than the Birmingham City managing director, Karren Brady. Trouble was expected before the start of the game from right-wing Birmingham fans and other 'fascist' and British National Party supporters (as well as some Birmingham 'Zulus', a group of black hooligans) who were thought to have targeted Irish pubs in the area and Celtic fans drinking in them. In response, various groups – *Tiocfaidh Ar La*, Anti-Fascist Action, Red Action and Celtic Soccer Crew – overlooked their differences to form a defensive alliance for the day. At the ground, 6,000 Celtic fans were said to have been taunted by a Red Hand of Ulster banner waved by English fans and chants of 'no surrender to the IRA'. Certainly the provocative symbols did not appear from nowhere, but were part of the pre-match preparations. Celtic supporters who complained of the role of the Celtic 'casuals' were told by their defenders that without them they would have been massacred by the 'fascists'.[22]

Two summers before, in 1993, Rangers fans made the headlines as they went 'on the rampage' before and after a pre-season friendly against Sunderland. All the 42 people arrested were Rangers fans, 30 of whom were from Glasgow; up to 10,000 were estimated to have made the trip. Shortly after the Sunderland troubles, when the scarred faces of two brothers involved were graphically portrayed in the tabloids, the *Daily Record* ran an exposé of some Rangers 'casuals', an Inter-city firm of the better-dressed hooligans whose main aim at matches was to cause trouble.[23] Despite the 'mod' image the 'casuals' like to affect, there was something rather passé about it all, reminiscent of an attempt to revive the fashions of another time. Rangers made the obligatory statement that the culprits would be booted out of Ibrox, but a more refreshing response came from other Rangers fans who supported all attempts to get rid of such trouble-makers. Today's Rangers fans are better behaved than those of the days before Souness, and by signing Catholics Murray removed the most obvious stigma of the club's sectarian past: where he has been less successful is in improving the behaviour of his own playing staff.

GUARDING GAZZA

The skills that take young men to the top of their profession in a highly competitive and physically demanding game like football are not those that guarantee a life of peaceful grace and elegance off it. More money than they know what to do with it, a mind-numbing mix of booze and celebrity, and especially in Glasgow the too-close attentions of a public that does not always respect the players' privacy – and players who do not respect the rights of others – are always liable to end in blows. Inevitably the sectarian element crops up, with provocation about being an Orange/Fenian bastard leading to a brawl.

One of the more disgraceful of these was a mere three days after the Dunblane massacre in March 1996, and involved a group of Rangers players and their friends celebrating in a Renfrewshire pub after a St Patrick's Day game against Celtic. At the game that day, the two teams and the packed stadium had joined the rest of the country in a silent tribute to the victims of the recent tragedy, but all of this seemed to have evaporated in what followed. A certain John McKee, sporting a tattoo of the Pope, a tricolour and the date of the Easter Rising on his arm, is alleged to have requested/demanded that the group stop singing sectarian songs and in the outcome was set on by some of them. Appearing in court the following January was Rangers' Charlie Miller and 'Gazza's best pal and former minder Jimmy "Five Bellies" Gardner'.[24] It was alleged that they were to the fore in beating up McKee, by which time the other Rangers players in the pub had left. Very little of this was noticed by the staff, who seem to have been smitten by a severe case of the Three Monkeys' affliction. Of those accused only 'Five Bellies' Gardner was convicted, but the reputed best friend of Scotland's wealthiest footballer was unable to pay the £500 fine.

Drunken excesses are never pretty, are positively ugly when they degenerate into brawls, and potentially criminal when they continue behind the wheel of a car. Several Rangers players have been convicted of drink driving offences in recent years, as though they did not have enough money to hire a chauffeur, let alone a taxi, or even buy one, or a fleet of them. The club does not tolerate drink driving, but seems to be more lenient concerning the drunken excesses of its players in other ways, dismissed by one top official as mere 'youthful pranks'. After one particularly vulgar exhibition at the Britannia Intercontinental hotel in London, in February 1996, where Gascoigne led a drink-and-vomit spree while his wife gave birth to his first child (at another venue), Rangers vice-chairman Donald Findlay was reported to have excused it all as a 'harmless weekend break'.[25]

No one at Ibrox seems to have seen any relationship between such behaviour and a lack of professionalism that several foreign stars, and not just Boli, have commented on, and which could have played some part in the succession of injuries suffered by the club, or the poor performances in Europe. On the contrary, Gascoigne suggested that the club – which reacted angrily to his 'revelation' – encouraged the players to drink and let their hair down after a game. This was in a 'fly-on-the-wall' television documentary for Channel Four, 'Gazza's Coming Home', that came out in the autumn of 1996; later it was admitted that he downed large whiskies before games and even at the half-time interval. Gazza's reputation was highlighted in the opening credits of the TV film where an artistically presented banner draped over the fence at a game (not Ibrox, probably Italy) proclaimed:

GAZZA'S BOYS . . . are here . . .
SHAG women . . . DRINK beer

It was Gascoigne, too, whose off-field behaviour brought more unkindly light on himself and the club when, hard on the heels of having had himself ordered off for a pointless attack on Winston Bogarde of Ajax in a Champions League match in Amsterdam, photographs of his battered and bruised wife appeared in full colour on the front pages of newspapers and television screens throughout the land. It was not the first time that Gascoigne had been accused of assaulting his wife, and not for the first time that he had expressed remorse and promised not to do it again. The role of the club as an arbiter in what some saw as a private matter, others as a national disgrace, was delicate. The video on Gascoigne covering his time at Ibrox and which ended, ironically, with his wedding, revealed a somewhat sympathetic figure, a young man with genius in his boots but nothing in his head, no more aware of what to do with the mansions and limousines his millions had given him than how to relate to others who did not appreciate his childish humour: a man more at home with drunken footballers or their hangers-on than with his wife and children.

All of this was reflected in his public and on-field behaviour: the petulant responses to his overworked elbows and flailing arms, the adolescent humour that had him belching at radio journalists in Italy and belting balls at those in the media he did not like in Scotland. There was also the sadness behind the smile, and the genuine humour, such as when he 'yellow-carded' a referee when the cautionary card dropped out of his pocket and Gascoigne returned it to him, but not before he had mimed the caution, a gesture that the referee apparently saw as an insult to his pride so he gave Gascoigne a real booking. And always with the ball at his feet a thing of wonder, of joy to his own supporters and a source of admiration even to his opponents.

Rangers opted to stand by the boy with the ball at his feet, as did England manager Glenn Hoddle, and Gascoigne went unpunished in football terms for a domestic crime that took up more media attention than all the other atrocities that were going on around the world at that time. What Bill Struth would have said about the wife-beating incident we can only guess, but we can be sure that he would have taken it upon himself to do all that he could have to find Gascoigne a decent tailor.

Indeed, Gascoigne's dress sense seemed to be of more importance than his behaviour to the Rangers vice-chairman, Donald Findlay QC, whose image at the club had been growing steadily since he had taken up that position in 1992. Findlay was one of Scotland's most brilliant defence lawyers, and a Rangers fan who was proud to call himself a 'Bluenose', although he rejected any accusation of bigotry. At the 1995 AGM, Findlay showed that he was a worthy representative of some of the older traditions within the club when he not only expressed his delight about going on to eight Championships in a row, but looked forward to nine and then ten, proudly accepted that 'no one likes us, we don't care', and, to wind up the proceedings, led the gathering in one of the fans favourite songs: 'There's not a team like the Glasgow Rangers'.[26]

A man with his own peculiar sense of humour, he was not perhaps entirely kidding when he claimed, in an interview with Anne Simpson of *The Herald*, that if 'Celtic never won another game it would be a source of enormous rejoicing to me'.[27] Tongue in cheek he said that although St Patrick's day was his natural birthday, his 'official birthday is the 12th of July'. For Findlay it was all match-day banter, a 90-minute exchange of hatreds that was forgotten as soon as the game was over.

The quiet man at Rangers, the man who brought Gascoigne to Ibrox, Walter Smith, later admitted that he might have made a mistake in signing the player. This came when Rangers had effectively won their ninth successive flag and after further incidents in which Gascoigne, while recovering from an injury, went on a 'transatlantic bar crawl' in the course of which he wore Celtic scarves in a Manhattan bar and had an alleged altercation with a young woman in a London street after a night out with some showbusiness friends. In April 1997 Walter Smith admitted that his signing of Gascoigne had turned into a nightmare: 'When I signed him I was 100 per cent clear about my judgement, but the percentage drops with every incident that happens. And so does the level of backing at this club'.[28] He was fined a derisory £30,000 for not looking after himself while injured.

It is all a long way from the days when a Rangers player could be sent on his way for falling in love with a Catholic: whether or not this is progress is a more open question, although for those who believe in winning at all costs it is an irrelevance. Certainly if Rangers had dismissed or suspended all the players who had committed serious breaches of discipline in the last year or so their playing strength would have been considerably weakened. When it came to the crunch, however, a hat-trick in a key game could make up for any misdemeanours on or off the field. That genius and loutish behaviour need not go together can be found in many examples through football history, from Eusébio and Pele on the one hand to Bobby Charlton and Franz Beckenbauer on the other, while at Ibrox Brian Laudrup has shown a class on the field that is matched by the dignity of his behaviour off it.

PROBLEMS AT PARADISE

The Celtic players at this time managed to keep out of the headlines, except when some of their foreign stars spoke to their home press and then had their words translated back into the Scottish tabloids. There was a long history of this, going back before Boli to Jan Bartram who told a Danish newspaper about life under Souness and the violence of the Scottish game. He did not last long at Ibrox (but then neither did several other imports at this time).

Celtic's imports seemed happy to adopt what they saw as the culture of the club and struck up an immediate rapport with the fans. They were also happy to report on life in Scotland. Dutch Catholic, Pierre van Hooijdonk, as well as giving the club headaches over his contract before he finally left for Nottingham Forest in March 1997, gave interviews for several Dutch newspapers in January 1996 in which he spoke freely of Scottish football and the 'religious' life of the city, all of which was reported in *Elf, de Volksrant* (6 January 1996) and *Voetbal International* (17 January 1996).[29] Van Hooijdonk commented on the hard nature of the Scottish game, claiming it was 'rugby with a round ball', and that the Ajax–Feyenoord derby was 'kid's play' in comparison to that of the Old Firm. But he was at pains to stress the intense commitment of the fans.

He denounced the hatred that being a Celtic player inspired, claiming that he had to go out in disguise when he left his house. He also said that while he had nothing against the Rangers players, he did not like them as a team, but was somewhat out of date when he claimed that Rangers would rather sign a Protestant than a Catholic, even one of the quality of Romario. His attitude to the Old Firm divide was not helped when he was spat at while sitting in his car at the traffic lights.

Inevitably these players would claim to have been misrepresented and the club would either accept this explanation or a mild apology. The local tabloids were all caught up in a circulation war that depended more than ever on exclusives, being first with mostly trivial information, and preferring sensation to analysis. Long gone are the days when reporters had one or more columns to develop their ideas; now they are down to one or two sentences in a paragraph in which lurid adjectives or nouns jump out at the reader in block letters, with inch-thick headlines that take up most of the page, along with a large photograph to save the reader from actually having to read very much.

The silence of the press over Rangers' attitude to Catholics in the days when Rangers ruled had little to pride itself in, while the Catholic press, with 'Man in the Know' through to the 1930s, showed a grotesque bias in the other direction that makes fascinating reading today. There were other aspects of life then that were also kept under wraps by both the Catholic and the Protestant press, issues far from football and then thought to be too delicate to trouble the minds of their readers. The recent exposure of sexual failings by men in positions of trust and authority is no reflection of a sudden increase in such activity, but merely of the media's concern to bring it to light. Scout and choir leaders have often been the subject of lewd gossip or court reporting in the columns of the best-selling *News of the World*; now that notorious Sunday scandal sheet has been surpassed from all points of view by newspapers on daily sale in supermarkets.

It was into this maelstrom of scandal that the Celtic football club found itself drawn, first and indirectly by allegations involving priests and bishops, at times no more than a betrayal of vows by falling in love with a woman, but more seriously when it involved the corruption of a minor. It was all grist to the anti-Catholic mill and the supporters of other clubs on the look-out for something to throw at Celtic. Then in mid-August 1996 the *Daily Record* brought the club right into the middle of it all, with accusations of a paedophilia scandal when it claimed that two people involved in the Celtic Boys Club had taken advantage of their position to harass young boys under their care. In unambiguous language the *Daily Record* accused the two men, on the basis of statements by former players who claim they were abused, accusations that were denied but which have since led to the arrest of the two men. The worst cases were said to have taken place long before McCann came on the scene, and Jock Stein, whose son George had played with the Boys Club, is alleged to have literally kicked one of the men out of his office when he heard of the rumours. McCann ordered an immediate investigation and promised that the club would do all in its power to sort the matter out. In the meantime one of the Rangers fanzines suggested that Rangers should start a 'Bears against Buggery' campaign.

Fergus McCann surely had none of this in mind when he set out to improve the quality of life in Scotland, but even the 'Bhoys against Bigotry' campaign and the Mission Statement that went with it, had reflections of Scotland's biggest historical hangover: for all its admirable intentions and practical application, the Mission Statement of the 'Bhoys against Bigotry' campaign is more in the tradition of Catholic charity than Protestant self-help. McCann and Murray have both shown surprising ignorance regarding the history of their club, with McCann claiming that Celtic have never been a Catholic club, while Murray, in rejecting the Lally award from the Glasgow City Council, said that his club was 'in the business of sport, nothing else'. That may be how he wishes it to be, but he is surely not so naïve as to believe that this is the case. However much McCann and Murray want to see the traces of their religious past expunged from their clubs, they can't close the door on history. The world of the 1990s is not the world of the 1970s, let alone the 1950s or even the pre-World War period, but despite their progressive new owners, both Celtic and Rangers are still two clubs linked to two different traditions, traces of which still remain. There was a time when they drew their strength and passion from this, now they have to overcome it.

9. No More, the Bygone Days of Yore . . .

In *The Old Firm* I traced the story of how Celtic and Rangers grew in opposition to each other as representatives of the two major communities in Scottish society: Celtic the team of the immigrant underdogs and the paranoia that this encouraged, but inspired by the 'Celtic spirit' and proud to be known as 'the people's club'; Rangers the team of the established Scots, proud of the 'Rangers tradition' and with the touch of arrogance that led them to being seen as the 'we are the people's club'. Celtic's image was more easygoing and rebellious in the way of the Catholic Irish, while Rangers reflected a dignified – some would say dour – image of a more austere Protestantism. Although the origins of these differences were religious, separate cultures had grown around them, developing into a 'cultural apartheid' that lingered on until the 1960s. This was reflected in both clubs: from playing styles, dress and stadiums to the literature associated with them, their supporters and their heroes. The caricature of the Rangers fans was once of aggressive loud-mouths happy to declare that 'no one likes us, we don't care', while Celtic pre-sented themselves as more happy-go-lucky, open and tolerant. In politics Celtic were inevitably involved in Irish affairs, tended to Labour sym-pathies, while Rangers were more Conservative, Unionist and Protestant, aggressively so in their Orangeism, more subtly in their masonic associations, and innocently in the bulk of the fans who followed the club for purely secular reasons.

By the 1980s much of this was a hangover from the past, but the club itself, with its belief that silence was the best policy in the face of its critics, did not help to remove the more negative aspects of its reputation. It would take more than Souness and the signing of Mo Johnston to change the traditions of generations, and while the troubles in Ulster drag on there will continue to be the echoes of the historical links between two neighbours that one historian has evocatively called 'intimate strangers'.[1]

There is a mystique that attaches to the awesome splendour of Ibrox stadium, dominating as it does the district in which it stands like a cathedral of old, while inside the mystery of what lies beyond the marble staircase has an aura that charges the faithful with a not entirely secular devotion. David Murray has found himself at home in the imposing grandeur of Ibrox, and there are some who say that however innocent of what are usually called West of Scotland prejudices when he arrived at the club, he soon became 'one of us'. Whatever cleansing influence he has been in regard to the moral welfare of the club, his improvements at the ground itself have made a grand stadium even grander. On view to the public he has set the Club Deck on top of the original Leitch Main Stand, provided facilities like the Argyle House restaurant in the new Govan Stand, and filled in the corners of the four stands, two of them now with the largest television screens in Britain. Out of view of the general public he has modernised the decor without infringing in any way on the understated opulence that was there before him. For health reasons, Souness replaced with showers the communal bath in which players once disported themselves in post-match frolics; Murray, for aesthetic reasons, has refurbished the furniture and fittings, retaining the rich panelling of the showpiece Blue Room, reminiscent (and not without accident) of the luxury liners that were the pride of Clydeside in the 1930s. The sumptuous leather armchairs have been recovered with a softer fabric and the carpet replaced: all in royal blue and all exquisitely done, while the still-to-be-completed Senga Murray mural depicting the history of the club looks over it all, no more out of place in its modern-ism than the Chagall ceiling at the Paris Opéra.

This is Protestant Scotland at its stylish best, and while the new stadium at Celtic Park, when completed, will make it one of the best in Britain, and although it is on the site of the Celtic glory days, there is little in concrete terms to remind the faithful of the club's history: the Jungle is gone, as are the floodlights which were for the poet Tom Leonard reassuring symbols that despite the gloom the game would still be played ('dork init/good jobe theyve gote thi lights'), while even the entrance to the Main Stand is barely a decade old. But whatever physical representations of the two clubs remain, they are as tied to their history as ever.

Since the Souness revolution the image of soccer itself has had a face-lift, so it is hardly surprising that the image of the two clubs and their supporters has also changed, much of this reflecting the changed fortunes on the park. More surprising, perhaps, is what has not changed.

POLITICAL COLOURING

Michael Kelly, the man who in name and in his more recent battles can claim to speak on behalf of the club that has been associated with his family since Celtic were founded, has no doubt about what the club stood for. They represented the Irish in Scotland and defended the underdog. They were anti-establishment and stood for 'social justice and opposed discrimination'. Throughout their history Celtic had fought 'against poverty and discrimination and for social justice'.[2] They were the victims of an intolerant Protestantism, and so the immigrant Catholics and their descendants developed a paranoia against the 'establishment', represented above all in the eyes of Celtic by the Scottish football authorities. In October 1992, Liam Brady, 15 months into his job as Celtic manager, said: 'I was told when I joined about Celtic's "paranoia". Now I know it is true. We are hard done by. Religiously and politically, there are people against us.'[3]

The reputation of Rangers as being Conservative, royalist and Unionist has been encouraged by some of their best known players and managers, their most outspoken fans, including the bulk of the con-tributions to *Follow, Follow*, and the official histories of the club, especially Allan and Allison. All of this has been given a ringing endorsement by Robert McElroy in his book which, if not an official history, speaks with the authority of a man who has devoted much of his life to Rangers, recording its deeds in intimate detail, at first through statistics and a self-edited journal, *The Rangers Historian*, but now in the best history of the club to date, written with the help of the journalist Bob Ferrier, son of one of the great players of Scottish football – Bobby Ferrier of the outstanding Motherwell team of the inter-war years (the only one to break the Old Firm dominance of the Scottish League between 1904 and 1948), and who was deprived of a Scottish cap by the accident of being born in England where he lived for all of three weeks.[4] McElroy claims that for over 120 years Rangers have become

> institutionalised as the flag carrier of what a majority of Scots would consider to be national virtues – Protestant, Monarchist tradition [*sic*] and Unionist in the literal sense of the Union of Great Britain and Northern Ireland. Red, white and blue are the Rangers colours.[5]

Presumably this applies to the directors and management of the club, which can fairly clearly be established, but also to the supporters, whose political opinions are harder to ascertain.

A researcher from Caledonian University, Joseph Bradley, set out through a series of questionnaires distributed at football matches in 1990, to make a profile, among other things, of the political beliefs of the fans of Scotland's Premier League clubs.[6] The evidence he thus adduced generally justifies the popular preconceptions. Celtic fans claimed to be overwhelmingly Labour voters, about 85 per cent, Rangers fans only 33 per cent. A mere 4 per cent of Celtic supporters voted Scottish Nationalist, against nearly 14 per cent for Rangers, and while only 3 per cent of Celtic fans claimed to be Conservatives, a large 32 per cent of Rangers supporters were proud to call themselves Tories, which is well above the figure for Scotland as a whole. The only club to match Rangers and its Tory following was St Johnstone, with just over 29 per cent (only 12.5 per cent of Hearts fans claimed to vote Tory: indeed there is little in Bradley's findings to justify their being called 'The Wee Huns'). The closest to Celtic's Labour sympathies was Kilmarnock with nearly 58 per cent, while Hearts claimed 45 per cent. The highest nationalist support came from Dundee United (41 per cent), Motherwell (37.5 per cent) and Aberdeen (33 per cent).

These figures clearly establish Celtic as the team of the Labour Party, while the new Labour Prime Minister, Tony Blair, is said to have expressed a sympathy for the club while a pupil at Fettes College. A more spontaneous expression of Celtic's political sympathies came when Prime Minister Thatcher visited Hampden in 1988 to see the Scottish Cup final between Celtic and Dundee United, and was greeted with a storm of red cards and Irish tricolours. On a three-day trip to Glasgow in March 1990 the Prime Minister made the draw for the Scottish Cup and then paid a special visit to Ibrox. She came as a supporter of the Anglo-Irish agreement that was hated by the Loyalists, and so her support from the other end of the political spectrum had diminished. Not so in *The Rangers Historian*, however, which fell over itself in a fit of forelock-tugging and general obsequiousness, praising the 'finest' Prime Minister of 'the last 70 years', along with Winston Churchill and Harold Macmillan, also, and not coincidentally, prime ministers who had honoured Ibrox with their presence. McElroy duly set out the Conservative Party credentials of Murray, Butcher and Woods as typical of the club, while in another part of the publication the editor castigated a 'minority of Rangers fans who disgrace the Club's colours with extreme Left-wing propaganda'. He also lambasted the left-wing bias of the anti-Tory press in the west of Scotland, with particular reference to Labour MP Brian Wilson. Rangers, he insisted, had always been a 'True Blue Conservative organisation', a 'vast number' of supporters were Conservative and Unionist and the club itself had proudly opposed 'the devolution proposals of the then Labour Government' in 1979. Celtic, on the other hand, were dismissed as a club to which 'Socialists have always more readily identified themselves', some of its players (John Colquhoun, Brian McClair and Billy McNeill) being so wicked as to 'promote their socialist views, using their prominent positions in Scottish football to influence the youth of today'.[7] Something the Tory-loving Rangers players never did.

No wonder then, that some Rangers supporters have been driven to near dementia by the reputation people like McElroy have foisted on the club. It also seems clear that in a Scotland that has recently removed the Tories to rump status, and as supporters of the monarchy lose faith in an institution that stands out (the Queen apart) as an insult to decent family values, the majority of Rangers supporters are far from being the Tory lickspittles McElroy likes to portray them as.

One Rangers fan, the historian Graham Walker, author of various works on Scottish and Irish politics, as well as several newspaper and journal articles on Rangers, has tried to show another side to the club. In a more academic discussion, '"There's not a team like the Glasgow Rangers": football and religious identity in Scotland', he sets out to redress the image of Rangers as an institution that 'perpetuates all that is reactionary in Scottish life'.[8] Walker agrees with the editor of *Follow, Follow* that most Rangers fans are right-wing Labour, but unlike the more traditionalist Dingwall, Walker would prefer that Rangers fans were more nationalist and less tied to the narrower aspects of Unionism. He is perhaps a little over-optimistic, however, in his appraisal of the liberal tendencies of Rangers fans, the most vociferous of whom fit only too closely into the stereotype. Rangers still await a history that will emphasise the other side to its more familiar triumphalism, and while most fanzines generally have a left-wing bias, this is not a characteristic of any of the Rangers fanzines – although *Follow, Follow* has included material expressing views at odds with those of the editor. Until such a history and such a fanzine appear, however, Dingwall and McElroy will speak as the voice of the average fan.

Whether Celtic has the 'socialist' sympathies McElroy attributes to the club or not, the Labour Party allegiances of the fans are reflected in some ways at board level. Many directors have expressed Labour sympathies, from McCann on the one hand, to Michael Kelly and Brian Dempsey on the other: Kelly was a prominent Labour Councillor, Dempsey is the son of a well-respected Labour politician. That men of such wealth should retain Labour sympathies is more surprising than that the millionaires at Ibrox have right-wing sympathies. Souness and Butcher were fairly outspoken in their right-wing beliefs, while Celtic heroes like Stein and McNeill did not object to being called socialists. Souness, like club captains Greig before him and Butcher who followed him, is an ardent royalist. One of his gifts to Ibrox was a full-length portrait of the Queen which he had hung up in the dressing-room, and while he is no longer there to urge the players to look on it as an inspiration for victory, the Queen is still there to gaze down on the players in their various states of undress. Butcher's less imposing portrait of the Queen, a bust only, is still above the door where he placed it for players to make their reverences on the way out to the field. One has to wonder what the foreign players think about it all, and for the Catholics it hardly makes up for not being allowed to bless themselves where and when they please.

David Murray, although a capitalist, clearly right-wing and a Unionist, fits into no pre-existing caricature. Unionism comes in many varieties, and it is on the Union of the crowns (1603) and the parliaments (1707) of Scotland and England that the material – and in many ways moral – success of Great Britain has been founded. Scots have gained more than they lost from the Union, certainly in colonial ventures, but above all in the end to wars between the two nations that has allowed energies to be used elsewhere. The treatment of the Catholics in Ireland, on the other hand, has been appalling, a permanent blot in the British government's treatment of a subject people through to the creation of Northern Ireland in 1921. Unionists defending Northern Ireland's refusal to be forced out of the United Kingdom today, however, need not be narrow reactionaries, although they often are, and Unionists in Scotland can retain a cultural independence that has nothing to do with politics. Unionism and loyalty to Scotland need not contradict, as is nowhere better represented than in the case of David Murray. He has chosen not to follow the path of the tax exile, but instead has stayed in Scotland and provided work for thousands of Scots.

Like Brian Meek, Scotland's wittiest and most polished Conservative journalist, as well as other Rangers directors whose company Meek was once tipped to join, and manager Walter Smith who exudes good grace and tolerance in the public eye, Murray and the new Ibrox present an image of Rangers of which any fan can be proud. Unfortunately for Rangers at the official level, the public image of the club is more likely to be associated with the hirsute visage of vice-chairman Donald Findlay QC. Here is a man who has openly expressed his contempt for Celtic, proudly conjured up images of 1690, and who is happy to boast that 'no one likes us, we don't care'. Those who know Findlay privately will tell you of his sense of humour and a support for the underdog that does not discriminate between Catholics and Protestants, but while many Scots will have no trouble remembering his defence of one of the most vile Protestant killers, few will be able to recall the last Catholic activist he defended. What Findlay does in his professional and private life is his own affair, whether it be defending alleged criminals or chairing the 'No, No' campaign in the recent devolution referendum; but rightly or wrongly, his words and actions cannot easily be dissociated from his position at Rangers Football Club. In this regard he is Dingwall with a more polished accent, McElroy with a better education, reminders that for all the good Murray and others have done in raising the profile of the club, parts of its past keep resurfacing to tarnish the image.

RANGERS, FREEMASONS AND HEAD-CASE HISTORY

The association of Rangers and its followers with the freemasons and the Orange Order is unofficial but clearly established, and these serve as the essential links with its anti-Catholic past. It had long been whispered, proudly by insiders and less respectfully by outsiders, that not only were Rangers an all-Protestant club, but that every player was a freemason: if not one when he joined, he became one soon after. It was in this way that the ban on Catholics was perpetuated. Much of this, in the nature of things, was based on hearsay, as the club, in the best traditions of freemasonry, maintained what it believed to be a dignified silence. Again Ferrier and McElroy have at last made an open affirmation of links that the club need scarcely have been ashamed of:

> The Union Flag, the 'Union Jack', was inevitably the flag of establishment Rangers, the club of the Protestant faith, of the monarchy and the union, not to mention of the masonic order and the Orange movement.[9]

In the flurry of press activity that followed the signing of Maurice Johnston, one newspaper contacted Don 'The Rhino' Kichenbrand, one of Rangers' two known or suspected Catholics since the First World War. Kichenbrand, from his home in his native South Africa, was happy to reveal how his religion was concealed from the club, and went on to tell how he had been inducted into the Lodge. The *Daily Record* of 12 July 1989 spilled the beans with a banner headline declaring that: 'One of Rangers biggest stars was a SECRET CATHOLIC', before going on to reveal the 'Amazing confession of an Ibrox legend'. For three years from his arrival at Ibrox in 1955, it declared, Kichenbrand 'lived a lie', but kept his promise not to reveal the error the scout had committed by not establishing the young South African's religion before he signed him. All at Ibrox assumed Kichenbrand was a staunch Protestant, but to be on the safe side he accepted without demur the proposal that he become a freemason. When he left the club it was assumed that he had been kicked out because he had fallen in love with a Catholic, but Kichenbrand claims that this happened after he had left the club. It was only then that he married Josephine, a Catholic, 'in a Dublin chapel'. Kichenbrand's testimony gives truth to the rumours freely circulating – proudly by some Rangers fans – that anyone at Ibrox who fell in love with a Catholic would soon be on his way out of the club.

That Rangers still liked their players to be members of the Brotherhood can be inferred from one newspaper report concerning the sometimes drunk and disorderly Duncan Ferguson, whose unruly behaviour was so bad that he could not be nominated for membership of the Lodge. The freemasons, indeed, pride themselves on their behaviour and social responsibility. The popular image is of a closed society whose members help each other, granting promotions to brothers in the professions and supporting each other in business. This has certainly happened, but in violation of the strictest code of the Brotherhood, and like the Rangers Football Club, the freemasons have not helped their cause by maintaining a principled silence on the matter. But the Brotherhood, like Rangers, is no longer the closed body it once was, emphasising that while it has secrets it is not a secret society. Indeed in tune with the times that have seen Ibrox opened up to Catholics, freemasons have presented themselves to the public and opened up their lodges for inspection. Part of this is in a drive for new members, but it is also a reflection of a more open age. The freemasons still insist on the moral probity of their members, that they be upright citizens, true to each other and loyal to the state. Their associations with Rangers are doubtless still strong, but not complete.

Freemasonry and the Catholic Church have been enemies since the days of the Enlightenment of the eighteenth century, when the burgeoning movement, because of its beliefs in religious tolerance, social equality and intellectual progress, was banned by the Vatican. Freemasons were blamed by the Church for weakening the moral fibre of the French people, so that they fell easy victims to the false principles that led to the French Revolution in 1789: from that time on Catholicism and freemasonry became implacable enemies. In Protestant countries, where Catholics were distrusted for what some saw as their subservience to a foreign power, and where the confessional was seen as a threat to the secrets of the Brotherhood, freemasons often became part of the Establishment. Freemasonry was originally an essentially aristocratic body, becoming more middle-class by the end of the nineteenth century and popular among the small business classes. In Scotland it was more working-class than in most countries; it was also more anti-Catholic.

In the more liberal atmosphere since the 1960s some Catholics were inducted into freemasonry, believing that they could do so without threatening their mortal soul. Pope John-Paul II, in keeping with his attempts to undo what he saw as the damage of Vatican II, has reaffirmed the ban on Catholics who become freemasons, but has not decreed instant excommunication. In the last decade some Protestant churches have turned a dyspeptic eye on the Brotherhood: the Methodists condemned it in 1985; the Free Presbyterians then described it as 'anti-Christian and of the works of darkness'; while even the Church of Scotland, after a two-year study, pointed out the incompatibilities of aspects of masonic worship and that of Jesus Christ, but while warning its followers about this, it did not forbid them to be members.[10] The role of freemasonry in Scotland continues to exert a more powerful influence than in most other Anglo-Saxon countries, and only in Scotland was attention drawn to the alleged masonic links of the Dunblane killer, Thomas Hamilton, with the implication that it was these links that helped him avoid detection in the years leading up to his abominable crime.

The historian John Roberts, in his book *The Mythology of the Secret Societies*, opens with the statement: 'Though sometimes amusing, it is always disturbing when intelligent people seriously talk nonsense.'[11] Among the people Roberts had in mind was Britain's nineteenth-century prime minister, Benjamin Disraeli, a man 'otherwise shrewd and intelligent', but someone who was obsessed with the machinations of freemasons and secret societies. Indeed freemasonry, or more accurately anti-freemasonry, has resulted in a rich tradition of what might generously be called 'head-case history'. In common with best-sellers along the lines of 'I spoke to a Martian', authors like Nesta Webster have sold tens of thousands of copies of books claiming to explain the real reasons for the revolutions from 1789 to the modern age, and for many decades one of the best selling books on the French Revolution was the ravings of the Abbé Barruel, blaming its wickedness on the machinations of freemasons – along with Jews (inevitably), Protestants and cosmo-politans in general, the common enemies of the Catholic Church. Towards the end of the nineteenth century, the Frenchman Léo Taxil made a fortune out of books and public appearances exposing in lurid detail the secrets of the freemasons, and when he gathered another over-subscribed audience at the Grand Palais in Paris in 1898 to reveal 'the biggest secret of all', it turned out to be the only one his audience would not believe: namely that everything he had told them up until then was a pack of lies. The freemasons have also held a fascination for such renowned figures as General Franco in Spain, the dictator Salazar in Portugal and Marshal Pétain and his collaborationist government in wartime France, all of whom, along with Hitler, the Kremlin and the Vatican suppressed the organisation. Any organisation that attracts a swarm of enemies like that cannot be without its virtues.

More recently the works of Stephen Knight and Martin Short

'exposing' the masons have enjoyed immense popularity. Short's *Inside the Brotherhood: Further Secrets of the Freemasons,* took up in 1989 the work of Knight, who died in July 1985, aged 33, just 18 months after the publication of his exposé, *The Brotherhood.* Obviously to those who know about such things his death was no accident. One of the chapters in Short's book is on the alleged links between freemasonry and police corruption, and so it was not surprising, despite some of the egregious nonsense that appears in his book, that he was the first witness in the recent Home Affairs Select Committee inquiry into masonic connections with the police and the judiciary.

It is an old story, and as suggested above, while there are doubtless instances where police have betrayed the force, masons have higher duties to the laws of the land. In Scotland all of this was brought into proper perspective when Celtic fans, angered by a series of decisions that went against them, took up the claims of a masonic conspiracy among its referees. As suggested earlier, Celtic supporters often had good reasons to challenge the eyesight if not the morality of some referees regarding decisions that have gone against them in the past couple of years, but any accusations of a 'masonic conspiracy' have to be regarded in the same light as the ranting of a wide range of empty and discredited visionaries posing as historians for over a century and more.

Masons do have a duty to assist each other, but not in transgression of laws either moral or man-made. Some individuals have broken this code, and critics of the Brotherhood would say that they all do, but a single swallow does not make a summer any more than one bent mason makes a conspiracy. Nevertheless, there was a tasty titbit to feed the paranoia of the persecuted in the officially sanctioned Rangers audio-tape that came out in July 1993, incorporating the comments and memories of many individuals associated with the club. One of these was Bobby Brown, the golden-haired goalkeeper of the Iron Curtain defence and later a manager of Scotland. He tells the story of a former referee whose proudest boast was that in 18 years of refereeing he had never officiated at a game in which Rangers lost. Brown recalled the case of a Queen of the South game where the referee deliberately disallowed a last-minute goal that would have won the game for the Dumfries club. It was at Palmerston Park, and with the score 1–1 and Rangers facing a corner, Brown asked the referee how long there was to go. He was told not to worry. The home team scored from the corner, but to the mystification of everyone the referee awarded a free-kick to Rangers. No sooner was it taken than the whistle blew for time. It was two years later, at a Lodge presentation, that the now retired referee made the boast claimed by Brown. Brown's imagination was perhaps working a wee bit overtime on this occasion, certainly so if his reminiscences of the 1948 Scottish Cup final against Morton are anything to go by – and journalists trying to track down the game against Queen of the South were unable to find it.

HELLO! HELLO! CAN YOU STILL HEAR US?

Before Souness came to Ibrox the Orange associations of Rangers were loudly proclaimed in songs, chants and images of King Billy fording the river Boyne in 1690. Ibrox was the regular venue for the annual religious service of the Order, at least until 1987 when the new management at Ibrox turned down its request – although a few years later this was to be regarded more favourably. At the same time steps were taken to clear out the vendors of Orange literature who plied a vigorous trade outside the ground, although this was as much to clear out unwanted commercial competition as undesirable messages.

Rangers' associations with the Orangemen of Ulster are very much a part of the historic past, today most likely to be seen displayed by marchers at The Walk, either openly or under the regalia, where some marchers can be seen to wear a Rangers replica strip. We would not expect Rangers today or even a couple of decades ago, to send a director to Ulster to address an Orange Order social gathering, as James Bowie did in 1930, praising the Order for its 'traditions' and 'principles'[12] or to send a team to Belfast to help raise funds for the Orange Order, as they did on several occasions before the 1960s. One of these benefit matches, played on 10 May 1955, was to help finance extensions to the Sandy Row Orange Hall. In the programme for that game there is a brief history of the Orange Lodge in Belfast which includes this verse from the 'Orange Poet':

> *To guard the faith which Luther preached*
> *The rights which William won*
> *The Orangeman relies upon*
> *His Bible and his gun.*

No more, of course, would Celtic, whose trips to the South were as frequent as Rangers' to Ulster, today associate itself with the rabid support of Man in the Know for the IRA, and his summary of a 2–0 victory by Celtic over Rangers: 'Rebels 2, Black and Tans 0'. Today (although on recent form the scores might be reversed) you would be more likely to see: 'C.R. Smith (or Umbro) 2, McEwan's Lager 0'. And certainly no Catholic priest today would openly associate himself with the club and the IRA the way young Father McRory did, an ardent Celtic supporter and Irish nationalist, and who became a hero in his parish of Calton at the time of the 'Duke Street shoot-out' in 1921.[13]

The Orange Order has not been receiving a good press in recent years in Scotland, as no more today than in other times does its members abide by its strictures on drunkenness and bad language. Its followers are more into slogans and mythologising, particularly since the role of Catholics among King Billy's troops at the Boyne is now so well documented, as is the praise showered on him by the Vatican and the goodwill of Catholic Spain. In the more irreverent reporting of recent times his sexual proclivities have found their way into the tabloid press, luridly in headlines proclaiming him to have been a 'rent boy', and more accurately in reports casting doubts on his heterosexuality. None of this reflects on his undisputed valour in battle, and all of it is irrelevant to the man's main claim to fame as the champion of Protestantism. Perhaps the time has come, however, now that Rangers have Catholics helping them to win titles, to acknowledge that Catholics actually played a significant role in the establishment of Protestant hegemony in Britain: moreover, and as befits the multinational Rangers of the present day, that in addition to Catholics and some home-grown talent among King Billy's troops at the Boyne, were the Dutch, French Huguenots, English, Danes, Prussians, Finns and Swiss.

THE BEST FANS IN THE WORLD

In 1984 the reputation of the Rangers supporters was at an all-time low, saddled as they were with a club being berated for its bigotry and performing poorly on the park. Both Rangers and Celtic had their hooligan fans, but over the previous 20 years the worst examples of spectator violence had involved those of Rangers. Since then it has been the Celtic supporters who have been more in the news for the wrong reasons. The civil war at Parkhead showed an admirable commitment to the club by its fans, but it also threw up an unflattering exchange of insults as Celt was pitted against Celt.

Michael Kelly once believed that Celtic supporters were superior in morals and behaviour to the Rangers fans, but when his family was subjected to threats and insults by those who opposed his activities on the board, and articles sent to him through the mail included a box of excrement, he had to revise his opinion. And Kelly himself, a passionate supporter of the club, reveals the terrible hatred that existed between his father and his father's brother, Celtic chairman Bob Kelly: for decades they passed each other in the directors' box at Parkhead without exchanging a single word.

Few clubs have had an entire book devoted to their fans, but Gerry McNee's *And You'll Never Walk Alone*, published in 1972, celebrates the adventures of the Celtic fans who travelled with the club in its triumphal run before and after Lisbon. This is the same McNee who went on to write a history of Celtic and a biography of its legendary centre-forward, Jimmy McGrory, but who has since earned the impartial hatred of both sets of fans. In his later career McNee was assaulted by a Celtic manager, threatened with physical violence by a Rangers manager and now, through his provocative comments in the press, and on radio and television, has set himself up as a safety-valve for the release of the emotional excesses of Bears and Tims alike. To some Celtic people he is seen as a traitor, as he is now prepared to lump some of the Celtic support with the worst of the Rangers, an indication either that the behaviour of the Celtic fans has deteriorated since the 1970s or that McNee has grown wiser with age.

Since the success of Nick Hornby's *Fever Pitch*, a brilliant attempt to unravel the complexities of his life through his obsession with football and Arsenal in particular, a few others have tried their hand at books in a similar style. They have generally found that it is not as easy as Hornby makes it seem. One of these was by a Celtic supporter, David Bennie, whose memoirs of a Celtic fan, *Not Playing for Celtic*,[14] did nothing to enhance the literary reputation of Celtic followers. In addition to his pretentious style, Bennie reveals himself as someone who added little lustre to the image of the club's followers, especially in the two instances he recounts of attacking wee boys: on one occasion he threw a half brick at a couple of youngsters who had mocked him on his way back from a bad day at Parkhead, knocking one of them off a wall; on the other occasion he battered a wee boy's head for annoying him outside his recently deceased father's house. And if Paul Gascoigne is to be believed, a Celtic fan who drew alongside him in his car after the flute-playing incident at Ibrox promised to find out where he lived and to go there and slit his throat if he did it again. Empty threat or real, Gascoigne admitted to nearly soiling his pants at training the next day.[15]

John Cairney, television idol of the 1960s, one of Scotland's great actors and Burns interpreter without equal, in his private life a Celtic fanatic who bears no ill-will towards Rangers, found to his horror when he watched the first Old Firm game of the 1997–98 season at Ibrox, that the Celtic supporters around him made the experience almost unbearable, positioned as he was between 'two hate-filled teenagers who were never seated or quiet throughout' in an atmosphere that was less 'electric . . . than a stressful, obscene tension'.

Rangers fans inside Ibrox have now been so successfully tamed by the club's police liaison officer that Alistair Hood now rates on a par with the Pope as the most unpopular icon at Ibrox. The clean-up at Ibrox has not been without its critics, who have not only lost the East Enclosure to seating and season-tickets, but have seen their places usurped by the camel-coat brigade, denounced in the fanzines as fair-weather followers of the club. Even before the closure of the East Enclosure the class war within Ibrox was already evident as chants broke out during the more boring episodes of games where the team was once more toying with a luckless opposition. This was directed against the season-ticket-holders of the Copland Stand along the lines of: 'Can you hear the Copland sing . . . You can't hear a fuckin' thing.' The atmosphere at Ibrox has been denounced as funereal except for the big games against Celtic or Aberdeen. Fans who could not afford season-tickets have been reduced to being away followers of the club, leading to the claim that there was more atmosphere at away games where Rangers were playing than at 'iceberg' Ibrox.

Gone with the atmosphere are serious outbreaks of hooliganism at Ibrox and Celtic Park – the last notable incident was at Celtic Park in the days of the civil war when fans turned on the directors with their Mars attacks in January 1994 after another humiliation by Rangers and, more seriously, one Celtic fan attacked the Rangers goalkeeper. Hooliganism, like sectarian or bigoted behaviour, can never be entirely eliminated. To the extent that the comparative silence at Ibrox is through the elimination of the more odious anti-Catholic sentiments ('If you hate the fuckin' Fenians, clap your hands') then this is surely to be applauded. But there is reason to regret that more than bigotry has been thrown out with the filthier bath water of the more rabid Bears. Songs about being up to one's knees in Fenian blood challenge decency, although it is a great song – witness the way it has been taken up by many supporters elsewhere. While sectarian killings in Ireland and England continue, however, songs and chants in praise of the killers are somewhat sick. 'The Sash' and one-time favourite, 'No Pope of Rome', on the other hand, have little to do with present-day realities and as such can be seen as more humorous than provocative. At least they have more to do with Scotland than such contemporary Ibrox favourites as 'Rule Britannia' and 'Swing Low, Sweet Chariot'. They also come from the fans themselves, a form of DIY entertainment with more to recommend it than canned music deliberately turned up to drown them out and to direct them in what some disembodied presence thinks they should be doing.

It is all part of the general cleansing of the game for the benefit of its new middle-class clientèle: seats that must be sat upon, directions that must be followed by occasionally thuggish stewards, polite applause at the risk of being thrown out if you get too carried away, and respect for the wonderful sponsors without whom you would not be able to see the millionaire foreigners on show on the field. Some clubs have been worried by the loss of atmosphere, and many spectators have reacted against the new authoritarianism, highlighted at Old Trafford where a near civil war has broken out between fans who refuse to sit down when ordered to do so by the stewards, and whose response to directives over the tannoy is to deliberately disobey them: the whole East Stand standing up when told to sit down.

THE NEW VOICES OF THE FANS

Rangers may have continued since the Souness days to trump Celtic in the signing of new players, and their commercial developments have put Celtic in the shade, but there is one area in which the Parkhead club is still well ahead of its rival, and that, Bennie notwithstanding, is in the various books and other literary expressions of what the two clubs stand for. In works devoted to them, Rangers have constantly continued to come second to Celtic: *The Rangers Historian* first came out in September 1987, four years after the first issue of *The Celt*; *Not the View* first came out at the beginning of November 1987, then Rangers followed at the end of that season with *Follow, Follow.* (*World Shut Your Mouth* was a Rangers fanzine that actually preceded *Follow, Follow,* but it had a mercifully short life.) When Rangers produced the admirable theatrical production of its history, *Follow, Follow,* which played to appreciative audiences in the summer of 1994, they were following in the footsteps of *The Celtic Story,* produced to coincide with the club's centenary. In most of these productions Celtic have projected a more open and good-natured image. The dramatised Celtic history, for instance, begins and ends with the theme of helping the less privileged, the Rangers play ends on a note of worshipful reverence to Bill Struth and David Murray with the message that 'the club is always bigger than the man'.

The Rangers' aural history produced by Roddy Forsyth, however, is a refreshing break from the more usually wooden treatments: it actually admits that the club was founded in 1872, treats the Mo Johnston signing with candour, and, still fresh from the stings of Souness's departure to Liverpool, is refreshingly frank on his impact on the club.

In terms of club histories and books about the clubs, however, Rangers are still a long way behind Celtic. Pat Woods in particular, in various combinations with Tom Campbell and Kevin McCarra, has produced several excellent books which can now, with the old board gone, even be purchased through Celtic outlets. His most recent publication, with

California-based Jesuit priest Peter Burns, bon viveur and top sleuth on the trail of masonic malevolence, is a celebration of the famous 7–1 League Cup victory over Rangers in 1957. *Oh, Hampden in the Sun . . .* is not just a recounting of a treasured triumph, rather it is a living archive of a period now long gone. Missing among the myriad stories surrounding that event is Rangers fan Andy Cameron's recollections of how he and a mate had stuck it out to the end, ever hopeful, at least until there were only a couple of minutes left, of an equaliser. On their way home from Hampden and finding themselves surrounded by a triumphal group of Celtic supporters chanting the score, Andy's mate whispered out of the corner of his mouth: 'Don't let them see that it annoys you.'[16] One can hardly wait for the next Celtic tome, perhaps a book on Patsy Gallacher's winning goal in the 1925 Cup final. In the meantime, *Oh, Hampden in the Sun . . .* is a reminder of the grave error made by Graeme Souness back in that otherwise glorious triumph for Rangers over Celtic in August 1988, when he chose, with the score at 5–1 and half an hour still to go, to rub in Rangers' superiority with arrogant control of the ball rather than banging it into the net.

Other Celtic fans have set their thoughts down in print, most notably David Potter although there are many others, resulting in a minor industry in books about the club, most of which are of a very good quality and carry on the tradition of respect without subservience. Rangers have at last had a book written about them, which, once it has trumpeted its political message in the Introduction, goes on to tell a story that rises above the more usual hagiography. Because the Ferrier/McElroy history is based on systematic research, McElroy has been forced to admit that much of what was published about Rangers by people with no connection with the club, and which the more inward-looking fans found hard to take, was correct. The Ferrier/McElroy history is essentially a statistical work with an account of just about every game Rangers have played, and it is written for Rangers fans, but it is based on years of persistent effort at the grass-roots and it does take time off from the more usual hyperbole in praise of the club to mention a few of its negative aspects.

Criticism of Rangers in the official club newspaper is as non-existent as ever. *Rangers News* might sell more copies than the *Celtic View*, and it is certainly a more glitzy production – but it is still aimed at a more juvenile readership. Although it has been attacked by the fanzines as '*Pravda*', the *Celtic View* is still more open to the fans and its articles are of a more independent and critical nature. Its worst critics, indeed, are the Celtic fans themselves: the Rangers paper is so bland that there is nothing to criticise.

The most interesting development in football literature in recent years has been the fanzines: the voice of the fans increasingly ignored by the clubs as they aim at a more profitable market. Devoted to the club, but independent of it, some fanzines have become profitable in their own right, and even without selling their soul. A written form of the 'phone-ins', the material in the fanzines is generally less bigoted than the opinions of those letting off steam before a radio audience. Amidst their irreverence and foul language the fanzines often come up with more serious discussion of the game than can be found in the tabloids. The daily press itself is renamed according to the bias of the fanzine: the *Daily Record/Rebel/Ranger*, the *Sunday Mail/Mason/Liam*, the *Evening Times/ Tims*, *The Sun/Hun*. It would appear from this, and the shared cries of foul by both Rangers and Celtic fans that the tabloids are at least maintaining a reasonable balance of objectivity.

In the fanzine market, Celtic and Rangers are well to the fore, although Scotland's best fanzine, *The Absolute Game*, its future in some doubt at the end of 1997, studiously tried – impossible task – to ignore the 'Awful Firm'. That Rangers have an independent and critical publication at all is an immense step forward from the pre-Souness days. The club to some degree has put itself out of reach of the worst criticism by its continued success on the field and in improving the stadium, but for the fans being squeezed out of Ibrox and made unwelcome by their unsuitable behaviour in the eyes of the new regime, the fanzines are a means of keeping in touch. As the voice of the East Enclosure, *Follow, Follow* has engaged in several campaigns on behalf of the less privileged fan: to save the enclosure from being converted into an all-seated area; for the preservation of the *Wee Blue Book*, and constantly and increasingly so in recent years against the greed of the club. But it has all been doomed to failure. For both Rangers and Celtic fanzines, the staple is still slagging each other off. The vituperation in *Not the View* tends to the humorous, that in *Follow, Follow*, more to the vituperative, although it also has its moments of pure humour in the cartoons, drawings, and extracts from other papers and occasional stories. The big guns are the regular contributors, where the Govanhill Gub and the Major (Forza Prod, Forever Orange) are open in their expression of Protestant bias and hatred of Celtic, while the Dowanhill Hack (who claims to be neither a Rangers supporter nor a right-winger) and Rantin' Robert [Burns] provide more balanced abuse.

Grandmaster Suck (Dingwall) provides the editorial comment for *Follow, Follow*, and from the start has vigorously denied all accusations of bigotry. He has been inflexible in his attacks on racism, and whenever he is accused of being bigoted in his attitude to Celtic he claims that it is only the club's IRA sympathies and its support for terrorism that he is attacking; that any bigotry at Ibrox or in his fanzine is of the '90 minutes variety'. He also justifies his attacks on the 'Beggars' at 'Mother Teresa's Pleasuredome' (one of the new names when 'The Piggery' became clearly unsuited to the renovated Paradise) as a sarcastic rejoinder to the constantly reiterated cant about Celtic having 'the best supporters in the world'. Yet this is the fanzine that has opened an article with the claim that Celtic, a club 'steeped in bigotry and support for terrorism', was 'founded by bigots, for bigots, with the purpose of bigotry its main aim'.[17] On another occasion he refers to the 'rotten pus which Glasgow still unfortunately spews forth from time to time under the guise of Celtic Football Club'.[18] In response to the cretins who on its 20th anniversary disrupted the silence in memory of the Ibrox disaster, Dingwall's rage was vented on the press for ignoring what happened and the BBC for turning its cameras away, but the central blame he laid on Celtic for being a club that 'provide and encourage the atmosphere of hatred of Protestants in which such behaviour is accepted as normal'.[19] We do not expect fairness or modest language in fanzines, and with the Gub and the Major we know where we stand, but it would not be out of place now and then for Dingwall to show some restraint in equating every Celtic fan with gun-happy terrorists and to give up the ludicrous notion that the club is in thrall to the IRA. It would also be refreshing if *Follow, Follow* showed more concern for the game beyond Ibrox and Rangers' away matches.

There have been other Rangers fanzines, such as *The Teddy Bear, Hello! Hello!, Aye Ready* and *No.1*, but none of them has achieved the consistency of *Follow, Follow*. *Aye Ready* makes the odd good point, but on the whole the humour is rather crude. *No.1* is equally crude, but has some excellent drawings. One of these is a spoof on 'Oor Wullie', where a remarkably accurate drawing of 'Oor Billy' has PC Murdoch replaced by Herr Hood and where the up-to-date scamp of Scotland's conservative Sunday paper is allowed more throaty expressions than 'Crivvens', 'Jings' or 'So help ma Boab', at the same time as he is able to run about chanting, in reference to the troubles plaguing Parkhead at the time, 'Who shagged a' the weans?'

Gerry Dunbar's *Not the View* has retained a humour over the years that is in the best of the fanzine traditions. Just as it came out in protest at the official club paper, the *Celtic View*, so Matt McGlone's *Once a Tim*, as mentioned elsewhere, came out in protest against the old board. When the old board was replaced, claims McGlone, much of the purpose of his fanzine was gone, and so in what some Celtic people saw as controversial circumstances, he accepted a position as regular columnist for the *Celtic View*. McGlone claims that there was no point in continuing to criticise the club under the new regime and that his critical independence has in no way been challenged it. In tune with this electronic age, a Celtic fanzine called *Bhoyzone* which first appeared on the Internet, has lived up to its early promise, although it could well be subtitled *Fergus's View* or *McCann's Mouthpiece*.

Another Celtic fanzine, *Tiocfaidh Ar La*, would justify many of Dingwall's criticisms if it had any respectability with the club – but it doesn't. Its ideals are set out in the meaning of its title ('Our day will come', a Provo slogan) and its contents combine cheery chatter about the club and how it is performing on the field with equally cheery chatter about the latest IRA bomb outrages. One of its main aims is to gain political status for IRA prisoners and it regularly donates money to the 'men behind the wire'. It is also anti-fascist and anti-racist, as well as socialist, ideals that some might think are not altogether in consonance with the goals and methods of the IRA. On the other side of the political fence, the *Blues Brothers* fanzine is a clear indication of the right-wing sympathies that bind Rangers to stablemates, Linfield and Chelsea. In several issues of *Follow, Follow*, the links between some Chelsea fans and Rangers were discussed at length, and generally condemned. At Chelsea itself, the club is split between a strong minority of right-wing racist fans, who have sought close links with Rangers fans, and others of a more liberal disposition, who founded the Chelsea Independent Supporters Association. Dingwall's rejection of the Chelsea advances was practicable: the morons were trying to infiltrate Rangers so that they could run amok in Europe under this cover.

OF SCHOLARS AND COMEDIANS

If the growth of the fanzines is a recent development in writing about sport, so too is the intrusion of academics. When *The Old Firm* came out in 1984 the number of consciously serious works on Scottish football could be counted on the fingers of two hands; now you almost need a computer to keep up with them. Among these, the Old Firm has come under some discussion, in particular from the sociologist Bert Moorhouse and the psychologist Gerry Finn, both of whom have poured scorn on my history, albeit from different perspectives: Finn is obsessed with what he sees as the sectarianism that oozes out of every pore of the Scottish body politic and has denounced me for failing to point this out; Moorhouse believes that sectarianism exists only in journalists' headlines and my fevered imagination. Alas, that truth does not lie halfway between extremes!

Moorhouse is so convinced that sectarianism in Scotland is non-existent that he would like to see a moratorium on the use of the term: he is right, of course, that this and other emotive words have been overused or misused, that there are too many glib references to 'wars' and 'blood baths', although he does not always distinguish between what the writer is saying and what he is reporting other people as having said. Moorhouse goes on to dismiss all suggestions that Scotland has ever had a population in which Catholic and Protestant differences have played a significant role. Like Margaret Thatcher and her claim that there is no such thing as 'society', that everyone is out for himself or herself and that is the way it should be, Moorhouse would have us believe that there is no such thing as 'community'. Despite holding such beliefs he seems to believe that he is the only person who has ever said anything sensible on the subject. Nevertheless, Moorhouse has written several excellent articles on Scottish football, and even when he discusses the Old Firm he makes many shrewd points, often in an arresting way. He has a tremendous capacity to gather material from all the scraps of the contemporary scene and present them imaginatively – including long extracts from the script of TV interviews complete with the interviewee's stuttering and repetition, even if this has little to do with his argument. But in the final analysis it is hard to take seriously someone who seems to think that the history of Rangers and Celtic, covering a century and more, should be written in terms of 'wine bars, mortgages, bureaucracy, contractual ties, office blocks, isolation, drugs and tourism'.[20] Until recently, these contemporary concerns would not have meant a thing to most Celtic and Rangers fans.

In complete opposition to Moorhouse, Finn denounces all those who do not agree that Scotland is saturated in sectarianism. In his relentless search for all that points to Catholics having suffered terribly at the hands of Scottish society, he tends to fall himself into the paranoia more apparent in less rational critics. In his work outside the Old Firm, Finn has no doubt made significant contributions to scholarship, but in his specific attempt to denigrate my work on the Old Firm he resorts to distortion and misrepresentation that many fanzines would be too ashamed to publish.[21]

Another academic sympathetic to Celtic who has devoted a large part of his work to the Old Firm is Joseph Bradley. In his book *Ethnic and Religious Identity in Modern Scotland: Culture, Politics and Football,*[22] Bradley justifiably points to the sloppy use of the term 'sectarian', and he performs a useful service in showing by assiduous research using questionnaires the responses of interesting cross-sections of the population regarding Protestant and Catholic identity in Scotland. In his analysis of the material, however, Bradley reveals touches of the persecution complex more readily associated with Parkhead. He shows that Celtic supporters are overwhelmingly Catholic, at 93 per cent a much higher figure than I would have thought is the case. He also shows that they identify more readily with Irish symbols and (Catholic) Irish causes. This is fair enough. What Bradley, in his condemnation of Protestant Scotland, fails to appreciate, however, is that while a few Scots might get irritated by this allegiance to foreign symbols, the vast majority might find no interest in them at all. It is one thing to be anti-Irish or anti-Catholic, another to find it all irrelevant – there is, after all, little reason why any Scot should get excited about Padraig Pearse, the harp, the shamrock or St Patrick. And in his anxiety to brand Protestant Scotland with anti-Irish racism, Bradley has at times allowed his wishes to override his scholarly rigour.[23]

The entry of academics into the world of the Old Firm has probably done little harm, and certainly it is good that the world of academe should at last be taking seriously such a superficially trivial subject as football. Academics often seem to make much of little, unlike the great comedians who make profound observations under the guise of humour. However that may be, one of the more hopeful signs that Old Firm antagonisms are not as bad as they once were can be seen in the way in which the subject is now more openly treated in the media, often as a source of humour. It is only in the last decade or so that this has changed.

Rikki Fulton was breaking new ground when he lampooned Rangers' sectarianism in his television show in 1979, and in 1984, Scottish Television took a risk when it allowed Robbie Coltrane as 'Mason Boyne' to poke some wicked fun at the followers of William. In the beginning 'Naked Radio' had no football content, but after a few years this changed, when Celtic fan Tony Roper and Rangers fan Jonathan Watson showed that the Old Firm was far from being an untouchable source of humour. From 1986 they broke away to perform their best-selling annual tapes, *Only an Excuse*. Their appeal was based on that of the phone-ins and the fanzines. Others have followed where they led.

The Old Firm now even appears in cartoon strips. 'Mick' and 'Billy' were introduced to *Evening Times* readers on 29 September 1995 by two friends who transferred to comic form their real life attachment to Celtic (Mick Foy) and Rangers (Billy Riddell). One of Scotland's great cartoonists, Malky McCormick, did not spare the Old Firm, even in the pre-Souness days, but it was an exception back in the immediate post-war years when the *Sunday Post*, in celebration of the return of peace, made so bold as to include a reference to the Old Firm in *The Broons*, when the Bairn held up a placard on which is written 'Up the Rangers!' but was careful to add at the same time, 'Up the Celtic!'.[24] (During the war, in an

'Oor Willie' strip about Halloween in November 1940, one of the guisers playing Lord Haw-Haw sneering about how Britain was falling apart, referred to the 'civil war between two tribes, the Celtic and the Rangers.'[25] The fighting in Europe did nothing to quiet passions at home at this time, and Rangers and Celtic were involved in several nasty incidents; a year later 'Rex' of the *Sunday Mail* departed from his more usually rose-tinted reporting to condemn the management of the two clubs for the 'religious heat' they encouraged to bring crowds to their games.)

Various entertainers have acknowledged their allegiance to one or other club, but generally have not brought this into their public performances. Lex McLean and Glen Daly played before their own, but the more international Andy Stewart generally kept his Rangers sympathies off-stage, the odd song notwithstanding. Andy Cameron, however, has openly used his support for Rangers as part of his comedy routine, always, however, in a non-sectarian way, while off the stage he was one of the few prominent Rangers supporters to oppose the club's stance on religion before 1986. His tongue-in-cheek dream is of an Ibrox heaven in which Rangers beat Celtic 8–0 each week, with the occasional mid-week game where they win 9–0. Rod Stewart's support for Celtic has seen him make the odd transatlantic flight to see them play, while among the other superstars, Sean Connery has angered some Celtic fans by appearing to transfer his allegiance to the directors' box at Ibrox, a presence not at all appreciated by the Rangers diehards. Broxburn-born Michael Caton-Jones has made a name for himself on the other end of the camera, establishing himself as one of the world's top film directors, most recently with *The Jackal*; a hyperactive brain and an overactive social life stood in the way of his football career, but success in Hollywood and the millions that came with it have not taken him away from his socialist leanings and Celtic obsession.[26] It was only later in his career that Billy Connolly introduced jokes about Celtic and Rangers, and while he openly admitted his love for Celtic at the time of the club's centenary, and helped them open the new stand in 1996, football has not been an important part of his repertoire.

Other pop stars have declared their allegiances to one or other club, such as Wet Wet Wet to Rangers, Simple Minds to Celtic, but only Celtic can boast of a star from the other end of the musical scale who has worn his heart on one of his scores. James MacMillan was still in his thirties when he achieved fame as a composer, one of his concertos achieving the unlikely feat for a modern work of being played more than 30 times around the world in the 1995–96 concert season alone. Said to be a 'passionate and life-long adherent of socialism, Catholicism,

Scotland and Glasgow's Celtic football team',[27] MacMillan was so furious after another fiercely fought failure by his team that he was inspired to compose a piece called 'The Berserking'. Put to words by Billy Connolly or better still if Tom Leonard was to give it lyrics along the lines of his splendid voice poems, this would surely offer a welcome replacement for 'The Fields of Athenry'. Another performer at Celtic and Rangers functions, usually held in the street and always unofficial, was Pastor Jack Glass, leader of the Church of the Twentieth-Century Reformation Movement. His fire-and-brimstone denunciations of those who paid no heed to his version of the Truth once commanded widespread media attention. It is perhaps a sign of the times that he has now been relegated to occasional appearances in late-night television and the odd notice in the Tom Shields diary column in *The Herald.*

Barely a decade on from the arrival of Souness at Ibrox and Rangers could parade a team of foreigners most of whom are Catholics. Celtic have stepped out into the community to take up the fight against bigotry, while their team, like that of Rangers, is comprised of many ethnic hues. Both clubs have made immense strides in their efforts to expunge the worst blots from their past. If bigotry or sectarianism still attach themselves to Rangers and Celtic, it can now be claimed, as it never could be in the days before Souness, that the problem is in society at large and so has little to do with the clubs. Neither bigotry nor sectarianism can be completely removed from Scottish society, any more than prejudice can be eliminated from any society. It is a problem that will always hang around the two clubs, but it is one that they cannot ignore. The challenge for the multicultural future of the Old Firm is to treat their traditions, now shorn of their ancient hatreds, as a celebration of differences rather than as a challenge to battle.

10. Rangers, Celtic and Scottish Society

In the early 1980s players of Afro-Caribbean background were coming into prominence in the English leagues, although exotic imports like the Argentines Osvaldo Ardiles and Ricardo Villa, who had played with Tottenham Hotspur since 1978 and starred in the memorable FA Cup final replay of 1981, were rare birds. There had been black players in English football since early in the century, from Walter Daniel Tull who played for Northampton Town in the years before the First World War (in which he lost his life) to Jack Leslie of Plymouth Argyle between the wars and Lindy Delaphena of Middlesbrough after the Second World War. A few blacks appeared in the 1960s, but it was only in the late 1970s that the sons of the West Indian immigration from the post-war period began to make their impression on English football: in 1978 Viv Anderson became the first black to play for England and in that same year Laurie Cunningham went from Nottingham Forest to Real Madrid for £800,000. By the early 1990s black players, although comprising only 1.5 per cent of the population, made up 12 per cent of the players in the top English League, and the proportion keeps getting bigger. By then such famous names as Jamaican-born John Barnes and up and coming Ian Wright, among a host of others, had been joined by blacks from African countries as well as Afro-Caribbeans.

In Scotland there had always been a few foreigners to grace the game, in the case of Rangers mainly South Africans, Scandinavians and Ulstermen, and in the case of Celtic mainly Irish, from both sides of the border. But they were seldom English and rarely black, although Gil Heron for Celtic and Mohammed Latif for Rangers made brief appearances. Rangers signed another black player earlier in the century, but he was killed before he could play for them. This was Walter Tull, mentioned above, who arrived in Scotland to undertake an officer-training course at Gailes, near Irvine in Ayrshire. His brother, living in Glasgow and Britain's first black dentist, persuaded him to sign for Rangers, but he was called to the front before he could play for them and was killed in the last stages of the war, leading his men into battle.[1] With the arrival of Souness, Scotland, better known for exporting star players than importing them, began to reverse the flow. Today players of all colours and nationalities are to be seen in all major English and Scottish teams. This acceptance of players beyond a narrow national base is a reflection of the multiculturalism that has been one of the more positive aspects of the globalisation of culture in this era. Today foreigners, if not in a majority, are often the best players in the top teams in England and Scotland.

Multiculturalism is the acceptance of people of various ethnic backgrounds into the host culture, a celebration of difference and diversity. From the beginning of this century Scotland has had its Italian ice-cream sellers, and for many a visit to the 'Tallies' was a highlight of the weekend walk; Chinese restaurants have been with us almost as long, although it is only more recently that they have become, along with Indian food, as local as fish and chips; and Glasgow's Italian community has come a long way from the tricycles in the park selling ices on a Sunday to regular cafés – now they provide some of the best Italian food in Europe. Lithuanians, Poles and other central Europeans have settled into the population, and like the Italians, their religion is no problem. In Scotland Jews have not had to suffer the overt anti-Semitism that has been their lot in too many other countries. Coming from a wide range of backgrounds, with strong communities in the Gorbals and Garnethill, Glasgow's Jewry, according to Kenneth E. Collins, participated in a 'wider society which it found, on the whole, to be tolerant and welcoming'.[2] The worst trouble the Jews found was from the missionaries of the Church of Scotland and the Roman Catholic Church, who 'poisoned Jewish-Christian relations for many years'.[3]

That the Jewish population of Scotland was never more than 15,000 can account in some measure for the absence of widespread anti-Semitism. This has perhaps also been the case with regard to racism against the small numbers of Scots of Afro-Caribbean or Asian background. There has been prejudice, and there has been violence against Scots from such backgrounds, most recently in the cowardly attack on young Stephen Roberts, a black player who scored the winning goal in a penalty shoot-out for Campsie Black Watch in the Golden Goals Under-21 cup final in June 1997, but historically Scotland's ethnic animosities have been directed mainly against Scots of Irish-Catholic origin. Even the English, Scotland's largest immigrant group, have had little to fear so long as they kept their accents under control.

SECTARIANISM IN CONTEMPORARY SCOTLAND

Depending on your sources, the prejudice against Scots of Irish-Catholic origins is a living scar, a figment of paranoiac imagination, or a relic of Scotland's past. For some it is a 90-minute prejudice, alive and screaming for the duration of an Old Firm game, forgotten as soon as it is over as Rangers and Celtic fans share a few pints while they discuss the finer points of the game and then return to work happily alongside each other on the Monday. Even those who have never seen Rangers and Celtic fans share a pint after a game (just about everybody) would claim that serious prejudice ceased somewhere in the 1960s. But there are others, mainly Catholics who have been the victims of prejudice, who believe that prejudice has never ceased to exist and that it has manifested itself in venues other than football: and for those involved in football, for much longer than the 90 minutes of a game.

Two of the foremost scholars on the subject, Steve Bruce and Tom Gallagher, emphasise the decline in sectarianism, but Callum Brown believes that their opinions are rather optimistic. Brown agrees that there has been a decline in the importance of religion in political parties, and that the influence of the old sectarian institutions has lessened, while religiously oriented street gangs have all but disappeared, but he believes that this is to 'underestimate the vibrancy of the popular culture of bigotry'. Prosperity and better education have made the overt expression of bigotry less acceptable, but it reappears in other forms, and is still 'a factor in the day-to-day life of working-class Scots'. Some might wonder whether the bigotry of the working classes is merely more visible than that of the 'hooligans in high places', but it seems, at least on the part of the Protestants, to have lost any serious religious content. Brown's final comment on the issue is to point out that when the Rev. Ian Paisley led some demonstrators in the early 1980s to protest against the admission of 'the Pope – the Protestants' anti-Christ – to the palace of world Presbyterianism in Edinburgh', only one hundred turned up.[4]

Whatever the reality of the situation, sectarianism in Scotland is still a live issue. Whether or not it is a real one or a media beat-up is another matter. Before the 1980s serious discussion of the Old Firm rivalry on radio or television was either scarce, produced by a foreign film company or dutifully careful in its analysis to tot up an evenly balanced number of opinions for and against each side. Failure to do so could evoke pique in the strangest of ways: Archie Macpherson, the television commentator, was once threatened by a Celtic director with dire consequences if he did not do something about his bias, revealed by his more frequent references to Rangers players by their first name than to those of Celtic.[5]

Foreign coverage of the Old Firm rivalry was often merely sensational, as in the *Stern* article of 1981 with its graphic photographs of Old Firm extremism and the claim that the sectarian fighting at these games had resulted in the biggest number of deaths and injuries at European football matches. A recent home-based film on the subject, shown on Channel Four on 12 November 1995, was more in line with *Stern* than some of the more balanced attempts at discussing the issues on radio and television. *Football, Faith and Flutes* was produced by the Glasgow-based media company Wark Clements, but it is hard not to question the west of Scotland credentials of the producer when he claims that his film about bigotry and football was the 'big untold story about Scotland'. Moreover, in his diary of the events covering the making of the film,[6] Alan Clements seemed to have been more concerned about sensation rather than analysis: he expresses his delight at turning up groups or individuals who would say what he wanted them to say, and thanks Fergus McCann for refusing to enter the discussion programmed to follow the screening, because of the publicity this was sure to provoke. On the other hand, the abuse Clements suffered, including the vandalising of his car, showed that the subject matter had touched a raw nerve.

McCann's initial willingness to participate while Rangers would have nothing to do with it has a familiar ring going back to the days when Ibrox was a Catholic-free zone. It is still to be regretted that Murray and McCann do not appear together or make more joint comments when it comes to the issue of sectarianism, but this particular programme was perhaps not the place to start. Since the coming of Souness and the signing of Johnston, Rangers no longer have the albatross of their anti-Catholic signing policies hanging about their neck and need no longer be embarrassed about making public statements in this regard, a task left in the pre-Souness days to the hapless Rev. James Currie, who did his best to deny the obvious. McCann's appraisal of the programme in a statement to the press, branded it as 'a gross caricature of the extremist attitudes of two unfortunate individuals and others in a drunken state . . . a manipulated example of tabloid television which responsible people should deplore'. This may well have been a fair judgement of the film, although it might better have been made in the post-viewing discussion; or at least, since Murray had refused from the start to take part, through a representative of Celtic – and preferably one from Rangers.

'Unfortunate' is perhaps a reasonable enough description of the two main football fans referred to, although, as in the rest of the film the Catholics come over as more civilised than their Protestant counterparts. Sam the Rangers fanatic reveals the UVF initials tattooed on the inside of his lower lip and expresses his hatred of all Fenians. He describes his despair as he wakes up each day in his home in Parkhead and sees Celtic Park, which he claims is a 'breeding ground for Republicanism, Catholicism, Sinn Fein, the IRA and everything I oppose'. Rather than find a house where he won't meet this eyesore on a daily basis, he expresses his hope that one day the stand at Celtic Park would collapse and bury all who were under it. Paddy, Sam's reverse image – at least so far as the totems are concerned, for he was less rabid in his bigotry – claims that as a Catholic he had to hate Protestants, and that as a Celtic supporter he had to hate Rangers. In another segment of the programme, which includes the respectable side of Orangeism with its members at prayer before a parade, there are also scenes of some suitably decked out Orange women singing (to the tune of the 1970s pop song, 'Chirpy, chirpy, cheep, cheep') such choice ditties as:

> *Last night I saw my daddy makin' a bomb . . .*
> *. . . woke up this mornin' and the chapel was gone . . .*

– and in reference to the 1981 hunger strike, 'Could You Go a Chicken Supper, Bobby Sands'. (Since much of the footage was out of date, both clubs having denied Clements access to their grounds, it would have been little surprise to hear the Celtic fans singing, to the tune of 'The Farmer Wants a Wife', 'Fagin Shagged the Queen'.) In the film, Catholics are seen visiting the Carfin grotto, and a father preparing his wee boy for the Volunteer Billy Reid Republican Flute Band piously tells the cameras that while he wanted the British removed from Ireland he did not want to be associated with the 'football hooligans who sing Irish rebel songs at matches'.

From a footballing point of view there is better insight into the thinking of fans at Old Firm games in Stephen Walsh's *Voices of the Old Firm*. This was made into a very good radio programme narrated by David Francey and presented on Radio Five on 25 and 26 December 1995. Here a whole range of Celtic and Rangers supporters freely expressed themselves on what it was like to be a fan of the Glasgow giants over the last four decades: the bigotry is there and the hatred, and even the downright callous or inane, but so too is the humour and the simple devotion and the day-to-day cares of a section of society that has an obsession with football.

Every society has its pathological criminals, and in Scotland this can occasionally be given a sectarian label. On 7 October 1995, a young man returning from a Celtic–Partick Thistle game at Parkhead was murdered in an unprovoked attack near Bridgeton Cross. Mark Scott was wearing a Celtic jersey under his sweater and had to undergo a barrage of abuse along with his two friends as they passed a group of youths outside a pub and betting shop. Uneasy, they walked on, when suddenly one of the youths, well known for his hatred of Catholics, and whose father and uncle were in gaol for serious crimes associated with the UVF, came up from behind and slit the 16-year-old's throat. Despite the defence of Donald Findlay, the evidence against the unrepentant Jason Campbell was overwhelming, much of it from witnesses who had looked on in horror as the crime was committed. Young Mark Scott's funeral was attended by Celtic manager Tommy Burns, chief scout David Hay and several Celtic players. In the meantime Rangers and Celtic scarves carefully entwined and left as a gesture of reconciliation near the scene of the crime were disentangled, while floral tributes in memory of the young victim were scattered by vandals who used them as footballs.[7]

As Campbell's trial came to an end in mid-March 1996 another young Celtic fan was brutally murdered, this time a 15-year-old boy who had signed 'S' forms with Celtic, and having starred for Scotland Under-15s when they had beaten Belgium the previous week, had had hopes of making the big time. Lawrence Haggart was beaten to death in his own home, with suggestions of sectarianism or hatred of Celtic in the way the killers had burned the feet of a young lad with a bright football future.

Neither of these two acts had anything to do with Rangers or Celtic or football or even religion, and when in October 1997 Henry McLeish, the Scottish home affairs minister, appeared to bestow political status on Campbell's crime by having him transferred to the Maze prison near Belfast, where he would have had an easier time among criminals of the same political persuasion, the shocked response of the Scottish public forced Donald Dewar, the Scottish Secretary, to intervene and reverse the decision. The crimes committed against Mark Scott and Lawrence Haggart were the acts of depraved individuals beyond the ken of any civilised society. But they should give pause to those who boast of their sectarian hatred and make it felt in the worst of their songs and chants. And in that mad month of March 1996, just a few days after the Dunblane massacre, and on the same day as Lawrence Haggart died, Celtic and Rangers fans battled in the streets of Thornliebank, while a Rangers footballer was involved in the infamous 'Five Bellies brawl' inside a pub in Renfrewshire.

Scotland has been spared the Ulster violence, and some would claim that the concentration of Ireland's sectarian hatreds around a football match in Glasgow has served as a safety-valve in this regard. However that may be, the Ulster violence has been restricted to the arrest of the occasional gun-runner from Scotland, although more recently, in

December 1995, one Ulsterman and two Scots were convicted of being part of a terror ring supplying guns to the Ulster Volunteer Force: photos of the convicted men showed them defiantly trumpeting their contempt for the verdict.

There had been a time when IRA and UVF supporters used Celtic Park or Ibrox as cover for their illegal activities, but that is well in the past and this never had the support of either club. In colour photos for weekend magazine supplements or television interviews or trials, spokesmen for the IRA or the UVF have often been happy to be seen wearing the colours of Celtic or Rangers, and through to the present day, demonstrators for either cause in Glasgow, Belfast or Derry proclaim their allegiance by wearing Rangers or Celtic tops. It is in Ulster, too, that the most extreme reactions to the internal affairs of Parkhead and Ibrox have been voiced. Scotland, however, has been spared the bombings that have scarred the lives of too many people in certain parts of England. The London government is the main target for the IRA terrorists, even if hundreds of innocent individuals in England have had their lives ruined by the bombs and bomb threats; to bring a bombing campaign to Scotland would only further convince the vast majority of Scots, Catholics and Protestants alike, that they want none of Northern Ireland's violence transported to Scottish soil.

THE MONKLANDS MAFIA

The issue of sectarianism with regard to Protestants and Catholics in Scotland keeps popping up in the strangest of places, as in the minor furore that arose when a bursary fund that had been operating since 1868 came under fire in April 1996 because its long dead benefactor, the thread-maker, John Clark, had stipulated that no Catholics should be allowed to apply for it. More ecumenical in his exclusiveness, Clark also banned Moslems, Buddhists and atheists from his bursary. There were calls for the 'bursary for bigotry', advertised at Strathclyde and Glasgow universities, to be banned. And the Orange Order can always be relied upon to make what they see as a principled stand on behalf of those they have chosen to defend. One such case was in January 1996 when a Catholic bishop had to cancel a visit to the Harthill Primary School to speak to the dozen or so Catholic children who were about to take confirmation and their first communion. Objections were raised, including one promise that if Bishop Devine did turn up there would be a flute band to meet him. As the *Sunday Mail* reported it, '12 little kids had to trek through snow to meet their bishop' instead.[8] Even Glasgow's finest could find themselves with strained relations as policemen who, in their private life supported Rangers, chivvied any Catholic colleagues who happened to be on duty and had picked up a Rangers player driving around drunk at the time.[9]

In recent times, however, the Monklands East by-election of June 1994 has raised the greatest outburst of sectarian breast-beating outside football. This by-election, called following the death of the leader of the Labour Party, John Smith, on 12 May 1994, brought to light grievances that had been simmering beneath the surface of local politics for years about bias in the way the Labour-controlled Monklands District Council had run its affairs – above all that Catholic Labour councillors had favoured family and fellow Catholics. In a report issued shortly after the poll, Robert Black, professor of Scots Law at Edinburgh University, came to no fixed conclusion, but presented a litany of the complaints that had been made and in so doing allowed those who wanted to prejudge the issues to regard them as truth. His report was in turn criticised in a fuller investigation by William Nimmo Smith QC, who cleared the Monklands councillors of nepotism and religious bias, charges more than just a little redolent of religion on the eve of the Reformation, and apparently not altogether out of place in 1990s Airdrie and Coatbridge.

The Monklands East seat covered the two adjacent towns of Protestant-dominated Airdrie (whose football team has been accused of operating a no-Catholics policy) and Catholic-dominated Coatbridge (whose football team, Albion Rovers, despite a proud history and boasting Jock Stein among its playing talent, has almost passed out of the memory of Scottish football fans).[10] A faction within the Coatbridge Labour council was accused of discriminating against Airdrie, showing favouritism in regard to employment, job allocation and the issuing of licenses, all of which would have been branded as a masonic conspiracy except that the main actors were Catholics. The by-election campaign gave an opportunity for these resentments in the running of local government to come to the fore, and sectarianism was shown to be a reality in parts of Scottish society and in areas far removed from football. Resentment against the perceived bias of Catholic Labour councillors from Coatbridge, itself said to be a payback after previous discrimination by Protestant councillors from Airdrie, led to Protestant working-class voters preferring the Scottish National Party to Labour, whose candidate, Helen Liddell, came within 1,640 votes of losing what had been one of the safest Labour seats in Britain. Whatever the outcome of the official findings, at the core of discontent was the belief by many citizens of Airdrie that the Catholic-dominated Monklands District councillors discriminated against the people of Airdrie. It was more than another incident to add to the long-running saga of tales of suspected corruption in local government that can be found in all places and at all times since such democracy has been in existence, for in addition to the perennial accusations of jobs for the boys was that of religious preferment.

The Coatbridge councillors were castigated as the Monklands mafia, and in the by-election campaign a few of the more zealous workers on behalf of the two main parties played the sectarian card – albeit against the advice of the leaders, who knew better than to fish in such murky waters. Voters were made aware of the religious beliefs of Labour's Helen Liddell, as it was pointed out that she was called Reilly before she was married and had gone to St Patrick's High, a Catholic school. On the other hand, some over-zealous Labour workers tried to spread the story that if the Scottish Nationalists won they would put an end to separate Catholic schools. One Conservative voter was threatened that if he voted for the SNP his 'vote against the Union' would be disclosed the next time he went to Ibrox to support Rangers. All of this was helped along by Tory imports from England anxious to distract attention from the sleaze activities that had become a permanent feature of their own party.

For those who liked to believe that sectarianism in Scotland was merely a matter of history, it was time to revise their opinions. Among these was the chief political editor of *The Scotsman*, Peter Jones. At the end of the campaign he wrote an article in which he criticised both George Galloway of the Labour Party and Alex Salmond of the Scottish National Party for the way in which they had reacted to the sectarian issue.[11] This they had done in *Flourish*, the monthly journal of the Roman Catholic Archdiocese of Glasgow, where Galloway blamed the SNP for bringing sectarianism into the campaign, while Salmond claimed that it was the conduct of the Labour councillors, and not their religion, that was the issue. The one was saying that sectarianism was an imported issue and was overturned by the result, the other that it did not exist at all.

Jones denounced both of these claims and appealed for a recognition that sectarianism did exist and had to be confronted. He claimed that the Monklands by-election was one of the first in which religion rather than social class, home ownership or age has decided people's voting preference: while 80 per cent of Catholics voted Labour, 65 per cent of Protestants voted SNP. For them, if not for the Black report and the Smith inquiry into the affair, religion was clearly an issue. For Jones, who once thought that 'real sectarianism in Scotland today had been locked away into the cul-de-sac of ceremonial marching bands and distasteful football songs', it was time for him and others like him to admit that they were wrong. Much of the old discrimination was gone, but much of it lingered on, and not only in Monklands.

THE CATHOLIC CHURCH AND THE SECULAR STATE

The Catholic Church no longer has the power it once had, either over its members or over society at large; even in Ireland it has lost much of its previous power to impose its religious morality on public policy. This has been in the face of resistance within the Church itself, which has never pretended other than that it has the right to a role in political as much as in moral matters, even in societies where the bulk of the population is non-Catholic and prefers that politics be secular and religion remain a private affair. The insistence of the Catholic Church, even in this secular age, on telling its members how to act on certain issues, has often been to the annoyance of Catholics themselves, and this even on issues with which they are in agreement with their Church. Despite this, Scots who hold such secular views have been denounced in some circles not only as being anti-Catholic, but as being anti-Irish and racist. Gerry Finn claims that people who hold such views are merely putting forward a recycled version of an earlier racism, while Joseph Bradley, another researcher unwilling to recognise the socially divisive policies of the Catholic Church, seems to have swallowed Finn's assertions.[12] Finn and Bradley are in the company of another academic, Willy Maley, who is also happy to add the tag of 'racist' to people whose objection to Catholicism has nothing to do with Catholics or the Irish, but much to do with the Church's interference in political and personal matters.

Abortion is a delicate subject, and Catholics have no monopoly on the outrage that it should be legalised, but it has generally been accepted that this is ultimately a matter for the woman and her doctor to decide. It is natural that the Catholic Church should make its opinion known on this matter, and should advise its members accordingly, it is another matter when it tries to impose this belief on non-Catholics or when it blackmails a political party into conforming with its religious beliefs on the issue. This was the case in July 1991, when an article in the journal of the then Archbishop (now Cardinal) Winning, threatened the Labour Party with a loss of Catholic votes if it went soft on the issue. In a banner headline, *Flourish* declared that, 'Abortion is a political test', and Archbishop Winning issued voters a 'challenge', the clear implication of which was that Catholics should reconsider voting for the Labour Party unless it came into line with the Church's policy on abortion.[13] We can expect a similar intrusion into private morality and the issue of suffering and terminal illness when the euthanasia debate comes to Britain.

The most sensitive issue for the Catholic Church today, as it has been since the time of mass literacy, is that all Catholics must be educated in Catholic schools: it was this that forced Mussolini to come to an agreement with the Church in 1929, and the only time the Vatican spoke out against the Nazis was in 1937 after they had ignored the provisions of the Concordat between the Church and Hitler that guaranteed the Catholic Church the right to independence in how young Catholics were being educated – and the only time a member of the Church used his office to thwart Nazi policy (as distinct from individual clerics and other Catholics who risked their lives in opposing the regime) was when Bishop Count Galen of Münster spoke out against the euthanasia programme. Since 1918 when the Labour Party won over the support of Catholics in Scotland with its support for the Conservative-dominated coalition government's introduction of fully funded Catholic education in Scotland, Scottish taxpayers have been helping to provide for the maintenance of a particular religion. This is an issue that has been sanctioned by time, and no party is seriously committed to changing it in its fundamentals. In recent years, however, as school numbers drop off and it has been necessary for some schools to merge, the opportunity to bring children of different religions together in the same classrooms has been strenuously resisted by the Catholic hierarchy (and minorities among the Protestants). This perennial source of conflict was brought to a head in a series of public debates in the middle of 1991.

It was at this time that the irrationality of the divided system was brought to the fore, as parents of either denomination refused to have their children mix with those of the other sort. Or even, as happened at a school in Glasgow's Easterhouse, Catholic and Protestant kids were taught under the same roof, but by different teachers acting under a separate administration. This situation arose when St Colette's RC school was destroyed by fire in 1986 and the pupils had to be accommodated in the non-denominational Commonhead school. The system actually seemed to work quite well, but at a time of cutbacks in education spending, the duplication of resources was something of an anomaly.[14]

Cardinal Winning has no doubts on the schools issue. He would not be in his present position if he thought otherwise, as the education of its young by its own priests is one of the most fiercely guarded demands of the Catholic Church. This is not for educational, but religious reasons. Cardinal Winning has made this quite clear on many occasions, claiming that without Catholic schools he would lose Catholics to the faith. At the time of the problem discussed above, Winning declared openly:

> The Church would not be as strong as it is without Catholic schools . . . I know other denominations are envious of our schools and the great rapport we have with our kids. We would be foolish to throw away an asset like that.[15]

Catholic schools in Scotland are under no threat from any of the political parties: the only threat they are under is from a society that is increasingly free from bigotry and sees that one of the few ways in which bigoted attitudes grow is when children are brought up in ignorance of each other's way of life. Anyone who supports apartheid in education has little grounds for complaining of bigotry in society at large. This is neither an anti-Catholic nor a racist statement.

The recognition of freedom of conscience and opinion and the removal of religion to the private sphere are among the essential tenets of the modern democratic state. To hold to such beliefs is not to be anti-religious, and those who accuse critics of the Catholic Church's interference in secular affairs as bigots are really reflecting on themselves. Finn and Bradley's narrow views were taken up from a different angle by Willy Maley in a newspaper article entitled: 'Of saints, scholars and sectarians' that appeared in *The Herald* of 29 June 1991. Maley argues that 'reading between the lines' in regard to separate schools, 'integration' and 'secularisation' were an attempt to get rid of Catholic schools by a process of acculturation and assimilation. Attributing motives that may be applicable to some, but certainly not to all or even to a majority, he then slews off on a non sequitur to declare that private schools are as 'divisive and exclusive as Catholic education'. This is certainly true, but the education of the rich and the privileged is not directly subsidised by the taxpayer. Maley also claims that 'anti-Irish racism and anti-Catholicism are inseparable in a Scottish context', a statement as unacceptable as his related one that the Catholic Church and socialist republicanism are not mutually exclusive: the socialism of the Catholic Church is that of Rerum Novarum, proclaimed in 1891 and practised by Mussolini a few decades later, while the socialism of James Connolly was damned by the Church along with that of all other political socialists, Catholic or otherwise, who dared to suggest that the fate of the people should be in their own hands.

There are no doubt Scottish Protestants who fit Maley's accusation, and no doubt he could find many of his examples at Ibrox or even in the columns of the broadsheet press, especially when the controversial writer John Macleod comes spewing onto the middle pages with a mind that is still locked somewhere in Scotland's medieval past. Much of what Macleod has to say was true once upon a time, and some of it is true today, but for him the Catholic Church remains, Vatican II notwithstanding, the same as that which happily sent heretics to be burned at the stake. Like Sam and Paddy in *Football, Faith and Flutes*, Maley and Macleod speak from oddly similar viewpoints.

CATHOLICS, PROTESTANTS AND PATRIOTS

Maley, who seems unwilling to distinguish between integration and assimilation, or at least chooses to overlook them in the Scottish situation, takes a swipe at Graham Walker for daring to suggest that 'Scotland is a Protestant country'. He makes the assumption that this statement leaves no room for those who are not Protestant. Here we have one of the ironies of multiculturalism, when the host country is turned on by those it had hoped to integrate and finds itself forced to justify itself before the more recent immigrants: Christians defending Christmas and Easter against Muslims; Protestants in Scotland having to apologise for having been there for a few hundred years and feeling that somehow the country of their forebears has something to do with them. Even the supporters of Glasgow Rangers, no blushing violets in defending their own position, have been assailed to such an extent that they now exhibit on occasion a paranoia more usually associated with their rivals on the other side of the city.

Scotland is many things. It is Protestant, but far from exclusively so. There was a time when this was a defining or a dominant characteristic: a Scotland where in his pre-teen years the young male went to Sunday School and the Life Boys, then when he was older to the Boys' Brigade followed by church service. At school he learned of the good work of missionaries like David Livingstone, the inventions of a host of people who can be found on tea-towels anywhere in the Scottish tourist market, the novels of Scott and the poems of Burns. At home he would be taught the virtues of hard work and the lessons of the Bible, all translated into simple language in the couthie columns of the *Sunday Post*. (Women, of course, did what they were told.)

Little of this has much attraction for Catholics whose heart is in Ireland, and even those whose heart was in Scotland would have been offended by Oor Wullie's comment in the middle of the Second World War[16] when he listed first among the great Scots, 'Bruce and Wallace and the Rangers . . .' (it is always overlooked that Bruce and Wallace were Catholics). Even the message of Burns, one of whose closest friends, William Maxwell, was a Catholic, has more in common with two great enemies of the Catholic Church: socialism and freemasonry. But the Catholic of the 1990s is as different from the Catholic of the pre-Vatican II days as the hardline Protestant is of the pre-Souness days at Ibrox. As Bradley rightly says, there are many layers of Irish identity; what he seems less willing to recognise is that there are also many layers of Scottish identity.

The portrait of the Protestant in works of literature has often been that of the bigot or the narrow killjoy: the Orangeman in Hector McMillan's *The Sash*; the despair of the central character in Gordon Williams' sympathetic novel *From Scenes Like These*, and the narrow honesty of the innocent in the short stories of Alan Spence, brought together in his book, *Its Colours They Are Fine*. The world of the Protestant work ethic is presented in dark hues in the works of A.J. Cronin, more sympathetically in works like John Blake's *The Shipbuilders*, or the film loosely based on it that came out in 1949, *Floodtide*. These are the people who made Scotland into a country whose contribution to the developed world was immense. It was the Protestant Scots, educated in the religion of the Book, whose restless energies took them to the far-flung corners of the globe: engineers, clerks and tradesmen in the service of the industrial revolution, missionaries, civil servants and educators in the spread of the Empire, whose most lasting and perhaps greatest memorial is in the game they took with them (along with some Englishmen and others) to play in their leisure time – the contribution of Scots, both Catholic and Protestant, in the spread of association football is echoed in the names of teams and competitions and the foundation members of associations established throughout the world in the years up to and beyond the First World War.

By the 1960s the success of Scotland's Catholic football club was paralleled by the success of Scottish Catholics throughout the business and professional world, and this, along with the greater loyalty retained by Catholics to their religion, challenged the certainties of Scots who still believed in a Protestant ascendancy. For those who felt marginalised, comfort could be found in Rangers Football Club, or the control of local councils such as that of Airdrie. Since Souness, Protestant pride has been regained, although in the new-look Rangers there is less emphasis on the old Protestantism, and even less on the Scottishness that Rangers once boasted in opposition to the Irishness of their Catholic rivals.

It is one of the ironies of Scottish identity that its two biggest football teams are its least Scottish: Rangers with their British rather than Scottish identity, their red, white and blue of the Union Jack, the Queen and the National Anthem; Celtic with their green and white of Ireland, the Pope and the Republic. In contrast to countries like Belgium, Italy and Greece (but not Spain) where the immense differences between regions and communities are overlooked when the nation is represented in the colours of the national football team, support for the Scotland team has never been complete. Many Celtic fans have always been more likely to support club before country, now they have been joined by many Rangers fans. In the new Europe with its emphasis on regions rather than nation states, this has been emphasised, with the club taking pride of place over national identity. When Gascoigne scored that fantastic goal that sank Scotland's chances in the match against the Auld Enemy at Wembley in Euro 96 there were sporadic fights throughout Scotland as Rangers fans celebrating the goal angered other Scots fans – and even other Rangers supporters. Many Celtic fans, with no Republic of Ireland to support, supported no one.

There was a time, in the 1960s in particular, when what later became known as the Tartan Army was made up mainly of Rangers supporters, some of whom, unfortunately, could not stomach the sight of a Celtic favourite in a Scotland jersey. The disgust felt by these players at being abused by their own supporters is understandable, as is that of the Celtic supporters who witnessed it. Now the Scotland team of recent years is routinely dismissed as a Jacobite XI by the Rangers fanzines. The prominent Celtic supporter and now a writer for the *Celtic View*, Matt McGlone, spoke for many Celtic fans when he admitted to losing his last remnant of support for the Scotland team when he heard the Scottish crowd baying for Sandy Jardine to come on in place of David Hay during a Scotland international match, and Bobby Brown, the Scotland manager, caved in to the crowd.[17] Twenty years on and a Tartan Army less dominated by Rangers fans and Scotland was still not a top priority in the minds of many Celtic people.[18] Michael Kelly tells of the reaction of Celtic supporters, at an away match in Kirkcaldy, to the announcement that the Scotland rugby team had lost by a single point in the last minute of a Calcutta Cup match: to his disgust they immediately started jeering and taunting the Raith Rovers supporters.[19] On the other hand, in 1994 Scotland played Holland as part of the Dutch team's preparation for the World Cup in the USA, and this coincided with a visit of the Celtic Boys Club to the Netherlands for a youth tournament. The youngsters went along to cheer on the Scotland team, but were subjected to such a torrent of abuse from some Scottish supporters that they had to be removed by the Dutch officials and placed among the home supporters for their own safety.[20] None of this has been helped by the owners of the two big clubs, who, while they claim to be acting in the best interests of Scottish football, and not just the shareholders in their club and its followers, often give a good impression of wanting to have nothing to do with the game in Scotland.

In such circumstances it is easy to see how Rangers and Celtic can be scorned by other Scots, and while patriotism may be dismissed as the last refuge of the scoundrel, the rejection of one's 'native land' can just as often reveal a soul dead to more than just a field or forest. While Rangers and Celtic play within the Scottish system with only a secondary loyalty to Scotland, even more so as they rely on foreign imports at the expense of bringing on young local talent, they cannot expect to win over the support of agnostic Scots when they play abroad. It would be heartening if this were to be the case, and now that they have shed their religious baggage Celtic and Rangers should be able to enter Europe as ambassadors for the country as a whole. Neither the Unionism of Rangers nor the Irish associations of Celtic are necessarily antithetical to a Scottish identity – and above all in this age of multiculturalism. A Rangers fan who is British first and Scottish second is not in breach of loyalty to his own country, and there is no reason why Celtic supporters can't appreciate Irish culture, sing Irish songs and visit Ireland as a preferred place for holidays. This is the situation for many Catholics in Scotland and the 'Bhoys against Bigotry' campaign celebrates this. Scotland and Ireland have common Celtic roots and if it wasn't for religion would have very little to divide them – certainly not racism.

FAIR PLAY FOR JOCK TAMSON'S BAIRNS

The problem of new immigrants and their children holding onto their old ways and adapting to the new is one that has faced untold numbers of people in dozens of countries around the world. In Britain, football circles have come under criticism for the absence of players from an Asian background. The FA ran a conference at Oldham in October 1996 on the theme 'Asians in Football', concerned about the absence of Asians in the major English leagues despite there being Asian leagues and Asian teams in the country. The assumption was that it was prejudice against the Asians that had kept them out, under the excuse that gave the title to two Asian researchers' project: 'Asians Can't Play Football'. Much of this has echoes of the accusations of prejudice by Catholics of a few decades ago; but not all the blame rests with the host community.

Moves have been made to welcome Asians into the Scottish game, above all by Celtic, in line with their 'Bhoys against Bigotry' campaign, and *Scotland on Sunday*, who have engaged in active campaigns to integrate Asians through football. Even before they launched the campaign, Celtic worked closely with the recently appointed City of Glasgow's Ethnic Minorities Officer, Kash Taank, during the 1995–96 season. They helped him set up coaching sessions involving the club's players and invited groups to visit Celtic Park for discussions and as guests at some games. Celtic was the only high-profile club to become actively involved with the Scottish Asian Sports Association, and fully supported the plans to set up the Asian Soccer Academy in Glasgow, the first of its kind in the UK.

Scotland on Sunday began its campaign of 'Fair play for Asians' in its issue of 24 November 1996, and thereafter Jonathon Northcroft wrote regular articles trying to improve the opportunity for Asians to 'take part in football from the top level down'. Northcroft claimed that Celtic was the only high-profile club with initiatives targeting Asians, although he also pointed out that the only Asian playing in the Scottish League at that time was Rangers' Jaswinder ('Jazz') Juttla. He also noted that when the 'Let's Kick Racism out of Sport' campaign was opened in 1993, the Scottish League and the SFA thought that this had nothing to do with them.

Luckily not all of the clubs in the Premier League agreed, although not all of them entered the spirit of the campaign. Rangers struck the strongest possible blow against racism when Souness signed Mark Walters, but since then foul monkey chants have again filled the stadium, most recently directed at Celtic's Regi Blinker, especially whenever he lined up to take a corner near the Copland Stand in his first Old Firm game of the 1997–98 season. Little – if anything – of this was noted in official Rangers publications, and yet this is surely something that no one in sport can tolerate. Whether it is to be done by campaigns and words, or specific action, is up to those concerned. As Gerry McNee has pointed out, if someone like Richard Gough had gone up to Blinker and demonstrated to the fans that he was having nothing to do with racism, it would have been an action worth a million words.

Celtic and *Scotland on Sunday* have been combining both words and action. The newspaper backed a national sixes tournament to celebrate Asian football, planned to take place in Edinburgh in the spring of 1997 as part of a campaign called 'Fair Play for Asians'.[21] The idea was thought up by Sultan Mahmood, a designer retailer who has arrived in Edinburgh from Huddersfield and whose team, the Kurry Kickers, was just one of the many playing in the Asian leagues there. Mahmood's main wish is for the Asian teams to be integrated into the Scottish leagues and not to be forced into separate leagues as was the case in England. *Scotland on Sunday* claimed that Asians were forced out onto the margins of Scottish football by 'abuse, discrimination and ignorance',[22] and no doubt there is much truth in this: there are some communities, however, that prefer to keep to themselves. The absence of Asian footballers from the top grade is not necessarily an indication of prejudice against them. Some Asians, and Pakistanis in particular, do not see football as a high-status activity and encourage their male children into other pursuits: many of them find more important things to do than play football.

One of the few Asians to make the top grade in Scottish football was Rashid Sarwar, who made 21 first-team appearances for Kilmarnock between 1984 and 1987. By his own admission, football was not a driving obsession with him, and he pointed out that a couple of his mates who were better players than he was gave up football to concentrate on the family business. This has been reflected on the world stage, where Africa, despite a population that is a fraction of Asia's, has produced a multitude of top-class players; Asia by comparison has produced only a few. A Scots-Asian fan who wrote to *Not the View* saying how proud he was to have adopted Celtic as his team, confessed that although born in Scotland he was 18 before he knew about the Old Firm.[23] Admittedly his parents had preferred cricket, but any native-born sports-loving Scot who has not heard of the Old Firm by the time he is a young adult is surely living in another world.

Times change, and with the yuppification of football, the time might come when all these young Asians who can be seen kicking balls about the parks and wastegrounds of Scotland are encouraged to join the potentially lucrative and decidedly more socially acceptable status of professional football player. And in a world where Rangers employ Catholic players to help them win games, no team is going to turn down an Asian Maradona because of his ethnic origin. There are also signs of other cultural barriers coming down: Muslim women are no longer so prepared to abide by the strictures of their male 'superiors' who dictate that they should not be seen in immodest dress, such as a swimming costume, or gaze on immodestly dressed males, such as the bare knees on show at a football match. The one source of comfort to come from Australia's tragic elimination by Iran from France 1998 was when an estimated 5,000 Iranian women ignored the order to stay away from the celebrations for the heroes returning from Australia and burst past the guards set up to keep them out of the stadium.

There are Christians (and non-believers) today who find the Muslim attitude to women degrading, just as there are Muslims who believe that the adoption of liberal values by their womenfolk is a blasphemy. It is another version of the age-old problem of where religious belief ends and cultural contamination begins. Many who are uncomfortable with Muslim practices today need not be racists, although many are, just as Protestants who were once suspicious of Catholicism were not necessarily bigots, although many were. There are distinctions between culture, religion and race that can be easily confused, but this can never condone the open bigotry and racism that have too often scarred the face of football. On the other hand, if racism is to be measured by the exclusion of Asians from football, this must also have something to say about the countless numbers of blacks who are playing in football teams all over Britain today.

GLASGOW: DEAD BRILLIANT CITY OF CULTURE

Glasgow before the 1980s was a city with more than its share of problems. The transformation since the early 1980s has been little short of miraculous, as the city, despite some black spots that have won it recognition as being in need of special subsidy, not only smiles better but has presented its newly polished face to an admiring world. The savagely funny travel writer, Bill Bryson, thought no city more deserved its new reputation and although he didn't understand a word anyone said to him while he was there, still commented: 'Glasgow was named European City of Culture, and no one laughed.'[24] Glasgow was the Garden City of Europe in 1988 and it won the right, against tough opposition, to the stewardship of the Year of Architecture and Design in 1999. The 'no mean city' image of Glasgow is now a thing of the past as it enters the third phase in its history as a world power, tobacco and heavy industry now being followed by its role as a centre for tourism and the arts.

In common with the rest of Scotland, whose writers in the last decade or so have won Booker prizes and produced award-winning films and television series, rediscovered Charles Rennie Mackintosh and revolutionised its attitude to eating out, Glasgow with its freshly scrubbed tenements and spectacular examples of urban renewal prepares to host some of the top cultural events in Britain. There is nothing that can be done about Glasgow's weather or its geographical position, but it has always been within a short distance from some of the world's best scenery, while within its confines it has more parks than most cities of the same size, including public museums and art galleries that for more than a century have been open to the public free of charge. Now it has the Burrell collection in Pollok Park to add to the Art Gallery and Museum in Kelvingrove Park and the People's Palace in the Glasgow Green. And still the entrance is by voluntary donation. The new Glasgow is also reflected in the all-seated, all-covered stadiums at Celtic Park and Ibrox, with the difference that entry is restricted to those who can afford the high admission charges.

Glasgow still has its eyesores, as anyone walking from the city to Celtic Park can see, and there will be those who will have to make do with fish and chips and a carry-out rather than the gourmet delights of The Ubiquitous Chip and the other quality restaurants in the West End and elsewhere, but unlike those who have been priced out of the new stadiums at Ibrox and Parkhead, those who can't afford Chablis and choice seafood have not lost something that was once a cherished part of their life. It would be a welcome development if the dispossessed from Ibrox and Celtic Park were to reverse the trend of a century ago and

209

return to following the other teams in and around Glasgow – and elsewhere in Scotland. Such wishful thinking, of course, ignores the reality of life not only in Glasgow and with regard to the Old Firm, but in Europe and the world at large.

In the wider world of European football, the Scottish Cup and the Scottish League are minor trophies that serve as little more than springboards to greater things. Realistically, only Celtic and Rangers can hope to hold their own with the giants of the world game. Scotland, and Glasgow in particular, has its world-class opera, theatre, museums and galleries, but no urban culture is complete without world-class football entertainment. The stadiums in place at Parkhead and Ibrox are fit to set before the élite of the world game: now all we need is for Rangers and Celtic to provide the teams that the money and nervous energy spent on them warrant. Then Scotland, and in particular Glasgow, city of culture and home of football, will be back where it belongs.

Notes

1. The Greatest Club Game in the World?

1. Story told in the history of Rangers audio-tape that came out in the summer of 1993, narrated by Roddy Forsyth: 'Glasgow Rangers Revisited'
2. Stephen Walsh, *Voices of the Old Firm* (Edinburgh, Mainstream, 1995), p.222
3. Ibid. p.223
4. See in particular Vic Duke and Liz Crolley, *Football, Nationality and the State* (London, Longman, 1996)
5. For Jews in football see Bill Murray, *Football: A History of the World Game* (Aldershot, Scolar Press,1994), *passim*
6. See, for example, *Tiocfaidh Ar La*, Issue 8
7. This is recounted in several of the club histories. For an account in English see the excellent coverage of Spanish football in Duke and Crolley

2. A Catholic Comes to Ibrox

1. On Ure Primrose and Rangers, see Gerry P.T. Finn, 'In the Grip? A Psychological and Historical Exploration of the Social Significance of Freemasonry in Scotland', in Graham Walker and Tom Gallagher (eds), *Sermons and Battle Hymns: Protestant Popular Culture in Modern Scotland* (Edinburgh, Edinburgh University Press, 1990), pp.179–80. Finn has also pointed out that J.F. Wilson, the chairman of Rangers who supported Celtic in the 1952 Flag Flutter controversy, was a leading member of the Scottish Vigilance Society directed against the 'Irish enemy within'. Further work on the associations of high-ranking Rangers with such associations would be most interesting
2. The change was more a matter of style than a concession to essential truths. See in particular the opinion of two prominent academics who are also Celtic supporters: Pat Reilly in an illuminating article, 'The mirror of literature: the development of Catholicism

in Scotland since 1845', *Scottish Affairs*, 8 (Summer 1994), pp.86–95; and for a simple reminder that the Catholic Church is still unable or unwilling to compromise on Christian unity, Michael Kelly in his regular column in *The Scotsman*, 21 April 1997
3. For comments on Rush and Sheridan, see Rob Brown and David Cameron, *Scotland on Sunday*, 16 July 1989
4. Chick Young, *Rebirth of the Blues: The Story of a Rangers Revolution* (Edinburgh, Mainstream, 1987), p.26
5. Told to Pete Davies in his marvellous coverage of England's 1990 World Cup campaign, *All Played Out: The Full Story of Italia 90* (London, Mandarin, 1990), p.45
6. Stephen Walsh, *Voices of the Old Firm*, p.220
7. Joanna Macdonald in *The Herald*, 16 December 1996
8. *Shoot*, December 1996
9. *Daily Record*, 24 July 1989
10. 'Glasgow Rangers Revisited' audio-tape
11. *Follow, Follow*, No.8
12. *The Herald*, 12 July 1989
13. *Rangers News*, 2 August 1989
14. *Follow, Follow*, No.57
15. Bob Ferrier and Robert McElroy, *Rangers: The Complete Record* (Derby, Breedon Books, 1996), p.7
16. 'The Dowanhill Hack', *Follow, Follow*, No.57

3. The End of the Biscuit Tin

1. *Glasgow Herald*, 23 December 1986
2. Hugh Keevins, *Twists and Turns: The Tommy Burns Story* (Edinburgh, Sportprint Publishing, 1989), p.69
3. Michael Kelly, *Paradise Lost: The Struggle for Celtic's Soul* (Edinburgh, Canongate Press, 1994), p.150 on car phones, p.168 on catering
4. Tom Campbell and Pat Woods, *Dreams, and Songs to Sing: A New History of Celtic* (Edinburgh, Mainstream, 1996), p.250

5. Brian Wilson, *Celtic: A Century with Honour* (London, Willow Books, 1988), p.97
6. Kelly, *Paradise Lost*, p.14
7. Wilson, *Celtic*, p.108
8. For a brilliant evocation of the changes in Glasgow in the 1980s, see 'The Repackaging of Glasgow', in Ian Jack, *Before the Oil Ran Out: Britain 1977–87*, (London, Flamingo, 1987)
9. Archie Macpherson, *Blue and Green: Rangers v Celtic: A Personal Look at the Glasgow Derby* (London, BBC Books, 1989), pp.139–50 for a detailed and incisive analysis of the game and its outcome
10. *Mail on Sunday*, 5 March 1989
11. See especially *Follow, Follow*, No.9
12. Tom Campbell and Pat Woods, *A Celtic A–Z* (Glasgow, Greenfield Press, 1992), p.143
13. Callum G. Brown, 'Popular Culture and the Continuing Struggle for Rational Recreation', p.11, in T.M. Devine and R.J. Finlay (eds), *Scotland in the Twentieth Century* (Edinburgh, Edinburgh University Press, 1996), p.215
14. James E. Handley, *The Celtic Story: A History of the Celtic Football Club* (London, Stanley Paul, 1960), p.62
15. Wilson, *Celtic*, p.182
16. Kelly, *Paradise Lost*, p.56
17. Tom Campbell and Pat Woods, *The Glory and the Dream: The History of Celtic FC 1887– 1986* (Edinburgh, Mainstream, 1987)
18. In addition to *The Glory and the Dream*, Kevin McCarra and Pat Woods, *One Afternoon in Lisbon* (Edinburgh, Mainstream, 1988)
19. *Not the View*, No.17
20. Campbell and Woods, *Dreams, and Songs to Sing*, p.299; the date of the first offer and the year in which McCann went to Canada (1963 or 1964) have been challenged: the information given here comes from Campbell and Woods, but also from the account given by David Low, who was to become an intimate of McCann's, and who wrote, with Francis Shennan, a history of the McCann takeover. There were two other books on the issue (see Chapter Five), but to date the most important player in the takeover, McCann himself, has said very little publicly on his role
21. Kelly, *Paradise Lost*, pp.16–17

4. The Souness Legacy
1. *Sportsweek*, 11 September 1986
2. *Daily Star*, 17 April 1991
3. *Daily Express*, 17 April 1991
4. For Murray's frank appraisal of Souness, see 'Glasgow Rangers Revisited'
5. *Sunday Post*, 21 April 1991
6. *The Sun*, 25 October 1989
7. *Sunday Mail*, 30 August 1987
8. Sandy Jamieson, *Graeme Souness: The Ibrox Revolution and the Legacy of the Iron Lady's Man*, Mainstream, Edinburgh, 1997, pp.185–88
9. See the *Sunday Times*, 21 April 1991
10. *Follow, Follow*, No.13
11. Ferrier and McElroy, *Rangers: The Complete History*, p.131
12. For further discussion of this see Bill Murray, *Football: A History of the World Game, passim*, but especially pp.108–10
13. *Daily Mail*, 24 July 1996
14. Bob Crampsey, *The Scottish Football League: The First 100 Years* (Glasgow, Scottish Football League, 1990), pp.164–66
15. See for instance *The Herald*, 26 June 1992
16. Kelly, *Paradise Lost*, p.64
17. He said this in 'Glasgow Rangers Revisited', and in the *Daily Record* of 24 December 1993 Murray admitted that he would 'like to think that my connections with Rangers will become a family dynasty'

5. Uncivil War at Parkhead
1. Michael Kelly, *Paradise Lost*
2. ibid., p.172
3. *Not the View*, No.1
4. McGlone's relationship with Celtic and his role in toppling the old board is told in his highly readable *Emotionally Celtic* (East Kilbride, GD Communications, 1995)
5. Kelly, *Paradise Lost*, p.62
6. *Sunday Times*, 14 April 1991, where Jim Craig quotes him as saying that Rangers were '"too stupid and too slow" to make an approach for him'.
7. Kelly, *Paradise Lost*, p.98
8. David Low and Francis Shennan, *Rebels in Paradise: The Inside Story of the Battle for the Celtic Football Club* (Edinburgh, Mainstream, 1994)
9. Allan Caldwell, *Sack the Board: Celtic the End of a Dynasty* (Edinburgh, Mainstream, 1994), pp.21–22
10. Cyclops in *The Celt*, 32 (May 1991)

6. A New Firm: Murray and McCann

1. *Evening Times*, 7 February 1997
2. Article by Ken Gallacher in *The Herald*, 27 January 1997
3. See David Murray interview with Mike Aitken, in *The Scotsman*, 9 November 1994
4. On Sugar and other individuals who have made windfall profits out of their investment in (English) football, see David Conn, *The Football Business: Fair game in the '90s?* (Mainstream, Edinburgh, 1997)
5. *Daily Mail*, 23 January 1997
6. *Daily Record*, 23 January 1997
7. ibid
8. *The Scotsman*, 23 January 1997
9. ibid
10. See in particular the article by Christopher Sims in *The Herald*, 20 November 1997
11. *Evening Times*, 28 March 1997
12. *Evening Times*, 29 January 1997
13. *Daily Record*, 18 December 1996
14. Full details of the letter in the *Daily Record*, 6 February 1997
15. S.G. Checkland, *The Upas Tree: Glasgow 1875–1975* (Glasgow, University of Glasgow Press, 1976)

7. Nine Down, One to Go

1. Kenny Dalglish, with Henry Winter, *Dalglish: My Autobiography* (London, Hodder & Stoughton, 1996)
2. *Daily Record*, 9 January 1998
3. *Follow, Follow*, No.72; see also No.71
4. Quote paraphrased from Ed Horton, *Moving the Goalposts: Football's Exploitation* (Mainstream, Edinburgh, 1997), p83. This impassioned denunciation of the impact of television as viewed by an obsessive Oxford United fan overlooks some of the good that television has brought to football, especially in the way it has made games available to those with no chance of getting to the ground.

8. Bhoys, Bears and Bigotry

1. For further details on this see *The Old Firm* or any of the histories of the club by Pat Woods, but in particular his article, '1887 and all that', which appeared in the *Celtic View*, 2 February 1983. In Ireland those who accepted charity from Protestants in the Famine were condemned as 'soupers' for many decades thereafter, as Frank McCourt has recalled in his best-selling memoir of a Catholic childhood in Limerick, *Angela's Ashes: A Memoir* (HarperCollins, London, 1996), p.65 and *passim*
2. *The Scotsman*, 10 May 1997
3. There can be no doubting the seriousness with which McCann takes all aspects of the Bhoys against Bigotry campaign, as several bound cuttings of press and other extracts provided by Peter McLean make clear. The club has also, in collaboration with the Scottish Education authorities, compiled a set of primary and secondary class teaching aids on the theme of 'Youth against Bigotry'
4. *Tiocfaidh Ar La*, Issue 8
5. *Follow, Follow*, No.9
6. Campbell and Woods, *Dreams, and Songs to Sing*, p.323
7. Handley, *The Celtic Story*, p.173
8. Roddy Forsyth, *Blue and True: Unforgettable Rangers Days* (Edinburgh, Mainstream, 1996), p.25
9. *Daily Record*, 23 April 1990
10. *The Sun*, Nine-in-a-row souvenir pull-out, p.48
11. Forsyth, *Blue and True*, p.35
12. *Frankfurter Rundschau*, 13 January 1997
13. *The Sun*, 19 February 1996
14. *Evening Times*, 30 April 1996, which seems to be one of the few newspapers to comment on this
15. See, for example, the Celtic fanzine *Bhoyzone*, No.5, and following, where each game is listed and analysed
16. *Flourish*, February 1997
17. In the pub in Paris (The Auld Alliance) where I saw this game live, in the company of mixed Celtic, Rangers and French football fans, none of us saw any infringement by Cadete, yet when I first saw this in replay, a long time afterwards, I thought that Cadete *did* handle the ball. Instead of another one for the Lodge ('wan mair upfirthi luj' as Tom Leonard puts it in his poem 'Crack'), perhaps this was just another example of how the referee or his assistant will in the vast majority of cases see much more clearly than the fans
18. *Scotland on Sunday*, 29 September 1996
19. *The Sun*, Nine-in-a-row souvenir pull-out, p.20
20. *Ibid*, p.33
21. *Daily Record*, 12 October 1995
22. Apart from the press of the time, *Tiocfaidh Ar La*, Issue 14, gave its own, obviously

coloured, version of the events

23. *Daily Record*, 7 August 1993

24. *Daily Record*, 29 January 1997

25. *Daily Mail*, 19 February 1996

26. *Evening Times*, 27 October 1995

27. *The Herald*, 4 March 1996

28. *The Sun*, 22 April 1997

29. My grateful thanks to Else Bongenaar for finding these articles and sending them to me.

9. No More, the Bygone Days of Yore . . .

1. This is the title of Graham Walker's study of the two nations, *Intimate Strangers: Political and Cultural Interaction between Scotland and Ulster in Modern Times* (Edinburgh, John Donald Publishers, 1995)

2. Kelly, *Paradise Lost*, p.15, 179.

3. *The Independent*, 20 October 1992.

4. See Bob Ferrier's obituary on his father, reproduced in John Swinburne, *Motherwell Football Club: A History of the Steelmen, 1886–1986*, published by the club, 1985, pp.57–61. The son of an expatriate Scot who played for Sheffield Wednesday, 'Rabbie' Ferrier returned to his native Dumbarton three weeks too late to permit his son to play for Scotland. Bobby Ferrier spent his entire career with Motherwell, from 1918 to 1940, and the (George) Stevenson/Ferrier partnership is recognised as one of the greatest in the Scottish game

5. Bob Ferrier and Robert McElroy, *Rangers: The Complete Record*, p.6.

6. Joseph M. Bradley, *Ethnic and Religious Identity in Modern Scotland: Culture, Politics and Football* (Aldershot, Avebury, 1995), pp.68–71.

7. *The Rangers Historian*, 2: 10

8. Graham Walker and Tom Gallagher (eds), *Sermons and Battle Hymns: Protestant Culture in Modern Scotland* (Edinburgh, Edinburgh University Press, 1990), pp. 137–59

9. Ferrier and McElroy, *Rangers*, p.7

10. See the special four-part series on 'Freemasons in Scotland today', in *The Scotsman*, especially 'Part 4', 4 July 1996

11. J.M. Roberts, *The Mythology of the Secret Societies* (London, Secker and Warburg, 1972), p.1

12. Walker, 'There's not a team . . .', p.144

13. Bill Murray, *Glasgow's Giants: 100 Years of the Old Firm* (Edinburgh, Mainstream, 1988), pp.30–31

14. David Bennie, *Not Playing for Celtic: Another Paradise Lost* (Edinburgh, Mainstream, 1995)

15. *Gazza's Coming Home*, Channel 4 video

16. Story told in Roddy Forsyth's audio history

17. *Follow, Follow*, No.60

18. *Follow, Follow*, No.9

19. *Follow, Follow*, No.17

20. H.F. Moorhouse, 'Shooting Stars: Footballers and Working-Class Culture in Twentieth-Century Scotland' in Richard Holt (ed.), *Sport and the Working Class in Modern Britain* (Manchester, Manchester University Press, 1990), p.190. Moorhouse has published several articles since 1984, all of which he refers to in his successive works: five of these are listed in the bibliography to his article: 'From 'zines like these, tradition and identity in Scottish football,' in Grant Jarvie and Graham Walker (eds), *Scottish Sport in the Making of a Nation: Ninety-Minute Patriots?* (Leicester, Leicester University Press, 1994)

21. Among his publications, Gerry P.T. Finn has contributed an excellent article on freemasonry, 'In the Grip? A Psychological and Historical Exploration of the Social Significance of Freemasonry in Scotland', in Walker and Gallagher (eds), *Sermons and Battle Hymns*; and on Rangers, 'Faith, Hope and Bigotry: Case Studies of Anti-Catholic Prejudice in Scottish Soccer and Society', in Jarvie and Walker (eds), *Scottish Sport in the Making of the Nation*. He was to write three articles for the *International Journal of the History of Sport*, but the third of these did not appear. It is in the two published articles for that journal that Finn made his attacks on *The Old Firm* and *Glasgow's Giants*, together with other odd scraps of anything I might have said or was reported to have said, all of which he treats as being of equal value: 'Racism, Religion and Social Prejudice: Irish Catholic Clubs, Soccer and Scottish Society – I: The Historical Roots of Prejudice' (1991), 8: 1, pp.70–93; 'Racism, Religion and Social Prejudice: Irish Catholic Clubs, Soccer and Scottish Society – II: Social Identities and Conspiracy Theories' (1991), 8: 3, pp.370–97. It would take too long in a footnote to point out all the crass misinterpretations that make up these articles, so I will make do with one which typifies the rest. In the introduction to

Glasgow's Giants (p.13) I wanted to illustrate the ludicrous nature of some aspects of the Old Firm rivalry and gave three examples of this. Finn then ridicules me by ascribing to me the opinion of one of the people I was quoting. *IJHS*, 8: I, p.91

22. Bradley's book is unfortunately littered with serious faults in basic English and his documentation is often sloppy. While he is dismissive of earlier works on the subject, Bradley does not advance very far beyond them himself, and his history is patchy. His articles, usually made up of large chunks of material that have appeared in his book or his other articles, have appeared in various journals: Joseph M. Bradley, 'Religious Cleavage and Aspects of Catholic Identity in Modern Scotland' in *Records of the Scottish Church History Society*, vol.XXV (Edinburgh, 1995), pp.442–68; 'Ethnicity: The Irish in Scotland – Football, Politics and Identity', *Innovation*, 7, 4, 1994, pp.423–39; 'Football in Scotland: A History of Political and Ethnic Identity', the *International Journal of the History of Sport*, 12, 1, April 1995, pp.81–98; 'Integration or Assimilation? Scottish Society, Football and Irish Immigrants', the *International Journal of the History of Sport*, 13, 2, August 1996, pp.61–79.

23. Bradley, like several other writers more sympathetic to Celtic or the Irish, has seized on a cartoon from the *Scottish Referee*, which I reproduced in *The Old Firm*, and used it as an example of anti-Catholicism in Scottish society. He goes to great pains to point out how he discovered this cartoon, in his book and in all of his articles taken from the book (see footnote above). It would appear that he took it from *The Old Firm* and not at source. The giveaway for Bradley, and the others who did the same, is that he attributes my (ironic) title, 'Apes and Aryans' to the *Referee*. The cartoon was bad enough in its depiction of the sub-human Irish/Celtic player against the handsome Rangers player, but as I pointed out, only two such cartoons appeared, whether because readers objected or common decency took over, we don't know. And with some reflection, those writers who used this cartoon and blamed the *Referee* for the caption, must surely have wondered at its prescience, for while Nietzsche's works were being read by an élite

few, Hitler's rise to fame was still a couple of decades off.

24. *Sunday Post*, 13 May 1945

25. There is an excellent recapitulation of the *Oor Wullie* and *The Broons* comic strips in the 60th anniversary celebration that was brought out by the *Sunday Post: The Broons and Oor Wullie: 1936–96* (London, D.C. Thomson & Co Ltd, 1996)

26. See especially article in *The Scotsman (Weekend Magazine*, 29 November 1997)

27. *The Economist*, 1 November 1997

10. Celtic, Rangers and Scottish Society

1. *Daily Mail*, 19 February 1997

2. Kenneth E. Collins, *Second City Jewry: The Jews of Glasgow in the Age of Expansion* (Glasgow, 1990), p.14

3. ibid., p.11

4. Callum G. Brown, *The Social History of Religion in Scotland Since 1730* (London, Methuen, 1987), pp.243–7. Bruce and Gallagher have articles in Walker and Gallagher (eds), *Sermons and Battle Hymns*, and this should be consulted for a fuller bibliography of their works. See in particular: Steve Bruce, *No Pope of Rome: Militant Protestantism in Modern Scotland* (Edinburgh, Mainstream, 1985); Tom Gallagher, *Glasgow: The Uneasy Peace* (Manchester, Manchester University Press, 1987)

5. Archie Macpherson, *Action Replays* (London, Chapman, 1991), p.251. A prospective buyer of *The Old Firm* claimed to detect the book's bias by comparing the number of Celtic fans on the cover to those of Rangers

6. *Scotland on Sunday*, 12 November 1995

7. *East End Independent*, 12 October 1995

8. *Sunday Mail*, 26 January 1996

9. See, for example, *Sunday Mail*, 25 August 1996

10. It can also boast an impressive history written by one of its fans: R.W. Marwick, *The Boys from the 'Brig: The Life and Times of Albion Rovers* (Coatbridge Monklands Library Services Division, no date, but covers through to the 1985–86 season)

11. *The Scotsman*, 5 August 1994

12. Joseph M. Bradley, 'Integration or Assimilation? Scottish Society, Football and Irish Immigrants', *IJHS*, 13: 2 (August 1996)

13. *Sunday Times*, 7 July 1991

14. *Scotland on Sunday*, 5 May 1991

15. ibid.

16. *Sunday Post*, 10 October 1943
17. Matt McGlone, *Emotionally Celtic* (East Kilbride, G.D. Communications Ltd, 1995), pp.60–61
18. On this see also the work of Raymond Boyle: 'Faithful Through and Through: A Survey of Celtic FC's Most Committed Supporters', National Identity Research Unit, Glasgow Polytechnic, August 1991; '"We Are Celtic Supporters . . .": Questions of Football and Identity in Modern Scotland', in Richard Giulianotti and John Williams (eds), *Game Without Frontiers: Football, Identity and Modernity* (Aldershot, Arena, 1994), pp.73–101
19. Kelly, *Paradise Lost*, pp.148–9
20. As reported in *Tiocfaidh Ar La*, Issue 10
21. *Scotland on Sunday*, 1 December 1996
22. ibid
23. *Not the View*, No. 64
24. Bill Bryson, *Notes from a Small Island* (London, Doubleday, 1995), p.272

Bibliography

There has been a profusion of books on football since 1984, to add to the videos and fanzines that have also come on the market. I have indicated in the text the use I have made of fanzines, videos and the contemporary press. I have not always indicated where I have drawn on material from my other football books, where many points touched on in this book are explained in more detail:

Murray, Bill, *The Old Firm: Sectarianism, Sport and Society in Scotland* (Edinburgh, John Donald Publishers, 1984; 8th reprint 1997)
—— *Glasgow's Giants: 100 Years of the Old Firm* (Edinburgh, Mainstream, 1988)
—— *Football: A History of the World Game* (Aldershot, Scolar Press, 1994)
—— *The World's Game: A History of Soccer* (Urbana and Chicago, University of Illinois Press, 1996)

The explosion of publishing in books on football can be seen in the comprehensive guide to books on football that came out in 1995, complete with useful comments on the works listed, from general and club histories to fanzines and music and film.

Sedden, Peter J. (compiler), *A Football Compendium: A Comprehensive Guide to the Literature of Association Football* (Boston Spa, The British Library, 1995)

The following is a selective list of books dealing with the Old Firm, Celtic, and Rangers that have appeared since 1984; the above works should also be consulted for further information.

ON THE OLD FIRM

Macpherson, Archie, *The Great Derbies: Rangers v Celtic: A Personal Look at the Glasgow Derby* (London, BBC Books, 1989)
The Herald *Book of Old Firm Games: A Complete Record of all the Old Firm Matches Fought since the Second World War* (Edinburgh, Canongate, 1995)
Walsh, Stephen, *Voices of the Old Firm* (Edinburgh, Mainstream, 1995)

ON CELTIC

Burns, Peter, and Pat Woods, *Oh, Hampden in the Sun . . .* (Edinburgh, Mainstream, 1997)
Campbell, Tom, and Pat Woods, *The Glory and the Dream: The History of Celtic Football Club* (Edinburgh, Mainstream, 1987)
—— *Rhapsody in Green: Great Celtic Moments* (Edinburgh, Mainstream, 1990)
—— *A Celtic A–Z* (Glasgow, Greenfield Press, 1992)

—— *Dreams, and Songs to Sing: A New History of Celtic* (Edinburgh, Mainstream, 1996)

Forsyth, Roddy, *Fields of Green: Unforgettable Celtic Days* (Edinburgh, Mainstream, 1996)

Kelly, Michael, *Paradise Lost: The Struggle for Celtic's Soul* (Edinburgh, Canongate, 1994)

MacBride, Eugene, Martin O'Connor, George Sheridan, *An Alphabet of the Celts: A Complete Who's Who of Celtic FC* (Leicester, ACL and Polar Publishing, 1994)

McColl, Graham, *Celtic: The Official Illustrated History, 1888–1996* (Edinburgh, Mainstream, 1996)

McGlone, Matt, *Emotionally Celtic* (East Kilbride, GD Communications, 1995)

Potter, David, *Our Bhoys Have Won the Cup! 30 Times Scottish Cup Winners* (Edinburgh, John Donald Publishers, 1996)

Wilson, Brian, *Celtic: A Century with Honour* (London, Collins, 1988)

ON RANGERS

Ferrier, Bob, and Robert McElroy, *Rangers: The Complete Record* (Derby, Breedon Books, 1996)

Forsyth, Roddy, *Blue and True: Unforgettable Rangers Days* (Edinburgh, Mainstream, 1996)

Halliday, Stephen, *Rangers: The Official Illustrated History* (London, Arthur Barker, 1989)

Jamieson, Sandy, *Graeme Souness: The Ibrox Revolution and the Legacy of the Iron Lady's Man* (Edinburgh, Mainstream, 1997)

Young, Chic, *Rebirth of the Blues: The Story of a Rangers Revolution* (Edinburgh, Mainstream, 1987)

FURTHER BACKGROUND READING

Bradley, Joseph M., *Ethnic and Religious Identity in Modern Scotland: Culture, Politics and Football* (Aldershot, Avebury, 1995)

Conn, David, *The Football Business: Fair Game in the '90s?* (Edinburgh, Mainstream, 1997)

Devine, T.M., and Finlay, R.J.(eds), *Scotland in the Twentieth Century* (Edinburgh, EUP, 1996)

Gallagher, Tom, *Glasgow: The Uneasy Peace* (Manchester, MUP, 1987)

Jarvie, Grant, and Graham Walker (eds), *Scottish Sport in the Making of the Nation: Ninety-Minute Patriots?* (Leicester, LUP, 1994)

Macpherson, Archie, *Action Replays* (London, Chapman, 1991)

Marshall, William B., *The Billy Boys: A Concise History of Orangeism in Scotland* (Edinburgh, Mercat Press, 1996)

Walker, Graham, and Tom Gallagher (eds), *Sermons and Battle Hymns: Protestant Popular Culture in Modern Scotland* (Edinburgh, Edinburgh University Press, 1990)

Walker, Graham, *Intimate Strangers: Political and Cultural Interaction between Scotland and Ulster in Modern Times* (Edinburgh, John Donald Publishers, 1995)

Horton, Ed, *Moving the Goalposts: Football's Exploitation* (Edinburgh, Mainstream, 1997)

Index